T0302153

Decision Intelligence

Revealing the limitations of human decision-making, this book explores how Artificial Intelligence (AI) can be used to optimize decisions for improved business outcomes and efficiency, as well as looking ahead to the significant contributions Decision Intelligence (DI) can make to society and the ethical challenges it may raise.

From the theories and concepts used to design autonomous intelligent agents to the technologies that power DI systems and the ways in which companies use decision-making building blocks to build DI solutions that enable businesses to democratize AI, this book presents an impressive framework to integrate artificial and human intelligence for the success of different types of business decisions.

Replete with case studies on DI applications, as well as wider discussions on the social implications of the technology, *Decision Intelligence: Human–Machine Integration for Decision-Making* appeals to both students of AI and data sciences and businesses considering DI adoption.

Decision Intelligence
Human–Machine Integration
for Decision-Making

Miriam O'Callaghan

CRC Press
Taylor & Francis Group
Boca Raton London New York

CRC Press is an imprint of the
Taylor & Francis Group, an **informa** business

A CHAPMAN & HALL BOOK

First edition published 2023
by CRC Press
4 Park Square, Milton Park, Abingdon, Oxon, OX14 4RN

and by CRC Press
6000 Broken Sound Parkway NW, Suite 300, Boca Raton, FL 33487-2742

CRC Press is an imprint of Informa UK Limited

British Library Cataloguing-in-Publication Data
A catalogue record for this book is available from the British Library

ISBN: 978-1-032-38410-8 (hbk)
ISBN: 978-1-032-38409-2 (pbk)
ISBN: 978-1-003-34492-6 (ebk)

DOI: 10.1201/b23322

Typeset in Minion
by KnowledgeWorks Global Ltd.

Contents

List of Acronyms

AI	artificial intelligence
API	application programming interface
ARIMA	autoregressive integrated moving average
ASR	automatic speech recognition
BCG	business context graph
BPM	business process management
CDSS	clinical decision support system
CEO	chief executive officer
CNN	convolutional neural networks
CPG	consumer packaged goods
CRM	customer relationship management
CSO	combined sewer overflow
CSV	comma separated values
CTO	chief technology officer
CTR	click-through rate prediction
DBT	data build tools
DDN	dynamic decision network
DI	decision intelligence
DKN	deep knowledge-aware network
DSS	decision support system
ERP	enterprise resource planning
GCN	graph convolutional network
GPU	graphic processing unit
IDE	integrated development environment
JSON	JavaScript object notation
KCNN	knowledge-aware convolutional neural network
KPI	key performance indicators
LMS	learning management system
MAV	micro aerial vehicles

MDP	Markov decision process
MEU	maximum expected utility
MIP	mixed integer programming
ML	machine learning
MLP	multi-layer perceptron
MLR	multiple linear regression
NLP	natural language processing
NMPC	nonlinear model predictive control
OCP	optimal control problem
PAI	partnership on AI
PDF	portable document format
POC	proof of concept
POMDP	partially observable Markov decision problems
RAM	random access memory
RL	reinforcement learning
RNN	recurrent neural network
ROI	return on investment
RPA	robotic process automation
SQL	structured query language
SVM	support vector machines
TXT	text
WBS	work breakdown structure
XAI	explainable AI
XML	extensible markup language

Preface

I MAGINE, FOR A MOMENT, that you are making one of your life's most important decisions that needs a thorough analysis of information. Unfortunately, you don't have time to gather all the data and perform in-depth research. Instead, you install an affordable app on your mobile phone based on your friend's suggestion. The app allows you to ask questions in natural language and provides quick answers based on the analysis of massive volumes of data using highly sophisticated AI-powered models. As you ask a question, the app determines which data is most relevant, collects the data, selects suitable models and type of analysis, performs the analysis, makes predictions, evaluates the results, and finally provides you the answer in the form of a brief report, actionable insights, and a list of recommendations. Instead of basing important decisions on intuition only, you can now use the power of big data and AI to make the most optimal decisions most efficiently.

This might sound like a plot of a sci-fi fiction novel but it is not. Leading-edge technological systems that help us make better and quicker decisions are becoming a reality today – the emerging discipline is called Decision Intelligence (DI). For the most part, DI is the application of AI to enhance the quality and accuracy of decisions while making decision-making processes more efficient.

The purpose of this book is to help the audience get introduced to the emerging discipline of DI. They will explore various concepts related to individual and organizational decision-making, including how human and machine agents make decisions, what technologies, tools, and techniques are used in building DI systems, how to prepare an organization for DI adoption, and how to use DI to make the most optimal decisions ethically.

This book is based on the analysis of hundreds of pieces of research and literature in a variety of domains, including decision science, behavioral science, managerial decision-making, game theory, systems thinking, decision support systems, decision modeling, business intelligence, behavioral economics, artificial intelligence, and machine learning, to name a few.

INTENDED AUDIENCE

This book is primarily intended for undergraduate and graduate students in business analytics and other similar programs. In addition, it is also an excellent resource for:

- Technology professionals looking to understand DI and be able to use it

- Decision-makers responsible for DI planning and implementation

- Academic and industry researchers

CONTENT AND ORGANIZATION

Each chapter starts with an introduction and a conclusion to help the audience stay focused on the key ideas included in the chapter, what is coming next, and how all the chapters in this book fit together.

Chapter 1 sets the stage, introduces the concept of DI, and attempts to provide a comprehensive definition of DI that explains its true nature and purpose. The chapter also presents an overview of the DI landscape, why it matters, how it works, and how it fits in the organization's data architecture scheme. Next, different forms of DI are explained, followed by discussions on the state of DI adoption and the factors that influence an organization's decisions on DI adoption.

Chapter 2 compares human decision-making versus computer decision-making. While human decision-making is discussed with the help of behavioral economics, neuroscience, and neuroeconomics theories, computer decision-making is explained using design concepts, including hardware and software (programs), that make decision-making possible for computers. The chapter also covers key technologies, including AI, ML (machine learning), and RL (reinforcement learning), that power various decision-making agents and systems.

Chapter 3 stresses the need to see DI from the system's perspective. DI systems are the component of an organizational decision-making system. Organizations themselves are a system, a complex whole created by multiple sub-systems. The chapter explains how human and machine agents work together in an organization to achieve common goals and make decisions that benefit the organization as a whole. It describes different types of decision-making environments, advanced technologies (other than AI, ML, and RL) used in decision-making systems, and technological systems for decision-making.

Chapter 4 sheds light on the theoretical foundations of intelligent agents' design. This is where this book gets more technical. It shows how to design decision-theoretic agents for simple decisions using the concepts of expected utility and decision networks. Markov Decision Process model can be used to design agents that can deal with complex decisions in uncertain, sequential environments. Dynamic decision networks support decision-theoretic planning by allowing better visualization of the decision context. Then, it gets into the nitty-gritty of the algorithms that run intelligent agents and enable their decision-making and action-taking mechanism. Finally, it discusses multi-agent decision-making and various strategies agents in a multiagent environment use for decision-making.

Chapter 5 covers decision-making building blocks, tools, and techniques. It starts with a discussion on the importance of data and its management. Next, the chapter explains decision tables and decision trees as two important decision analysis techniques. The audience then gets exposed to decision modeling tools. Predictive modeling tools discussed in this chapter are regression, classification, time series, outlier detection, and clustering models. Prescriptive modeling is explained with emphasis on heuristics, optimization, and simulation models. Finally, the chapter describes how businesses use text analytics tools to make critical business decisions.

Chapter 6 shows how the concepts, technologies, tools, and techniques discussed in the previous chapters are used by real-life companies to create actual DI solutions. The chapter covers the current market players and emerging companies engaged in building highly innovative DI solutions and platforms. The solutions offered by Peak, Tellius, Xylem, Noodle.ai, Aera Technology, Diwo, and Quantelia are discussed from the technical viewpoint. It also lists several other companies making their way into the DI market with their propositions targeted to clients in different functional areas and industries.

Chapter 7 introduces the DI framework, a seven-step process that helps managers establish a systematic approach to decision-making. It aims to make individuals, teams, and organizations decision-smart. Decision-makers can use this framework to determine how much AI support versus people involvement they should use while making different business decisions. The framework is designed to promote the use of technology as much as reasonably possible so the people, the most important resource, will be allocated only to pursue the most critical and complex decisions.

Chapter 8 lists recommendations for DI adoption and delves into one of the most sensitive topics around AI – ethics. Different organizations have different DI needs. Some organizations need DI only for decision assistance, whereas others seek to use it for decision support, augmentation, and automation. DI adoption requires resources and preparation. One of the most critical tasks in adopting DI is determining whether your organization is ready for such a revolutionary change. This chapter guides you on DI readiness assessments using the DI readiness audit tool. The chapter then describes major ethical concerns for DI use. It explains how we can design better DI systems by addressing the issues related to bias in algorithms, data privacy and protection, data accuracy, and job loss. Finally, it sheds light on some large companies' initiatives to build and use AI systems ethically.

WHAT MAKES THIS BOOK UNIQUE

This book has been crafted with many distinctive features. Some of them are as follows:

Application cases show how the concepts explained within the chapters are used and applied by actual companies. These cases describe the technical details of topics that are otherwise difficult to comprehend. Using the application cases, the audience will be able to develop the skills required to understand, design, build, and manage DI systems.

Every chapter of this book is filled with *examples* to help the audience learn DI concepts in a convenient manner. The examples are used to explain most of the technical, mathematical, and economic concepts in detail.

End-of-Chapter Features, including *Case studies* and *Questions for Discussion*, provide the opportunity to build DI knowledge through group discussions. Case studies at the end of each chapter consist of thought-provoking questions that will prepare the audience to use critical thinking and solve decision-making problems more creatively. As they discuss end-of-the-chapter questions, they will be able to connect DI concepts with real-world decision-making problems.

Instructor Resources such as *Sample Course Syllabi* and the *Test Banks* built on Bloom's Taxonomy are designed to support instructor needs. The Sample Course Syllabi can be used to turn this book into a course that teaches DI concepts in a structured and comprehensive manner. The Test Banks include different types of true/false, multiple choice, and essay questions to evaluate student progress on various concepts at varying levels of difficulty. These resources can be accessed through the publisher's website.

Acknowledgments

First, I would like to thank William Woods University leadership for their immense support and encouragement of my research and writing pursuits. I would like to express my sincere appreciation to decision-making and big data specialists Dr. Stephen Forsha and Dr. Gulsebnem Sheb Bishop, whose valuable reviewer comments have helped me improvise the content and structure of this book.

A special thanks to professors Dan Klein and Pieter Abbeel from UC Berkeley, who inspired me to explore and learn various technical concepts related to the design of AI agents and allowed me to use some of their illustrations in this book. My sincere thanks to Shariq Mansoor, CTO and Founder of Aera Technology, for sharing with me his expertise and insights regarding the value and potential of DI for modern enterprises and the functioning of DI platforms.

I gratefully acknowledge the outstanding help provided by Randi Slack, my publishing agent at CRC Press. Her expertise, experience, and attention helped me keep this book's progress on track while making sure I met all publisher expectations and deadlines.

I thank my students for showing great interest in my research-based talks and discussions. Their enthusiasm and curiosity encouraged me to set high standards for the completion and success of this project.

Above all, I am deeply grateful to my family: my husband, Declan, and my children, Fatima and Yousuf, for their patience, understanding, love, and support that helped me stay sane throughout the process of writing this book.

CHAPTER 1

Decision Intelligence

Introduction and Overview

Advanced technologies such as artificial intelligence (AI) play a crucial role in how we humans as a species are evolving. We invented state-of-the-art solutions to gain and create knowledge, build systems, and design products, processes, and infrastructure that make our lives more convenient, better, and happier. Today, AI affects almost every aspect of our lives, including how we make decisions. The field of decision intelligence (DI) has emerged to democratize AI for effective decision-making. DI deals with applying technology, especially AI, to enhance individual and organizational decision-making potential. DI solutions integrate technological capabilities with decision-making theories, tools, and techniques to create systems that help us make better decisions more efficiently.

This chapter introduces the fundamental concepts of DI. We will discuss some key questions, including what DI is, why we need it, how it works, and how it looks within the organization's information and data architecture scheme. This chapter also covers the state of DI adoption across different businesses, highlighting factors that drive or restrain organizations from adopting DI technologies and frameworks for decision-making.

INTRODUCTION TO DI

"Democratizing AI is the very purpose of DI."

Our decisions shape our lives, institutions, and businesses. In addition, they impact the people and environments around us. Decision-making

DOI: 10.1201/b23322-1

is complicated and gets more challenging as our decision environments become more complex. With every increment of change, we add more complexity to our decisions. Today, we need different skill sets, effective frameworks, and advanced technological capabilities for decision-making. The good news is that we are already progressing toward creating a world where highly sophisticated AI capabilities will support our decision-making even in the most challenging situations.

In his interview with Tim Ferris,[1] former Google CEO and chairman Eric Schmidt shared that computers would become our enormously valuable partners in the future. Schmidt asked his physicist friend what they would like the computer to do for them. The response was not surprising – he wanted a *physics assistant*, a computer system that could read everything, figure out disagreements, and suggest things the physicist should consider or focus upon. Today, we have access to massive quantities of data and information but barely enough time to read it all. Most specialists, including biologists and philosophers, want assistance in reading volumes of information and generating new insights for better decision-making. According to Schmidt, AI's primary achievement in the next decade will be in helping humans generate insights. As a matter of fact, DI systems powered by AI are already integral to our decision-making today.

Cassie Kozyrkov,[2] Chief Decision Scientist at Google and a renowned DI advocate, describes DI as an academic discipline that brings together the best of data science, managerial science, and social science into a unified field. Concerned with all aspects of selecting between options, DI helps us use data to improve our lives, businesses, and the world around us.

DI is a relatively new technology discipline that integrates multiple academic and professional domains. It aims to help decision-makers enhance their overall decision-making potential by ensuring both efficiency and outcomes of their decision. This means DI enables faster, more accurate, and more impactful decisions that produce effective outcomes. DI can be seen via two separate lenses:

- A broad umbrella approach that augments technology with decision-making theories in different disciplines, including behavioral economics, human behavioral sciences, social sciences, neurosciences, and management sciences.

- A technological capability that combines various technologies, including AI, ML (machine learning), and automation, allowing data utilization in decision-making.

DI is a data-driven, efficiency-focused, and outcome-oriented practice. As technology companies are developing new DI solutions, they are also creating definitions that fit the commercial products they have designed for their clients in different market segments. Unfortunately, their explanations do not do justice to DI – one of the most promising capabilities of the future. Therefore, we need a comprehensive and compelling definition to describe DI's true nature and scope.

Defining Decision Intelligence

The primary focus of this chapter is on clearly defining the new discipline of DI. DI is in its nascent stage. It was Google that first popularized DI in late 2010. In her book *Link: How Decision Intelligence Connects Data, Actions, and Outcomes for a Better World*, Lorien Pratt[3] discusses some thought-provoking insights on DI. Pratt describes DI in quite a broad yet holistic manner but does not present its clear and comprehensive definition. Peak,[4] a DI solutions company, defines DI as the commercial application of AI to the decision-making process related to every area of business. DI is outcome-oriented and it must deliver on the commercial objectives of the organization. According to Peak, organizations use DI to improve their business performance and optimize every single department.

Another technology solutions company, Gartner,[5] defines DI a little more comprehensively. They explain DI as a practical domain, including a wide range of decision-making techniques. In order to design, model, align, execute, monitor, and tune decision models and processes, DI brings multiple traditional and advanced disciplines together, including decision management, decision support, and techniques such as descriptive, diagnostics, and predictive analytics.

Defining DI as merely a suite of commercial AI applications (software and solutions) is not appropriate. It uses concepts and theories in both human-related and technology domains. Today, our decision environments are much more complex than ever and AI cannot make all the decisions on our behalf. It is not that evolved or capable (yet!). Keeping humans in the loop when making important and complex decisions is essential. DI allows us to effectively allocate and divide decision-making tasks between humans and machines. Big-bet, highly complex decisions require more people or human involvement, whereas AI can handle most of the routine decisions and tasks in our stead. Considering this, we can define DI as follows:

> Decision Intelligence is a framework that integrates human and machine intelligence to enhance the outcomes of all individual,

team, and organizational decisions. It allows sharing the human decision-making load with AI-powered solutions and technologies. While AI deals with more routine and programmable tasks, humans will be able to channel their resources into making decisions that are more critical, complex, and require unique human capabilities such as creative problem solving, critical thinking, systems thinking, and emotional intelligence.

This definition communicates the true nature and purpose of DI. It is both a framework and a set of AI capabilities that enhance our decision-making potential. In Chapter 2, we will discuss why letting algorithms decide for us is a good idea in some instances. Algorithms running in AI systems are designed to mimic human intelligence. When it comes to accuracy and speed of decision-making, they are far better than humans. Despite the weaknesses and shortcomings of current AI technologies, a large number of businesses worldwide are harnessing their power for business success. They must have something substantial to offer! Chapter 2 will also explore how AI innovations in the past few decades have paved the way for what we call DI today.

DI Evolution and Landscape

The practical demand and the hype for making data-driven decisions have made AI a strategic advantage for organizations. During the last decade, enterprises have been heavily focused on acquiring AI-enabled tools and hiring data scientists to build the capacity for generating data-driven insights. These practices were focused mostly on using business intelligence (BI) solutions that enable users to collect, store, and analyze data to generate valuable insights into support decision-making. BI is a broad term encompassing several activities that often exhaust users with large amounts of data and cumbersome coding requirements. Furthermore, with BI, it is not always possible to generate good quality insights for decision-making in real time. To address the limitations of traditional BI, technology companies shifted their focus to building DI solutions designed to put AI directly in the hands of all decision-makers, including ones without high-level technical expertise.

Today, DI solutions offered by different providers use conversational, natural language input and feedback, provide semantic business context to data, and translate insights into recommended actions. Google explained DI as a single framework for finding optimal recommendations based on imperfect data. It emerged out of three key advancements in enterprise analytics: self-service analytics, big data, and ML.[6] It can be considered as a next-generation BI that is more focused on decision-making and improving business outcomes and process efficiencies in terms of rapidity, productivity, and cost control. To enhance our understanding further, let's discuss how DI compares against BI.

DI and BI share both similarities and differences. BI uses historical data to generate queries and create visualizations to support business decisions. Today, data is streaming from a seemingly endless array of applications and systems. BI doesn't inform which data is most relevant and useful for a particular decision, how the data will be used, and what accompanying technology will help make better decisions. It is notoriously difficult for analysts to figure out how to use this vast amount of information to inform business decision-making. This is where DI comes in handy.

One of the most challenging aspects of BI has been the overall user experience. The most common and popular BI tool is the dashboard – the key interface that provides data visualization and informs about the patterns hidden in the data. It is, however, not always easy to find a solution to a specific problem or decision from the generalized information presented in these dashboards. However, DI interfaces use more advanced technologies (such as natural language search and ML), modern data architecture, and parallel processing to present an interface that exposes decision-related insights instantly. Moreover, the interface generates recommendations on what decision would be the best in this scenario.[7] Where BI is a more generalized field, DI is more specialized and focused on helping you make more accurate, better, fewer, and faster decisions while improving user experience significantly.

So, DI evolved to address issues that BI couldn't. DI companies and their platforms are increasing at a swift pace today, with new solutions introduced every few months. The capabilities in these platforms constitute several software clusters created with proactive, intelligent systems, process-focused platforms, composite AI platforms, and visualization and automation functionalities. We will discuss the key DI platforms in Chapter 6. Hyon Park,[8] the CEO and Principal Analyst at Amalgam Insights, uses the term "last mile of analytics challenge" to explain how DI evolved out of the need to efficiently build the gap from data to decisions. The average employee today accesses massive amounts of data but they don't know how to find the most important data to make the best decisions in real time. We are failing to keep up with the pace of digitization and the amount of data empowering our systems. DI solutions offer operationalizing decision-making with the ability to quantify the business impact of decisions and make the whole process more reliable and consistent. Moreover, it provides the workflow we need today that is more exploratory, interactive, and diagnostic, supporting faster decision-making in real time. To augment human decision-making, DI solutions automate the production of insights to generate explainable, quantifiable, and actionable recommendations.

It is mind-blowing to see how fast this discipline is growing. DI revolution started in this decade and will be remembered as an important milestone, another remarkable innovation that changed the way humans make decisions.

As discussed earlier, the role of humans will always remain significant when it comes to decision-making. DI technologies augment human intelligence, ensuring that we make the best decisions for ourselves and our organizations. Since technology is saving so much of our time and resources, there is an excellent opportunity for humans to focus on building skills and capacities that will make us the best decision-makers the world has ever seen.

WHY WE NEED DI

DI to Optimize Decisions

There are basically two key approaches to making decisions – satisficing and maximizing. Satisficing seeks to find a decision outcome that is "good enough," whereas maximizing focuses on finding the best outcome possible.

Satisficing is quicker since it doesn't require a lot of information or data analysis to weigh decision alternatives. All a decision-maker wants is an outcome that satisfies the basic needs of a decision; it doesn't have to be the best outcome. Some of us are natural satisficers who make quick decisions based on our instincts and intuitions without spending too much time analyzing and comparing alternatives. It also depends upon resource availability, such as time, energy, and information. In an environment where resources are constrained, managers end up making satisficing decisions that may not produce the "best" outcome or maximum return. On the other spectrum, we have a maximizing approach that uses deliberation and detailed information analysis. Maximizers assess each decision alternative carefully and deliberately to find the decision that results in the best outcome. Maximizing requires resources and a strategic decision-making approach to accomplish the best results.

Each approach has its advantages and disadvantages. Where satisficing is quick and less energy-consuming, it usually gets you mediocre results. Maximizing leads to better outcomes but the process is often taxing. While choosing between satisficing and maximizing, we face a serious efficiency-outcome tradeoff. Choosing satisficing makes the process easy and efficient but we compromise the outcome. However, maximizing guarantees the outcome at the cost of the efficiency of the process.

There is another approach to decision-making called optimizing, where a decision-maker tries to find a balance between efficiency and the outcome. Optimizing helps you find the most favorable outcome, given your situation and constraints, while ensuring that the process is not too cumbersome and taxing. Most DI technologies are designed to help decision-makers find optimal outcomes while ensuring the efficiency of the process.

As informed by Karl Hampson,[9] Chief Technology Officer, AI + Data, DI focuses on injecting the right information into the right problem at the right time (or more accurately) at *"critical moments of truth."* DI companies are using creative ways of integrating design thinking principles with modern data platforms to create solutions that help companies make better and faster decisions. These solutions also help teams make fewer decisions and focus on important problems.

DI for Improved Business Outcomes and Efficiency

DI is essential for efficiency. It helps both – people and organizations. People save their time and energy, while organizations benefit from faster, more accurate, and high-quality decisions that help businesses reduce costs and increase profits, among other benefits.

According to Gareth Herschel,[10] Research Vice President at Gartner, DI is a business discipline that helps us understand how and why decisions are made and seek how to improve them. DI is about embracing change to better your decision-making. In Gartner's video, *How Decision Intelligence Improves Business Outcomes*, Herschel quotes the example of Brussels Bus Company which was struggling to keep its fleet on the road at one point. The problem, as they hypothesized, was "Cowboy Bus Drivers" – bus drivers who they thought were too aggressive, too hard on the gas, and too harsh on breaks. The assumption was that these drivers were causing buses to break down faster, costing the company huge amounts of money to maintain their fleets. The company then decided to look into the problem using DI. They took a step back, pivoted to take action, and used new data and insights to make better decisions. They looked at the data and found that their assumption was wrong – it wasn't the drivers. The city's terrain and geography wore out the buses in some parts of the city compared to others. This information helped the company to focus on the real problem. They were now able to maintain their fleets more efficiently and productively by ensuring that their buses were wearing out more evenly in different parts of the city. DI improves business outcomes by strengthening the decision-making potential of people.

In addition to improving the quality of decisions, DI also allows us to save time and energy. We cannot deny the fact that with AI capabilities, computers can perform a wide variety of tasks faster and more accurately than humans (we will discuss this further in Chapter 2). Organizations that are starting afresh might require an initial, high investment to build DI infrastructure but it helps them reduce their operational cost significantly. Organizations already using BI might already have legacy systems in place. They will not even need that big an investment since DI and BI have quite similar infrastructure needs. DI also helps us reduce process loss that contributes to a significant amount of waste of different types of valuable resources.

HOW DI WORKS AND HOW IT LOOKS

DI, as described earlier, is an approach that aims at enhancing your decision-making potential. The term is also coined for different forms of AI capabilities that aid decision-making in various contexts. According to Pascal Bornet,[11] DI can support business decisions on three levels – decision support, decision augmentation, and decision automation. The level of machine autonomy increases at each level. Decision support, according to Bornet, is the first level where humans use basic machine tools such as data exploration, analytics, and alerts to support their decisions. The second level is decision augmentation, in which machines analyze data and generate recommendations for human decision-makers. Machines are playing a more significant role already at this level. Finally, at decision automation, the third level, machines perform both decision and execution steps autonomously, reducing human involvement even further. Bornet's model provides valuable insights into how DI can be used for business decision-making.

After studying DI trends across hundreds of use cases in various industries, we can say that DI can actually take four specific forms that can be applied at different stages of the decision-making process. These forms are decision assistance, support, augmentation, and automation. They can also be considered as four levels of DI, where decision assistance is level one – the minimal or most basic use of AI technologies and decision automation is level four – decisions are automated completely using capabilities such as hyperautomation. The higher the technology use, the lesser the need for people involvement (involvement of people).

Before we dive deep into exploring these forms, it is essential to build some understanding of different types of business decisions and the decision-making process:

Types of Business Decisions

A decision is a choice made. Business managers and leaders face a large number of decisions every day. Many of these day-to-day decisions are based on personal judgment and intuition, which might be a suitable approach, given how much risk is involved in a particular decision. You don't need to analyze every single decision in your life. You don't have enough resources. However, important business decisions need deeper analysis and investment of resources to ensure a successful outcome. The key business decisions are categorized as follows:

- **Strategic decisions** aim toward achieving the business's purpose and vision. Some examples of strategic decisions include determining your value proposition, markets you want to cater to, and the competitive advantage you will leverage. With a long-term impact on the business, these decisions require leaders to focus on the big picture and use higher-level decision-making skills such as systems thinking and design thinking to devise a well-designed business strategy.

- **Tactical decisions** are made to achieve important business goals for the success of your strategic decisions. Some examples of tactical decisions include ensuring an efficient supply of goods, maintaining optimum inventory, and implementing a customer relationship management system.

- **Operational decisions** deal with conducting day-to-day operations of the business. With a short-term impact, these decisions are more structured and usually include procedures, rules, and policies created to achieve short- to medium-term objectives. Decisions related to reordering raw materials (when and how), adjusting your budget to inflation and rising prices, and deciding who will be addressing customer complaints next week are a few examples of operational decisions.

Decisions can be defined under several more categories, such as routine vs. nonroutine decisions, programmed vs. nonprogrammed decisions, structured vs. complex decisions, and decisions under certainty, uncertainty, and risk. We will cover these types of decisions in different chapters of this book.

Decision-Making Process

A typical decision-making process includes the following seven steps:

Step 1: Identifying the Problem

The decision-making process starts when a decision-maker realizes a problem that needs to be addressed. For example, you recognize that some people in your department are spreading rumors about the new organizational leadership. You realize that this might cause several problems for you, your department, and the organization. How you identify and frame the problem determines how you approach the next steps in the process.

Step 2: Gathering Information

In this step, information is gathered to answer some basic questions. The facts and data are collected to understand the decision's background, context, and ways to address the issue at hand.

Step 3: Identifying Alternatives

At this point, a few decision alternatives are identified. The more important the decision, the more alternatives are considered. Decision-maker comprehends the key information and examines how different courses of action can be used to address the problem under context.

Step 4: Evaluating Alternatives

Based on the available evidence, the worth of each alternative is assessed in terms of the impact it will have on the decision outcome.

The decision-maker weighs each alternative's strengths and weaknesses while also comparing their consequences and implications.

Step 5: Choose the Best Alternative

The best feasible alternative is chosen at this stage as a decision to be applied. The decision-maker considers several conditions and constraints to choose the best alternative.

Step 6: Implementing the Decision

In this step, the decision-maker acts upon the chosen decision and executes it. This is the operational part of the process that often requires the orchestration of different organizational resources and functions.

Step 7: Reviewing the Decision

The performance of the decision is monitored and the results are reviewed at this stage. This helps identify the consequences of the decision or the steps needed to improvise it further.

DI Forms

Figure 1.1 shows how the role of humans in decision-making changes as technology involvement increases, given which form of DI is used. The hatched boxes in the figure represent decision-making steps that can be handled by augmenting technology in the process. As technology involvement increases, human load decreases. The solid-colored (gray) boxes represent steps that require more people or human involvement. At the level of automation, almost no people involvement is required. Let us now explore different forms of DI and how they could help with each step in the decision-making process.

Decision Assistance

At this level, leading-edge technologies such as AI are only used to assist decisions, while humans have more autonomy over actual decision-making. Decision-makers use a variety of basic or supporting technologies, such as web-based tools and third-party applications embedded in software and devices, to find information that could be used in making important business decisions. Getting assistance could be as simple as using GPS by a delivery driver to find the best route to the client's location. People take responsibility for completing all the steps in the decision-making process, and technology mostly just helps with step 2, gathering information.

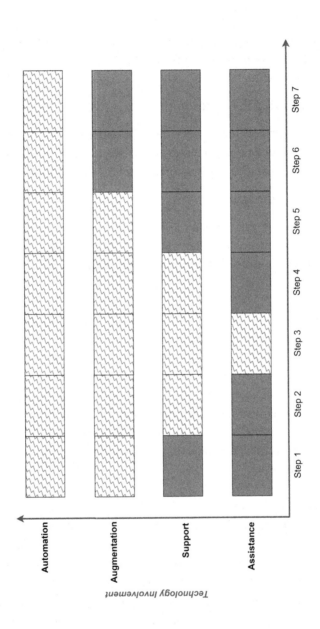

FIGURE 1.1   DI forms augmenting decision-making process

The information might also assist in steps 3 and 4, identifying and evaluating alternatives. However, the only purpose of incorporating technology at this level is to get access to valuable information that provides background information on the context of the decision and possible solutions. Decision assistance is largely sought for strategic decisions where people involvement and abilities are of utmost importance.

Decision Support

The next level (or form) is decision support, where decision-makers use specialized decision support technologies such as CRM (customer relationship management) systems, ERP (enterprise resource planning) systems, and traditional DSSs (decision support systems). Healthcare institutions such as hospitals use specialized DSSs for different tasks, such as performing diagnoses and getting patient care/treatment recommendations. A CDSS (clinical decision support system) is an excellent example of such aid. The system maintains clinical knowledge on different health conditions, which is matched to an individual patient's characteristics and assessment information to generate recommendations. Clinicians use these recommendations to make the most suitable patient treatment and care decisions. In the decision-making process, humans identify the decision but machines gather the data (step 2), identify alternatives (step 3), and often provide alternative recommendations or courses of action based on the evaluation of alternatives (step 4). Decision support can help mostly in operational decisions.

Decision Augmentation

Many of today's cutting-edge DI solutions are created for decision augmentation, where machines play a bigger, more proactive role in making predictions and providing recommendations based on the more profound analysis of large volumes of data. A typical DI platform or solution created for decision augmentation explores the data sources and gets the most suitable data for the decision. It then uses ML algorithms for prediction and recommendations. Among other tools, these platforms use search, exploratory analysis, trend analysis, forecasting, time series analysis, regression, classification, clustering, anomaly detection, natural language search, optimization, and recommendation systems. Some platforms also use a simulative analysis to provide information on the consequences of following different recommendations. Decision-makers finally decide whether or not to use the recommendations or which ones to act upon. They can accept recommendations generated by the platform or change them by working cooperatively with the system. Decision augmentation technologies use highly sophisticated AI algorithms and technological capabilities to provide more accurate and effective recommendations, often in real time, than DSSs.

The people involvement in decision-making declines as we increase the level of technological resources. With highly advanced capabilities, some DI solutions can even help in identifying decision problems. In addition, these platforms provide unprecedented agility making your teams remarkably well at decision-making. Decision augmentation can aid both tactical and operational decisions. Since the platforms mostly use big data to generate insights, this form of DI can also support strategic decisions.

Decision Automation

The most technology-intensive form of DI is when machines make autonomous decisions on people's behalf using a combination of tools and algorithms. Intelligent automation (or hyperautomation) is an emerging trend that streamlines and scales decision-making across organizations. It comprises AI, business process management (BPM), and robotic process automation (RPA) to create solutions that transform the outcomes of various business decisions. Intelligent automation primarily focuses on automating processes to free up resources and improve operational efficiencies.[12] Utilizing AI benefits through autonomous agents (such as industrial robots) is another good example of automating decisions and letting machines do more for us.

Automation can be used to eliminate repetitive tasks such as inventory scheduling, replenishing orders, reviewing loan applications, and processing refunds. It can make operational decisions highly efficient and streamlined. Intelligent automation systems also review their own performance to learn better ways of handling the situation. From identifying a decision to reviewing it, all the steps in the decision-making process are performed by machines with very little or no human intervention.

Infrastructure Design – Data Architecture for DI

Data is the crucial ingredient of any successful business decision. Therefore, organizations focused on data-driven decisions maintain a robust data architecture that helps align business data with business goals and strategies. A good data architecture helps organizations categorize, integrate, transform, and store data to enable the workflow required for analysis and modeling purposes. If your organization has already been using BI, you might only need a few upgrades to your existing data architecture. As mentioned before, many organizations might already have legacy systems to support the basic functionalities required for DI adoption and implementation. However, these legacy systems will require a new, modern data stack or a suite of tools to leverage the full potential of DI capabilities.

DI capabilities, just like AI, vary widely. It is like an ala carte menu. You choose what you want from a wide range of solutions and platforms available in the market today. Tellius,[13] a DI solution provider company, suggests mixing and matching best-of-breed tools to create your modern data stack to gather, store, transform, and analyze data more effectively. The architecture contains the following six layers (see Figure 1.2):

1. **Data sources layer**: it includes applications such as Salesforce and Google Analytics, databases, including Oracle and SQL Server, and multiple documents (flat files consisting of business transactions information. Examples include. csv and. txt files, semi-structured files such as XML, JSON, and Avro (formats), and social media data (examples include data collected from social media websites on public perceptions and customer satisfaction).

2. **Ingestion layer**: this layer with automated pipelines extracts data from various data sources. Tools such as Fivetran, Stitch, or Segment are used. This allows your teams to access and work with the freshest and most relevant data possible.

3. **Storage layer**: it usually comprises datastore, metadata store, and replication to support the availability of data whenever it is required. This layer is designed to support data security, scalability, and resilience. Proper business rules and configurations are maintained through the administration of this layer. The modern stack includes cloud data warehouses such as Amazon Redshift, Snowflake, and data lakes such as Amazon S3 and Databricks.

4. **Transformation layer**: raw data is cleaned up at this layer to facilitate further analysis. Tools such as DBT (Data Build Tools), a SQL command-line program designed to transform data, and Matillion (data integration and transformation solution that is purpose-built for cloud and data warehouses) are used.

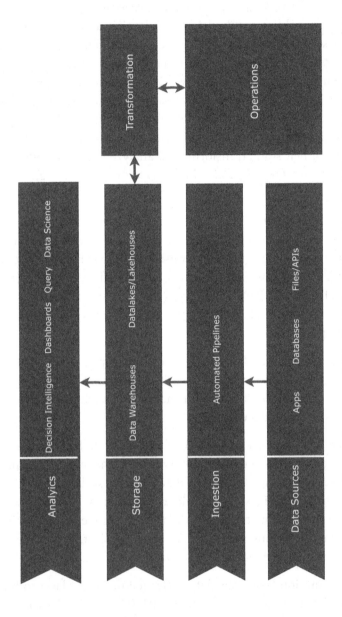

FIGURE 1.2   Data architecture with a modern DI stack (Credit: Tellius, Modern Data Stack Essentials: Next-gen Analytics & Decision Intelligence)

5. **Operations layer**: this layer supports tools such as Apache Airflow (open-source workflow management platform for data engineering pipelines) and Atlan that connect to the storage layer to help data teams access both internal and external data while automating repetitive tasks.

6. **Analytics layer**: in legacy systems, this layer allows the usage of a variety of AI, ML, and predictive analytics using programming languages (such as Python and R) with a combination of different APIs. In addition, analysts can use analytics dashboards and data visualization tools like Tableau, MS Power BI, and SAP Lumira that consume the data from data lakes for creating advanced analytics graphs and charts. The modern stack, however, uses ML tools such as Dataiku, a new form of augmented analytics called DI (integrated DI platform), dashboard tools, including Looker, as well as SQL query.

This book discusses DI adoption and implementation recommendations in detail in Chapter 8. In the beginning, though, it is important to know how to start with your DI adoption journey. Start with DI needs analysis – knowing your DI needs. They can be determined by reviewing your project strategy and goals, which will inform you about the type of impact your organization desires and what functionalities and solutions you will require, given your needs. Having clarity on the architectural design will help you create a more comprehensive DI adoption and implementation strategy.

STATE OF DI ADOPTION

In the previous section, we explored how different forms of DI are used for specific types of decisions and how each of these forms helps in the seven steps of the decision-making process. Your business situation also affects the decisions regarding which form of DI you should use. Still, in this age, many organizations use computer technologies very limitedly. Think about small businesses operating in local markets that don't go beyond using online searches, mobile apps, and spreadsheets. Decision-makers in these businesses make thousands of daily decisions based largely on their intuition.

Nevertheless, a large number of organizations today use BI capabilities such as data mining, reporting, warehousing, visualizing, and dashboarding to generate data-driven insights for decision-making. BI can easily be used without AI capabilities, but when combined, it can produce even better results faster. Many businesses are using AI to leverage the full potential of BI today. Think about financial institutions such as banks that seek to make their transactions secure against many criminal activities. Where BI provides the basis and descriptive analysis to generate insights, AI offers ML capabilities to detect fraudulent transactions by applying trained anomaly detection models.

In addition to using AI for analytics, some organizations also utilize it for building and maintaining autonomous, intelligent agents. The concept of intelligent agents is discussed in detail in Chapters 3 and 4. To get a basic idea, think of an industrial robot that operates autonomously. It receives information from the environment, processes it through its inbuilt algorithms, makes a decision, and actuates the action using its different body parts. This robot is an intelligent agent that works very similarly to humans but is merely an agent programmed to mimic our decision-making and action-taking mechanisms. Intelligent agents can also be software programs used for various decisions in product research and development, supply chain management, marketing and selling, and optimizing production and inventory.

Many organizations use DI in its different forms without calling it DI. Think about the biggest companies today – Facebook, Google, Apple, and Amazon. They are using AI to inform their decisions in almost all functional areas of business. For example, AI is used to generate insights on consumer behavior, design products based on actual customer preferences, target the right market segments for marketing campaigns, and optimize processes for higher effectiveness and efficiency. Furthermore, augmentation and automation of several tasks democratize AI and make it accessible to everyone in the organization. With only a few clicks, teams can build models, create visualizations, and share the results with their teams. They are no longer required to have skills for coding and programming in different languages. As a result, more and more organizations are now moving to DI. The rate and scale of adoption will increase at a much faster pace. DI companies publish content frequently to spread awareness about DI while also communicating its benefits for business decisions. They are focusing on making DI more explainable so people and businesses can quickly build trust in DI. Adopting DI is a major strategic business decision.

Factors Affecting DI Adoption Decisions

There are certain factors that affect DI implementation and adoption decisions in organizations. The scale and nature of business operations play an important role in determining the level of DI adoption. If the scale of your operations is small and most of the decisions could be made successfully without the use of cutting-edge technologies, then you will not even feel the need to implement DI solutions. This doesn't mean that your business doesn't actually need DI. It only means that you haven't perceived the need for its adoption.

Resource availability is another key factor. Many organizations, especially small businesses, cannot afford expensive technological capabilities. AI-based projects require advanced technological infrastructures such as GPU architecture, high-volume storage systems, high-performing scalable computing systems, and large volumes of data. Developing an AI-ready infrastructure and data management systems is not an easy task. Many organizations do not even know how to operationalize their data platforms at an enterprise scale. Others might avoid such projects since the process is cumbersome and time-consuming. In addition to investing in data and infrastructure, you also need talent acquisition, development, and training. Maintaining DI systems requires operational expenses that many small- and medium-sized organizations cannot afford.

Technology adoption decisions are strategic in nature, and therefore, top-level managers are often tasked to make or approve these decisions. Many leaders show reluctance toward acquiring revolutionary technologies such as AI for different reasons, including concerns for data governance, information security, ethics, or simply because they don't believe it is crucial for organizational success. Without top management's support, DI adoption can be a big challenge, if not an impossible pursuit.

People dynamics in the organization and organizational culture also affect the perceptions and attitudes toward using leading-edge technologies. Even though leaders' values provide the vision of organizational culture, it is the people, the teams, that shape the actual culture of the organization. People resist change naturally since it pushes them beyond their comfort zone. Some organizational cultures encourage maintaining the status quo while avoiding all disruptions. DI adoption could cause cultures to undergo a series of uncomfortable changes. For DI systems to work effectively, you need to break down the silos, build cooperation, and integrate all the enterprise data into a capacity that helps generate insights for high-quality decisions. Organizations in which teams prefer staying in silos will likely avoid DI adoption.

CONCLUSION

The concept of DI is relatively new but DI has been in action for many years. It reached the next level as machines built the capability to make recommendations using big data and AI algorithms. These recommendation systems are one of the most effective tools that help individuals, teams, customers, and other stakeholders make important decisions.

DI is not just a commercial application of AI to enhance business decision-making and grow revenue and profits. DI is augmenting natural human intelligence with AI for effective decision-making in different situations. We can never exclude humans completely when it comes to making critical business decisions. Although we have highly advanced and capable AI-supported systems at our disposal, we are not yet ready to let AI take full control over our decisions.

Decision-making could be an overwhelming task. However, with the application of AI-powered modern solutions (also called DI solutions), managers and leaders can reduce the time, effort, and energy on many less important decisions, freeing up these resources for the types of decisions that are extremely important. There are DI solutions available in the market to support almost all types of business decisions today. They use massive volumes of data to train highly sophisticated and effective models that can help decision-makers generate valuable insights based on the previous patterns identified in the data. The models incorporated in the software of these solutions are highly accurate and fast. Among all other benefits, they help save time, energy, and other resources that otherwise will be spent in decision-making.

DI revolution is only starting and we will see it growing very quickly worldwide. DI makes our lives easier. In addition, we can create a better world with decisions that produce optimal, the best possible outcomes for our businesses and all stakeholders, including our planet.

CASE STUDY: AI-POWERED RECOMMENDATION SYSTEM DELIVERING CONSISTENT ENERGY SAVING AT GOOGLE DATA CENTERS

Google is the world's largest corporate purchaser of renewable energy. The company seeks to act on climate change by minimizing its energy consumption at Google. Reducing energy usage has remained Google's major focus for more than ten years. Although their data centers were already highly optimized, in 2016, Google developed an AI-powered recommendation system jointly with DeepMind Technologies to safely deliver energy savings in Google's multiple data centers. Their AI agents, including the AI-powered recommendation system and the underlying control infrastructure, ensure the system's safety, efficiency, and reliability.

Google data centers power Google's services, such as Google Search, Gmail, and YouTube, with thousands of their servers. These servers generate a lot of heat that must be removed and controlled to keep servers running. Although the cooling can be done using large industrial equipment such as pumps, cooling towers, and chillers, data centers' dynamic environment presents three key challenges:

Operating equipment: the equipment, the environment, and the methods of operation interact with each other in non-linear and complex ways. Human intuition and traditional engineering based on formulas often do not capture information on these interactions.

System's response to change: data centers face many different operating scenarios and humans cannot develop enough rules and heuristics to handle each of these scenarios. Hence, the system fails to adapt quickly to internal and external changes such as changing weather and pressure conditions.

Architecture and environment: each data center is unique when it comes to its architecture and individual environment. A custom-tuned model created for one system might not apply to all the data centers. The centers as a whole need a general intelligence framework to understand the complexities of the system, including interactions between different data centers.

To address these challenges, Google started applying ML in 2014. As DeepMind joined in 2016, they started using a neural network system to create a more adaptive framework to optimize efficiency and understand data center dynamics. Their neural networks were trained on historical data collected by thousands of sensors within data centers. The data included information on variables such as temperatures, power, pump speed, and set points. The neural networks were trained on the average future Power Usage Effectiveness (PUE), defined as the ratio of the total building energy usage to the IT energy usage. Two additional ensembles of neural networks were also trained to predict the data center's future temperature and pressure over the next hour. These predictions were designed to simulate the recommended actions from the PUE model with due consideration of operating constraints. The model was then tested by deploying on a live data center.

The new AI control system directly implements the actions where the original recommendation system had the operators vetted and implemented actions. The system consistently achieved a 40% reduction in the amount of energy consumed for cooling. After accounting for electrical losses and other non-cooling inefficiencies, this equates to a 15% reduction in overall PUE overhead. In 2020, Google's AI-powered recommendation system was delivering consistent energy savings of around 30% on average. The average annual PUE for Google's global fleet of data centers in 2019 hit a new record low of 1.10 (compared to the industry average of 1.67). This means Google's data centers use about six times less overhead energy for every unit of IT equipment energy.

Sources:

DeepMind AI Reduces Google Data Centre Cooling Bill by 40%. (2016, July). Retrieved July 26, 2022, from https://www.deepmind.com/blog/deepmind-ai-reduces-google-data-centre-cooling-bill-by-40

Hölzle, U. (2020, February 27). Data centers are more energy efficient than ever. Retrieved July 26, 2022, from Google website: https://blog.google/outreach-initiatives/sustainability/data-centers-energy-efficient/

QUESTIONS

1. What are a few other possible applications of technology that Google developed for its data centers?

2. What forms of DI is Google using as its AI-powered recommendation system to manage data center efficiencies?

3. Search online and list three other companies implementing similar AI-powered technologies to augment human decision-making and run their businesses sustainably.

QUESTIONS FOR DISCUSSION

1. Is decision intelligence only a set of AI capabilities? Give reasons for your answer.

2. Compare and contrast DI with AI. What is the relationship between these two disciplines?

3. Why do companies today need to focus on replacing BI with DI?

4. Is it a wise idea to delegate all our decisions to technology? Describe the importance of keeping humans in the loop for decision-making.

5. Explain different steps in the decision-making process and how technology can help with each step. Use examples.

6. Discuss some business examples of satisficing and maximizing approaches to decision-making. How can DI help in finding a balance between satisficing and maximizing?

7. Survey the literature from the past two years to find how businesses in different industries are able to achieve better decision outcomes using DI.

8. Is DI only an outcome-oriented practice?

9. What forms of DI does your company or school use?

10. What DI form is most suitable for strategic business decisions?

11. Discuss five examples of each operational and tactical business decision that could benefit from decision augmentation.

12. Discuss the components of the modern DI stack in an organization's data architecture scheme.

13. What types of organizations will lead the way for DI adoption? Which factors will motivate them toward DI adoption?

14. Do you think DI is here to stay? What impacts will it have on the businesses of the future?

REFERENCES

1. Ferriss, Tim. (2021, October 27). Eric Schmidt – The Promises and Perils of AI, the Future of Warfare, Profound Revolutions, and More. Retrieved from https://www.youtube.com/watch?v=AGNImy8E02w

2. Kozyrkov, C. (2021, October 3). What is Decision Intelligence? Retrieved August 25, 2022, from Medium website: https://towardsdatascience.com/introduction-to-decision-intelligence-5d147ddab767

3. Pratt, L. (2019). *Link: How Decision Intelligence Connects Data, Actions, and Outcomes for a Better World*. Warrington, UK: Emerald Publishing.

4. Peak – The Decision Intelligence Company Using AI to Drive Growth. (n.d.). Retrieved May 12, 2022, from Peak website: http://peak.ai/us/

5. Definition of Decision Intelligence – Gartner Information Technology Glossary. (n.d.). Retrieved January 4, 2022, from Gartner website: https://www.gartner.com/en/information-technology/glossary/decision-intelligence

6. Park, H. (2021). Graduating Beyond Dashboards with Decision Intelligence: Get Immediate Business Return with AI-Powered Recommendations. Retrieved from https://campaigns.diwo.ai/almagam-insights-report

7. Reuter, C. (2020, September 28). Decision Intelligence vs Business Intelligence. Retrieved January 5, 2022, from Medium website: https://csreuter.medium.com/decision-intelligence-vs-business-intelligence-17e98e6194db

8. Elniski, T. (2022, May 9). How DI Solves the Last Mile of Analytics Challenge. Retrieved July 25, 2022, from Diwo website: https://diwo.ai/blog/how-di-solves-the-last-mile-of-analytics-challenge/

9. Team, E. (2020, September 20). Decision Intelligence vs. Business Intelligence: What Is Your Company Running On? Retrieved July 21, 2022, from insideBIGDATA website: https://insidebigdata.com/2020/09/20/decision-intelligence-vs-business-intelligence-what-is-your-company-running-on/

10. Gartner. (2022, June 20). How Decision Intelligence Improves Business Outcomes. Retrieved from https://www.youtube.com/watch?v=OFAxIPbUMyI

11. Bornet, P. (2022, May). Council Post: Is Decision Intelligence The New AI? Retrieved July 14, 2022, from Forbes website: https://www.forbes.com/sites/forbestechcouncil/2022/05/25/is-decision-intelligence-the-new-ai/

12. What is Intelligent Automation? (2022, April 28). Retrieved July 22, 2022, from IBM website: https://www.ibm.com/cloud/learn/intelligent-automation

13. Modern Data Stack Essentials: Next-gen Analytics & Decision Intelligence. (2021, November 23). Retrieved July 25, 2022, from Tellius website: https://www.tellius.com/modern-data-stack/

CHAPTER 2

Humans vs. Machines in Decision-Making

This chapter compares how machines make decisions differently from humans and the strengths and weaknesses of both – humans and machines in decision-making. With the help of multiple behavioral economics, neuroscience, and neuroeconomics studies, we will explore how humans make decisions.

To understand how computers make decisions, we will look into the basic design of computers, their components, and the capabilities that power their decision-making and action-taking mechanisms. We will also discuss the key AI technologies, including machine learning (ML), to understand how they enable computers to perform extraordinary tasks and surpass many human abilities.

HUMANS IN DECISION-MAKING

We, humans, are an extraordinary creation of nature. What differentiates us from other organisms on this planet is a small yet powerful organ in our body, our brain. The human brain is not just a physical organ. It is a device that supports the Mind, a set of faculties responsible for various psychological phenomena that enable decision-making, such as sensations, perceptions, emotions, memory, logical reasoning, critical thinking, and much more. Our minds produce thoughts and creative ideas that shape our decisions.

Human decision-making is explained under two types of theories. Normative theory: how people *should* make decisions, and descriptive

DOI: 10.1201/b23322-2

theory: how people *do* make decisions. Expected utility theory is a normative theory of rational choice that describes the process of human decision-making under uncertainty according to the principles of traditional economics. The expected utility of any action is a weighted average of the utilities of each of its possible outcomes. The utility of any outcome measures the extent to which that outcome is preferable or preferred compared to the other alternatives.[1] The decision-maker computes the probability of outcomes and then compares them with the expected utility. Their goal is to choose the alternative with the maximum expected utility.

Economics has been regarded as a non-experimental science. As cognitive psychologists studied human judgment and decision-making and experimental economists tested economic models in the laboratory, traditional economic views on decision-making started to transform. Economics research assumes that we are motivated primarily by material incentives and we make decisions in a rational way according to the laws of probability and standard statistical principles.[2]

However, real-world decision-makers are not economists. They are humans who do not calculate probabilities or make decisions according to the theory of expected utility maximization. According to descriptive theories in behavioral economics, humans code and interpret information in a conscious manner but other factors such as emotions, mental models, perceptions, and biases also affect their judgment to a great extent. Human decision-making is explained more accurately by descriptive theories (behavioral economics) than normative theories (economics). Normative theories, nevertheless, are important: they tell us how people should make decisions to maximize the utility of their outcomes. A large number of AI-powered agents are therefore designed on the principles of rational choice theories, aka normative theories. We will discuss this topic further in detail in Chapter 4. In order to understand human decision-making wholly and accurately, we need a multidisciplinary approach.

Behavioral Economics of Decision-Making

Behavioral economics combines economics and psychological concepts to analyze human behavior in the real world. It challenges the neoclassical economics assumption, which assumes that most people have clear, well-defined preferences and make well-informed, self-interested decisions based on those interests.[3] Several mental processes drive behavior in our minds. To understand human decision-making, it is important to know the thinking mechanisms of our brains. Renowned psychologist

Daniel Kahneman,[4] in his book *Thinking Fast and Slow*, explains two systems of thinking. One is automatic (system one), and another is reflective and rational (system two). The automatic system is quick and fast. It uses intuition for judgment. At the same time, the reflective system is more self-conscious and deliberate.

Our brain follows the law of least effort. It is lazy. It tries to save energy by avoiding tasks it can get away with. Since system one is fast and requires less effort, our brain tries to use and engage it for most cognitive tasks. On many occasions, our brain perceives problems simpler than they actually are. It calls system two only when system one experiences the complexity, the problem it cannot solve.

According to behavioral economics theories, people are incapable of analyzing complex decision situations fully, especially when the future consequences are uncertain. In such situations, we use some simple heuristics, the rules of thumb that work as quick information shortcuts. Unfortunately, relying on these heuristics can lead to systematic bias in our decision-making. Tversky and Kahneman[5] identified three key heuristics: anchoring, availability, and representativeness, and the biases associated with each. These heuristics emerge from the interplay between our automatic and reflective systems. Anchoring is also known as the first impression bias. It is our tendency to be overly influenced by the first piece of information we receive. The availability heuristic describes our tendency to place more value on the information that our brain can access instantly. This is often the most recent information we receive. Representativeness heuristics emphasize aspects of the event similar to the prototype of that event (mental representation of the event based on our past experiences) in our minds.

Human decision-making is influenced greatly by cognitive biases caused by information processing shortcuts, emotional and moral motivations, distortions in storing and retrieving memories, social influences, and the limited processing ability of the brain.[6] A brief explanation of some of these biases is as follows:

- **Overconfidence bias:** our tendency to be overly confident in our intelligence, performance, opinions, experience, and abilities.

- **Status quo bias:** our preference for choices that help us maintain our current state. Our preference for not doing something different from what we are doing today.

- **Halo effect:** creating the perception of someone based on one special characteristic that influences all subsequent judgments of other characteristics of the same person.

- **Planning fallacy:** blindly presuming that the end result will follow the plan; underestimating the time it will take to finish a task; not considering important elements of the decision during planning.

- **Framing effect:** when our choices are influenced by how the information is presented or framed.

John Manoogian III and Buster Benson have created a mind-blowing graphic representation of 188 cognitive biases of the human mind. That's true! 188 cognitive biases. The graphic can be viewed on their webpage: https://www.visualcapitalist.com/wp-content/uploads/2017/09/cognitive-bias-infographic.html.

Certain social and cultural conditions constantly prime our brains, according to Kahneman. This priming results in cognitive ease by invoking a common association that moves us in a particular direction. For example, why do we sometimes end up believing in falsehood, despite realizing that it might not be true? It is because the information is familiar to us and easy to process. One of the most staggering findings of Kahneman's studies was that people are not entirely rational. Instead of reducing risk to its acceptable levels, they have a propensity to value the elimination of risk. They show loss aversion when they fear losses more than they value gains. He also identified that, in general, people are poor statistical reasoners, especially in Bayesian terms. Even when supplied with compelling causal statistics, they tend to base their decisions on long-held beliefs that are mostly rooted in their personal experiences. The important reason why people avoid statistical thinking is that it is effortful. It requires resources and attention that only system two can bear.

Kahneman, Sibony, and Sunstein,[7] in their latest book *Noise: A Flaw in Human Judgment*, explain how noise in our brains affects our decisions. The credit for the rest of the content in this section goes to their book. It is an awe-inspiring resource to understand the concept of noise and how it affects human judgment and decision-making in multiple contexts. Noise is an undesirable variability in judgments of the same problem. System noise is the variability in judgments of the same case by different actors that should ideally be identical. Working in groups amplifies noise. Individual differences and dynamics among group members might result in higher noise levels. Simple factors that we take for granted might result in increased noise in group decision-making. These factors include who speaks with confidence, who speaks first, who speaks last, who is wearing a specific color, who smiles or not, body language, social influences, social pressure, polarization tendencies, and much more.

Occasion noise is the variability in judgments of the same case by the same person or group on different occasions. One important source of occasion noise is mood. Our moods significantly affect our judgments and decisions. It is a simple fact. When we are in a good mood, we are more positive. A negative mood has the opposite effect. We are more likely to accept our first impressions as true without challenging them when we are in a good mood. Some features of our cognitive machinery alter when our moods vary. Many other factors, including fatigue, weather, memory performance, and sequence effects, may trigger unwanted variations in the judgment of the same case by the same person. We are not the same person at all times. In short, we are noisy.

A published review of 136 studies informs that mechanical aggregation outperforms clinical judgment made by humans. The overall conclusion of this review included a diagnosis of jaundice, fitness for military service, and marital satisfaction, supporting the fact that simple statistical models beat humans in making accurate decisions. Goldberg based his research on how well a simple model of the judge would predict real outcomes. In this study, the judge was replaced by their own model. The results were surprising. Predictions made by the model outperformed predictions made by the actual judge. The accuracy of predictions improved when the judgment was made by the model of the judge and not by the judge themselves. Another review of 50 years of research published decades later concluded that models of judges consistently outperformed the judges they modeled.

What was happening? What caused such significant differences between the decisions of the judges and their models? The answer is simple: the models weren't affected by the noise that affected the judges' decisions. The models didn't capture the influences of momentary contexts and ever-varying mental states of human judges. As the models were employed, the noise was removed and it improved the accuracy of predictions. Removing noise also increases the validity of predictive judgments. Things got more interesting when Yu and Kuncel compared judges to a random linear model and not to their own models. Their findings were striking. When applied consistently to all cases, any linear model was likely to outperform human judges in predicting an outcome from the same information.

These studies establish that in the case of predictive judgments, models of reality, models of a judge, and even randomly generated linear models performed better than human experts. It is important to note that these models are not entirely noise-free. All models include noise. In machine models, however, noise could be controlled and eliminated by making a few changes in the algorithm. The studies confirm that the noise generated by human minds has a much worse impact on human decision-making than the impact of a model's noise on the model's decision-making.

How do you compare humans vs. AI systems in decision-making? AI uses ML to train the models on huge datasets. Due to their ability to process massive amounts of data, ML models outperform humans and even other simple models in making decisions. These ML models (if created right) use more accurate and fairer algorithms than human judges and are designed to detect all the possible valid patterns in the data. Sendhil Mullainathan, with his team, trained AI models to make bail decisions. Their model was trained to deal with nonlinear combinations and was able to handle higher complexity in data. It was designed to predict flight risk as a numerical score rather than a bail or no bail decision. The model's performance was tested against the performance of actual human judges and other simple models. ML model performed much better than human judges and was also more successful than other simple models at predicting which defendants are high risks.

Many studies have established that ML models make more accurate, faster, and more effective decisions than humans. Their capability goes well beyond the predictive power of humans and other models. They are superior because of the absence of biases and noise and because they can exploit much more information and use highly sophisticated algorithms to make decisions.

Neuroscience and Neuroeconomics Perspectives

Neuroscience provides a biological map of the Mind and tells where things happen in the human brain. We are born with brain architecture that supports decision-making through its multiple systems. According to Gutnik et al.,[8] the neural architecture of decision-making in the human brain comprises a highly complex and interconnected circuitry that uses various brain regions, including the prefrontal cortex, the amygdala, and basal ganglia.

Among other regions, decision-making engages areas of the brain involved in emotion.[9] Amygdala – an almond-shaped mass of nuclei inside each cerebral hemisphere – is involved with the experiencing of emotions. It is an important part of our limbic system, a set of brain structures located on top of the brainstem and buried under the cortex, responsible for emotional responses, hormonal secretions, and memory.[10] Several studies support the premise that emotions affect not only the quality of the decision but also our very basic ability to decide.[11] Christian Jarrett[12] informs that brain-damaged patients struggle to make the most elementary decisions due to the emotional struggles they face. Feelings serve as the basis for human reasoning.

The neocortex is the largest part of the cerebral cortex. This complex brain structure commands higher order functions such as sensory perception, cognition, and emotion.[13] Several studies inform how the emotional part of our brain (limbic system) influences the functioning of the rational part (neocortex). For example, in a study on how emotions affect logical reasoning, researchers found a clear effect of emotions on reasoning performance. Participants in a positive mood performed better than participants in a negative mood but the participants in a neutral mood outperformed both groups.[14] In another study, participants were found to make more risky decisions and were involved in more self-defeating behaviors when they experienced bad moods.[15]

Our emotions influence our decisions all the time. Think about decisions such as hiring a more attractive candidate or buying a red car because that's your partner's favorite color. A study performed at Case Western Reserve University[16] informs that when adults are presented with social or analytical problems (all external stimuli), they consistently engage the appropriate neural pathway to solve the problem. However, when a specific neural pathway is engaged, it represses the other pathway. The MRI images used to establish this research's findings showed that social networks in subjects' brains were activated when they were given social problems. This activation of social networks, however, deactivated networks associated with analysis. Also, when they were presented with physics questions (analytical work), their brains' analytical networks activated, deactivating the brain regions responsible for empathizing. The research also found that their brains naturally cycled between these two networks when subjects were lying in the scanner with nothing to do. When we are engaged in highly analytical tasks, our brain's empathy or feeling networks are repressed by the analytical networks. Social networks do the same. When you are feeling intense feelings, your social network is at work, suppressing the functioning of your analytical network.

Neuroeconomics analyzes brain functions behind decision-making and combines neuroscience, psychology, and economics to create powerful models explaining why and how we make specific decisions. Recent neuroeconomics research uses advanced imagery and biochemical tests to analyze brain activity and see what is happening in a person's brain while performing some mental tasks, including decision-making. Due to fundamental properties of the central nervous system, namely divisive normalization, some basic axioms of choice theory, such as the irrelevance of independent alternatives, are violated.[17] Among other discoveries, neuroeconomics studies provide insights into the problems and issues of human decision-making. Several studies established that humans might not even act to optimize utility in their decision-making. Their decisions are significantly influenced by emotions instead of reason and logic.

Jonathan Cohen,[18] Eugene Higgins Professor of Psychology, Co-Director, Princeton Neuroscience Institute, explains that economic models are based on two bad assumptions: one, we are one person (a single decision-focused agent) and second, we are evolved to deal with the circumstances that we are in. Our brains are not optimized to judge which alternatives or circumstances would be the most appropriate in any given instance.

The conclusions of behavioral economics, neuroscience, and neuroeconomics studies are similar: human decision-making has some serious limitations. It is imperfect because of our brain's biological design, limited processing power, neural mechanics, and flawed thinking process resulting in several types of biases and noise.

COMPUTERS IN DECISION-MAKING

This section will first discuss computer design aspects that enable computer decision-making at the most fundamental level – receiving and executing instructions using different hardware and software components. We will then explore the advanced AI technologies revolutionizing how machines help us make better decisions today.

We designed computer systems to mimic human brain function. Whatever computers decide or do is the outcome of the functioning of the algorithm fed into the computer system by humans. When a human makes a decision, their brain and Mind work together to execute various tasks required for decision-making. Computers do the same – the system receives the information, processes it with embedded rules and algorithms to produce the result (output).

In computers, information is processed in the Central Processing Unit (CPU), which is inevitably referred to as the computer's brain. While the other components perform more passive functions, the CPU does the active running of code and manipulating data. The code and the data that are being actively used are stored in the random access memory (RAM). The computer's persistent storage stores the bytes even when power is removed. Where hard drive stores bytes as a magnetic pattern on a spinning disk, flash drives (newer technology) store bytes on flash chips, making them work faster and more accurately while consuming less power. Due to the high flash technology cost, most computers still use hard drive storage.[19] Today, we have many more options, such as cloud technologies that offer even better storage alternatives.

Remember we talked about the circuitry in the human brain that connects different parts of the brain? The computers have kind of a similar mechanism called a motherboard – usually a rectangular board with integrated circuitry that connects different parts of the computer, including the CPU, RAM, and disk drives (hard disks or any others), and the peripherals connected through the expansion slots or the ports.[20] The motherboard uses thousands of its circuits to transfer information and power (electricity) between different parts. If the CPU is the computer's brain, the motherboard is its nervous system.

What about the software part of the equation? It is called the program. Computer programs work like human minds that support human thinking and decision-making. Traditional computer programs generally use heuristics and rules of thumb. It is appropriate to say that what a computer decides to do depends upon how it is programmed: its programmer's knowledge, level of expertise, the filters of their lifetime experiences, and mental models. The computer will do what it is asked to do through a set of instructions (programs).

Basic Programming Methods

When decision problems are simple, they can be solved with traditional methods and programs. Many applications we use for daily tasks are designed with simple heuristics and rules. For example, the flowchart in Figure 2.1 represents the blueprint of a simple decision that a computer tries to make with Boolean logic (values are either true or false). Flowcharts are a great tool to visualize the structure of the algorithm or a program. The Python program code (Figure 2.2) uses an if-else statement. In this instance, the programmer asks the user to input the number (start stage in the flowchart). If the number is greater than or equal to zero, the computer is instructed to print the result as "Positive or Zero." If this is not true (else), the result should be printed as a "Negative number." The program

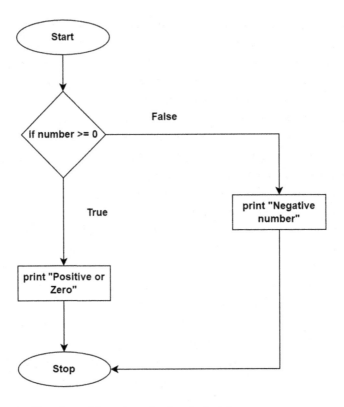

FIGURE 2.1   Flowchart: blueprint of a simple decision

will then be executed and stopped. In Figure 2.2, the user inputs number 8; the result generated by the program (output) was Positive or Zero.

We will now add a little complexity to this task by adding another condition. We want the computer to help us determine whether the number is positive, zero, or negative. The flowchart in Figure 2.3 represents how this new problem can be structured as an algorithm. Even though the level of

```
num = float(input("Enter a number: "))
if num >= 0:
    print("Positive or Zero")
else:
    print("Negative number")

Enter a number: 8
Positive or Zero
```

FIGURE 2.2   Program for a simple decision

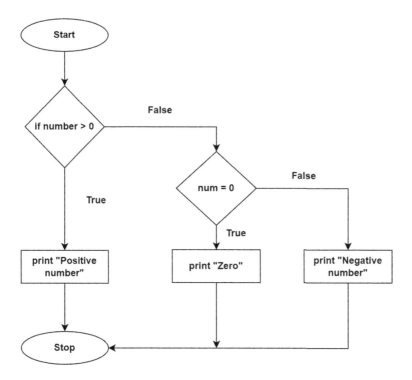

FIGURE 2.3   Flowchart: blueprint of a complex decision

complexity is not that high, we will still call it a complex decision to distinguish it from the previous example. The if statement evaluates whether
the number is greater than zero. If the test expression is true, the result
should be printed as a "Positive number." If the test expression is false, it
further tests whether the number equals zero. The result should be printed
as "Zero" if this expression is true. If this test expression is false, it finally
prints the result as a "Negative number," followed by the program's ter-
mination. This code uses an if-elif-else statement. This statement allows
the evaluation of multiple conditions but overall, the problem can be programmed easily with the help of a few lines of code as shown in Figure 2.4.

We use mathematical models and more advanced technologies for
highly complex and sophisticated problems.

The Evolution of AI-Powered Decision-Making

The codes exhibited in Figures 2.2 and 2.4 are examples of traditional programming methods instructing the computer to take a particular action if
specific values are inputted into the system. However, there is one down-
side to this traditional approach to writing programs. They grow larger as

```
num = float(input("Enter a number: "))
if num > 0:
    print("Positive number")
elif num == 0:
    print("Zero")
else:
    print("Negative number")

Enter a number: -32
Negative number
```

FIGURE 2.4   Program for a complex decision

you add more complexity, resulting in slow processing and sometimes not producing optimal results. To overcome such challenges, we turn to AI. It focuses on finding the best way to use just a few lines of code instead of vast programs. AI programs use sophisticated algorithms to produce more accurate and precise results even when the problem is highly complex to solve.

Artificial Intelligence is the science of creating technologies that enable machines to think and act like humans. It is about creating intelligence that, in reality, is not natural but, in some cases, better than natural human intelligence. The evolution of AI technologies has been marked by several winters – periods of no or very slow growth. Nevertheless, after decades of AI research, we have developed capabilities that can help us analyze large volumes of data, build sophisticated models, and deploy them to optimize our decisions and actions.

According to Wolfgang,[21] the roots of AI can be traced back to 1931, when the Austrian scholar Kurt Gödel showed that all true statements are derivable in first-order *predicate logic*. However, there are true statements that are unprovable in higher-order logics. This discovery opened new doors for deeper research into the understanding of logic and its use in solving problems of different orders. The following events, among others, are notable accomplishments in the history of AI research and development.

In 1943, McCulloch and Pitts introduced neural networks and made a connection to propositional logic.

In 1950, Alan Turing defined *machine intelligence* in his seminal paper published in Mind. He applied what was called the *Turing test* to determine if machines could win a game (the initial question was, "can machine think?"). He also introduced the concepts of learning machines and genetic algorithms.

In 1955, Marvin Minsky introduced a neural network machine that he developed with 3,000 vacuum tubes that simulated 40 neurons.

In 1956, the term *artificial intelligence* was first used in a conference at Dartmouth College organized by McCarthy. In 1963, McCarthy founded the AI lab at Stanford University.

In 1969, Minsky and Papert wrote about perceptrons in their book *Perceptrons*. They introduced a very simple neural network that could only represent linear functions.

In 1976, Shortliffe and Buchanan developed an expert system called MYCIN to diagnose infectious diseases. The system was able to deal with uncertainty. By 1982, an expert system called RI designed to configure computers was helping Digital Equipment Corporation save 40 million dollars annually.

In 1986, Rumelhart, Hinton, and Sejnowski, among others, were making progress in building more effective neural networks. During this year, the system Nettalk learned to read texts aloud.

In 1990, multiagent systems started gaining popularity. Various scholars brought probability theory into AI with *Bayesian Networks* concepts. By 1992, the advantages of reinforcement learning (RL) were demonstrated.

In 1995, Vapnik developed support vector machine (SVM) using statistical learning theory.

In 1997, popular chess world champion Gary Kasparov was defeated by IBM's chess computer Deep Blue.

In 2006, service robotics became one of the most focused AI research areas.

In 2009, we saw the first Google self-driving car driving on the California freeway. Autonomous robots were improving their behavior through learning.

In 2011, two human champions on the television game show "Jeorpardy!" were defeated by IBM's Watson that understood natural language and could quickly answer difficult questions.

In 2016, the Go program AlphaGo, developed by Google DeepMind, defeated a professional player in the full-sized game of Go. The program used deep learning techniques applied to Monte Carlo tree search, pattern recognition, and a novel combination of supervised learning from human expert games and RL from self-play games.

In 2020, Google's DeepMind AI launched AlphaFold, a deep learning program that predicts the shape of a protein, at scale and in minutes, down to atomic accuracy. It is a huge milestone that will revolutionize multiple health sciences and biology areas in the future.[22]

During the same year, the success of COVID-19 vaccine research proved the value of AI models in analyzing vast amounts of complex data related to coronavirus. Typically, it takes years, if not decades, to develop a new vaccine. With AI-powered models, the development of the COVID-19 vaccine was expedited, saving the lives of millions of people worldwide.[23]

In 2021, OpenAI developed DALL-E, a neural network that is able to create images from text captions. OpenAI's language transformer model is trained on 250 million pairs of texts and images collected over the internet. It can produce anthropomorphized versions of objects and animals, combine related and even completely unrelated things, and apply changes and transformations to existing images.[24]

In 2022, Neuralink lines up clinical trials to implant AI microchips in humans. These chips have already been successfully implanted in a macaque monkey's and a pig's brains. The chip implant is expected to restore full body functionality to someone paralyzed or with a spinal cord injury.

Machine Learning

ML is a form of AI that mimics intelligent ways humans learn to behave. It is usually called a subset of AI. Most of the AI programs that companies deploy today are most likely using ML algorithms so much that the terms AI and ML are often used interchangeably. ML algorithms have the capacity to improve on their own as they gain more experience and are fed with more data. ML enables computers to decide and act without being explicitly programmed for every single task. So, how does it actually work? It starts with collecting data in various forms, including text, photos, files, sensor data, reports, or transactions. This data is prepared to be used as training data – the information the ML model will be trained on. The prepared data is fed to a suitable ML model that trains itself on this data to find patterns or make predictions. The more data, the better your results will be. Some of the data is held out from the training data for evaluation and to test how accurately the model performs when it is shown new data. If the model fails to produce accurate results, programmers can tweak the model and even change the parameters to produce more accurate results and closer to reality.[25] ML systems could be descriptive (results explain what happened), predictive (predict what will happen), or prescriptive (make suggestions about what action to take).

ML is so pervasive today that you might not even know how many ways companies use this technology. Let's answer a few questions:

How does Netflix make those entertainment recommendations for you?
Their recommendation systems use various ML algorithms, including RL, neural networks, and ensembles, to make those recommendations.

How do your phones or computers auto-correct your incorrect spellings?

The auto-correct algorithms are implemented in your devices' programs that use Natural Language Processing (NLP) functionalities for spelling corrections.

How does Spotify decide which songs will go into its Discover Weekly playlists?

Spotify uses collaborative filtering, NLP, and many other algorithms and models to pick up songs that receive a lot of traction from users and the songs you have shown interest in. Among other technologies, Spotify uses deep learning and convolutional neural networks to leverage its huge data collections.

ML is making it all happen. Did you know that Netflix's personalized recommendation algorithms produce $1 billion annually in value by retaining customers?[26] Spotify's Discover Weekly feature reached 40 million people in its first year of launch.[27] Almost all big companies use AI and ML in one way or another. Would these companies achieve these levels of growth, efficiencies, and success without AI-powered systems? Certainly not.

Embodied intelligence takes AI to the next level. Like AI, embodied intelligence is created to mimic human ways of thinking, analyzing, deciding, and taking action. It is used in creating autonomous intelligent agents that use the embodiment of different parts that mimic the human brain, body, perceptual, and motor system. Think about autonomous cars and robots. They have physical bodies controlled by their cognitive system, which receives perceptual information from the environment and initiates a particular decision. The agent then executes the decision as an action performed by different parts of its body. We will discuss the details of these agents in Chapter 4.

The algorithms drive the actual functioning of neural networks and other ML models. Algorithms perform the actual ML tasks such as pattern recognition, enabling learning from data and improving the model. ML systems take their instructions through these algorithms. We will now discuss a few examples of ML algorithms in three ML subcategories – supervised, unsupervised, and reinforcement learning. We will also explore how classical ML models help decision-making and how deep learning further strengthens the capabilities of AI systems.

Supervised Machine Learning

Supervised learning models are trained on the *labeled* data. This means that the labels are already assigned to each data point in the database before data is fed to the system. During the training, the algorithm identifies the input features of the training dataset and learns which type of data belongs to a specific label. Based on this learning, the model makes a prediction.

Regression and classification are two types of supervised learning models. Regression models are used to make projections and predictions. They help us understand the relationship between dependent and independent variables. The most common regression algorithms include linear regression, logistical regression, and polynomial regression.

Classification is used when data has to be categorized in different class labels. For example, SVM algorithms can classify the type of iris (species of flowering plants) based on the variables in the dataset. Common classification algorithms include linear classifiers, SVM, decision trees, k-nearest neighbor, and random forest.

APPLICATION CASE 2.1: AUDIENCE TARGETING WITH SUPERVISED LEARNING

Using a publicly available sample dataset on Kaggle, Tellius[28] (a DI solution provider) performed audience targeting in the context of a consumer packaged goods (CPG) company to identify high-performing customer segments for a customized marketing campaign. The customer base for CPG companies is quite broad. It includes everyone who eats, drinks, and uses their products. Audiences in this industry are quite decentralized due to the availability of countless platforms, streaming services, digital media options, and consumers' ease of self-service and unsubscribing. Targeting the right customer segment to target specific marketing campaigns allows businesses to create more impactful campaigns resulting in high return on investment (ROI).

The dataset used consisted of customer demographic and purchase behavior information (products each customer purchased). Data exploration helped Tellius see the data summary with information on products that were most popular among customers. Their system applied a decision tree classifier algorithm to generate guided insights to create five distinct market segments. Tellius' Guided Insights tool automates AI and advanced statistical methods to solve complex business problems in minutes. Segment one included people whose total spending was more than $1,918, with more than four web purchase records. They were 4.6 times more likely to purchase than others. Buyers in Segment four were 3.5 times more likely to respond, were more frequent web visitors with lower total spending, and bought wine and meat most frequently. The results of this analysis and the insights generated can help any CPG company devise a successful and more focused marketing strategy.

Unsupervised Machine Learning

Unsupervised ML models work with data that is not labeled. Think about a dataset of 7,000 images of three different animals: zebras, male lions, and elephants. The images are not labeled and the system doesn't know which image represents which animal. How do you think the system will categorize 7,000 images into three different categories? Unsupervised learning deals with these types of problems. The system will identify unique patterns in the data, in this case, specific features of the three animals in each image, using clustering algorithms. It will then assign each image to a separate cluster. For example, all the images where the animal has black stripes will be put in a cluster called *zebras*, animals that are shorter in height and have manes will be added to the cluster *male lions*, and finally, all the animals that have a trunk and are huge in size will be added to the cluster called *elephants*. This is the purpose of unsupervised learning – to find out the natural clusters or dimensions in the data.

We are receiving large volumes of data in multiple formats and it is not easy to label each piece of data that is being ingested into the system. Moreover, this data is also coming in video, text, and audio formats. Unsupervised learning combined with other technologies such as computer vision, speech recognition, and NLP process these massive volumes of unstructured data to produce results that were never possible before. Common unsupervised learning algorithms include clustering (k-means, agglomerative hierarchical clustering, and mean-shift, among others), anomaly detection, autoencoders, and neural networks. It is applied mainly in fraud detection, recommendation systems, and customer and product segmentation. In the following application case, we will see how an online retail business can identify customer segments using k-means clustering algorithms in Python.

APPLICATION CASE 2.2: CUSTOMER SEGMENTATION WITH UNSUPERVISED LEARNING

Customer segmentation is the practice of partitioning a customer base into groups of individuals that have similar attributes. By dividing customers into smaller subgroups, it is easier for businesses to effectively allocate marketing resources to determine which segment should be targeted for a specific product offering. Recency, frequency, and monetary value (RFM) clustering approach is used for this analysis that is based on three pillars of customer attributes – *recency, frequency,* and the *monetary value* of the purchase.[29] The customers showing similar behaviors will be grouped together to create specific market segments.

The dataset was downloaded from Kaggle, containing 541,909 rows and eight columns. Exploratory analysis was performed first that helped identify the top ten selling products, as shown in Figure 2.5.

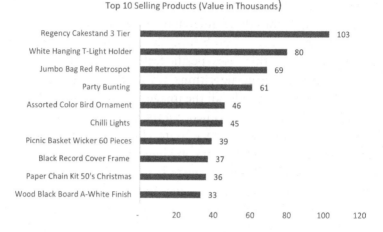

FIGURE 2.5   Exploratory analysis

The model was implemented with a k-means clustering algorithm that segmented customers into four distinct clusters. The number of clusters was determined using the elbow method. The following Python code was used to create the clusters and add the new cluster to the data frame:

```
kmeans = KMeans (n_clusters=4)
Ukdf_user['RecencyCluster']=kmeans.fit_predict
(ukdf_user[['Recency']])
```

The results can be seen in Figure 2.6. This table shows customers who made the most recent purchases, bought products most frequently and generated the highest revenue for the business (cluster 4). Customers in cluster 0 would be the most unattractive customers for this business since they have not been making any purchases recently, and the frequency and monetary value of their purchases are also quite low. The clusters were numbered based on their customer value, with 0 being the lowest value and 4 being the highest value customers. You can also visualize these clusters to compare recency-revenue, recency-frequency, and frequency-revenue for each cluster. The biggest dots in Figures 2.7–2.9 represent the high-value cluster, medium-sized dots show the mid-value, and the smallest dots represent the low-value cluster. To make visualization easier, you can assign colors to each of these clusters.

Overall Score	Recency	Frequency	Revenue
0	304.72	22.20	310.88
1	185.79	32.93	508.72
2	78.66	47.17	842.25
3	20.83	68.78	1,116.90
4	14.62	270.60	3,752.61

FIGURE 2.6   Summary of overall scores

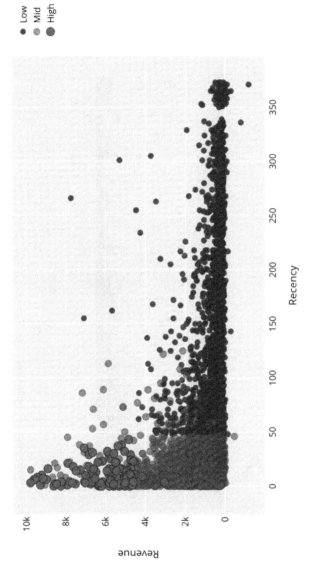

FIGURE 2.7 Recency-revenue-based clustering

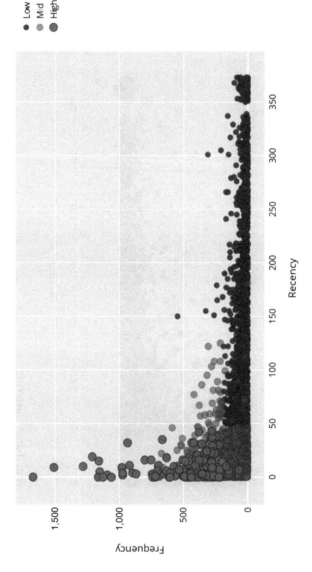

FIGURE 2.8 Recency-frequency-based clustering

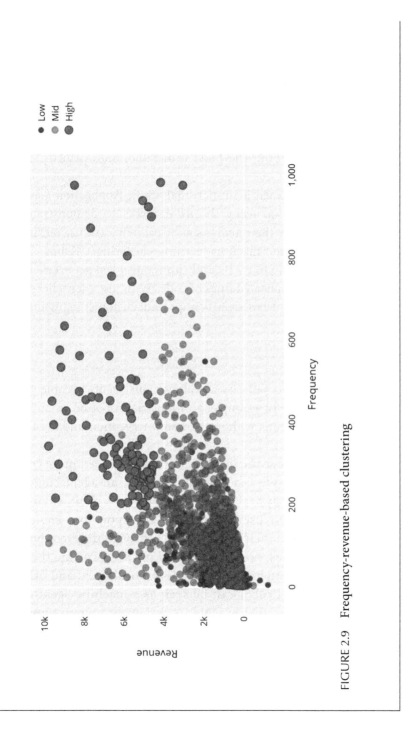

FIGURE 2.9 Frequency-revenue-based clustering

K-means clustering combined with the RFM can help companies identify market segments to allocate their resources more effectively. Businesses can profile their customers based on their demographic and behavioral predictors. For example, Best Buy identified that 7% of its customers accounted for 43% of its total sales. Using this information, Best Buy reorganized its stores to address the needs of its high-value customers.[30] Retailers can significantly maximize their ROI by correctly identifying the most profitable, high-priority customer segments.

Tellius has performed a similar analysis in Application Case 2.2 on customer segmentation using the RFM model to demonstrate DI use cases. You can access their analysis at https://www.tellius.com/use-cases/customer-segmentation-machine-learning-clustering/. Tellius' advanced technology allows you to create and run models and get excellent results without writing complicated lines of code. With just a few clicks and in a matter of minutes, you can identify important customer segments for your business.

Reinforcement Learning

RL is gaining more popularity as autonomous agents become commonplace. These agents (for example, an industrial robot or an autonomous car) can make decisions without human intervention and even act on a human's behalf.

You will notice that the terminology *agent* is used quite frequently in this text. As Russel and Norvig[31] explain, an agent could be any physical and non-physical entity that perceives their environments through sensors and use actuators to act upon that environment. Human agents sense their environments through different body parts (sensors) such as eyes, nose, ears, and skin. They execute their action through actuators, including hands, legs, vocal tract, and other body parts. An industrial robot can be seen as a machine agent designed with specific sensors that execute its action through various motors and other physical parts (actuators). Many non-physical entities, capabilities, or systems, such as decision support systems implemented entirely in software, can also be considered agents.[32] For example, software agents receive human input, file contents, and network packets as sensory inputs and actuate the result by displaying information on the device screen.

RL empowers intelligent agents (discussed in Chapter 3) to learn by trial, error, and practice. The model learns from incremental rewards for correct predictions and penalties for incorrect predictions. It is based on the psychological theory of operant conditioning that introduces the concept of reinforcement – we repeat the behaviors that are reinforced by positive rewards and avoid behaviors that result in negative consequences or punishments. While most of the other ML technologies only generate predictions, RL helps create systems with agents that make decisions on their own. Among other applications, RL-based agents are used in financial trading, content recommendations, gaming, marketing and advertising, autonomous vehicles, robotics design, and healthcare.

RL is most suitable for complex sequential decision problems. In such scenarios, optimal decision policies are usually unknown and difficult to determine. For humans, it is difficult to encode every instance, data point, and run computations to find the most optimal solution. Using RL, computers perform these tasks for us. RL approximates the optimal value function to predict the expected quality of an agent visiting a particular state in the future. It is based on the concepts of classical dynamic programming and Markov Decision Problems. Chapters 3 and 4 discuss these concepts in more detail.

Increasing volume, velocity, and variety of information are making our decision environments more dynamic and decisions more complex. Traditional RL might not work effectively in such scenarios. Therefore, deep RL came into existence. It is designed to handle decisions where the agent needs to learn from all the complex states and determine the most suitable path. The term "deep" refers to the application of neural network technology that allows RL algorithms to go through the deep layer architecture to estimate the states without the need to map every solution individually. This helps the agent create a more manageable solution space in the decision-making context.

RL algorithms that use models are called model-based and those that don't are called model-free.

Model-Based RL Algorithms   A model-based agent has access to (or they've learned) the environment model that guides its behavior. The model of the environment is a function that predicts state transitions and rewards. The agent takes action, observes the outcomes, including the next state and the immediate rewards, and then learns the most optimal behavior. University of California researchers[33] demonstrated how medium-sized neural network models could be combined with model predictive control (MPC) to achieve excellent sample complexity in a model-based RL algorithm. They explained how their work helped the model to produce stable plausible gaits to accomplish various complex locomotion tasks. OpenAI's Spinning Up documentation categorizes various model based and model free algorithms. Model-based RL algorithms include[34]:

- Learn the Model: World Models, Imagination-Augmented Agents (I2A), Model-Based Value Expansion (MBVE), Model-Based RL with Model-Free Fine-Tuning (MBMF).

- Given the Model: AlphaZero.

Model-Free RL Algorithms   The agents using model-free algorithms do not have any model of the environment to follow. Instead, the algorithms use different techniques for learning and optimizing policies for specific decisions. DeepMind Technology researchers applied a model-free method (without adjustment of the architecture or learning algorithm) to seven Atari 2600 games from the Arcade Learning Environment and found that it outperformed all previous approaches on six of the games. It also surpassed a human expert on three of those games.[35] They used an RL algorithm to control policies directly from high-dimensional sensory input. This model was a convolutional neural network trained with a Q-learning variant. The Model-Free RL algorithms include[34]:

- Policy Optimization: Policy Gradient, Proximal Policy Optimization (PPO), Trust Region Policy Optimization (TRPO), Asynchronous Advantage Actor-Critic (A2C/A3C).

- Q-Learning: Deep Q-Networks (DQN), Hindsight Experience Replay (HER), Categorical 51-Atom DQN (C51), Quantile Regression DQN (QR-DQN).

Classical Machine Learning
Classical ML technologies are designed mainly on statistical and probabilistic reasoning and therefore are less complex. The architecture of

algorithms is more rule-based and therefore requires less computational power than complex algorithms. Since they use a straightforward mathematical approach, they are simple to use and easy to understand.

Most supervised learning problems can be solved using classical ML methods such as regression, logistic regression, and classification, including decision trees and SVM. Classical ML methods are more suitable for problems that use simpler data such as numbers, categories, or text. In case data is more complex (such as images, videos, or audio pieces), classical approaches might not work that effectively.

APPLICATION CASE 2.3: CLASSICAL ML, MULTIPLE LINEAR REGRESSION ANALYSIS TO PREDICT BASEBALL PLAYERS' SALARIES

Have you ever wondered how much money baseball players make? What factors do decision-makers consider while determining their salaries? To create a model that predicts baseball players' salaries, you can use classical ML, a multiple linear regression model. For this analysis, the dataset was downloaded from Kaggle, consisting of 322 observations and 20 variables. Players' salary was chosen as the dependent variable.

Five features that showed extremely weak or no correlation with the salaries of the players were removed after exploratory and correlation analysis. For feature selection, the stepwise feature selection technique was used. In addition, forward and backward selection techniques were applied to ensure the right set of features was selected. The model with features selected by backward elimination performed the best after a few models were tested. A piece of Python code used for this model can be seen here:

```
X = bsalary[['AtBat','Hits','Walks','Years','CRuns',
   'CWalks','PutOuts']]
X = sm.add_constant(X)
y = y
model = sm.OLS(y, X).fit()
predictions = model.predict(X)
```

The r-squared value of this model was not quite high but it was still higher compared to other models with different features. Figure 2.10 shows the summarized results of this model. This classical ML approach determined seven variables (out of 19) that can help predict baseball players' salaries. Of course, you can try multiple models with different sets of features to solve the same problem and you might get even better results than this model.

```
                        OLS Regression Results
==============================================================================
Dep. Variable:              log_value   R-squared:                       0.536
Model:                            OLS   Adj. R-squared:                  0.523
Method:                 Least Squares   F-statistic:                     42.01
Date:                Sat, 10 Oct 2020   Prob (F-statistic):           4.17e-39
Time:                        14:26:32   Log-Likelihood:                -240.94
No. Observations:                 263   AIC:                             497.9
Df Residuals:                     255   BIC:                             526.5
Df Model:                           7
Covariance Type:            nonrobust
==============================================================================
                 coef    std err          t      P>|t|      [0.025      0.975]
------------------------------------------------------------------------------
const          4.5376      0.151     30.018      0.000       4.240       4.835
AtBat         -0.0027      0.001     -2.702      0.007      -0.005      -0.001
Hits           0.0123      0.003      3.838      0.000       0.006       0.019
Walks          0.0102      0.003      3.394      0.001       0.004       0.016
Years          0.0625      0.019      3.379      0.001       0.026       0.099
CRuns          0.0014      0.000      3.135      0.002       0.001       0.002
CWalks        -0.0011      0.001     -2.165      0.031      -0.002      -0.000
PutOuts        0.0003      0.000      2.305      0.022    4.82e-05       0.001
==============================================================================
Omnibus:                       20.310   Durbin-Watson:                   1.874
Prob(Omnibus):                  0.000   Jarque-Bera (JB):               49.164
Skew:                           0.319   Prob(JB):                     2.11e-11
Kurtosis:                       5.020   Cond. No.                     3.07e+03
==============================================================================
```

FIGURE 2.10   Classical ML – multiple linear regression model

Neural Networks and Deep Learning

One of ML's most promising computational models is the artificial neural network, also known as the neural network. Its design and architecture are inspired by the biological structure of the human brain. In our brains, neurons are closely connected and they communicate chemical signals through synapses between axons and dendrites. Artificial neural networks, however, communicate signals (numbers) through specific weights and activation functions (such as a sigmoid function) to activate artificial neurons. The networks adjust those weights using a training algorithm to solve a given problem.[36]

A perceptron or an artificial neuron represents the model of a biological neuron. It is the simplest neural network which comprised just one neuron that can be used for classification through supervised learning. While a neural network with a single layer can produce results, adding more layers to the network can help in optimizing and refining for accuracy. If a neural network consists of more than three layers inclusive of inputs and output, it can be considered a deep learning algorithm. The term "deep learning" comes from these networks containing several hidden, deep layers (see Figure 2.11). The term deep refers to the depth of layers in a neural network.[37]

Neural network innovations have been growing exponentially, and today, many different types of networks can be used for various purposes.

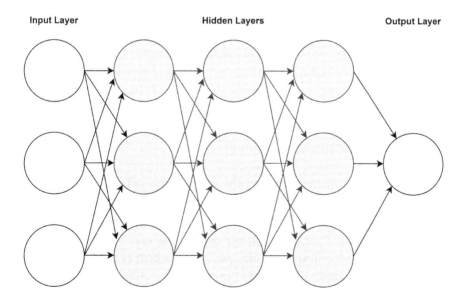

FIGURE 2.11   Deep neural network

The most commonly used deep neural networks are as follows:

- **Multi-Layer Perceptron (MLP):** as one of the most commonly used models, MLP consists of layers of interconnected neurons where the connections between the layers are assigned weights. It uses both forward and backward propagation. Data is transferred from the input layer to the output layer in the forward direction. The backpropagation technique is then used to optimize the weights in a backward direction of the network. MLPs can be used for a variety of tasks, including data compression, time series prediction, character recognition, and autonomous driving.

- **Convolutional Neural Networks (CNNs):** primarily used in computer vision-related tasks, CNNs consist of multiple convolution layers that extract distinct features from the image. The earlier layers take care of low-level details, whereas the deeper layers focus on extracting more high-level features from the images. The convolution operation uses filters that are initialized randomly and are updated through backpropagation. The key applications of CNN include image classification, video analysis, anomaly detection, drug discovery, and face recognition.

- **Recurrent Neural Network (RNN):** this unique model is distinguished by its memory feature, allowing it to take information from prior inputs to influence the current input and output. Unlike other models, RNNs share the same weight parameter within each layer. The backpropagation technique is used to determine the gradient and it is specific to the data that is sequential. They are widely used for language translation, NLP, speech recognition, and image captioning. So next time you ask Siri or Hey Google a question, it is RNNs working in the background.

Multiple layers incorporated in the deep neural network can process unstructured data, including images, videos, and audio. Deep learning has produced promising results in object detection, speech recognition and synthesis, machine translation, image processing, and NLP. One crucial function of deep learning is feature extraction which is used for pattern recognition and image processing. From building chips to help patients with spinal injuries to space exploration, deep learning algorithms are helping machines to grow more and more intelligent and help us solve a variety of problems in multiple domains. Deep learning can be combined with supervised, unsupervised, semi-supervised, or even RL techniques.

Although the history of deep learning can be traced back to 1943, it became a mainstream technology quite recently. By late 1900, computers had become relatively faster. The discovery of graphic processing units (GPUs) that enabled the processing of pictures increased computation speeds at significant levels. By 2011, these GPUs became even faster, allowing CNNs to train without needing layer-by-layer pre-training.

Today, deep learning drives many AI applications, including automation, robotics, and performing analytical and physical tasks without much human involvement. Deep learning is behind many products and services we use today. For DI, deep learning holds great promise. Its ability to process all types of data much faster will make it one of the mainstream DI technologies in the future.

HUMAN VS. COMPUTER – WHO IS BETTER AT DECISION-MAKING?

Early in this chapter, we explored concepts related to human decision-making. We also discussed the decision-making mechanism of computers and AI-ML technologies that drive their capabilities. As we deduce all that knowledge, do we conclude that computers are better than humans at making decisions? No, we cannot. Computers are certainly better at solving specific problems and making decisions in more structured environments. AI systems learn from experience with large volumes of data. Think about autonomous vehicles. Their history can be traced back to the 1980s, and after more than four decades, they are still not ready to be launched at a full scale. They are still in the learning and development phase. AI agents such as autonomous cars need to learn every possible instance and every piece of knowledge in their environments. This is not an easy task. The more complex the environment is, the more difficult it is for the agent to decide. Designing decision-making systems that work as effectively as humans in complex environments is difficult.

Human intelligence grows as we keep learning from our environments. Moreover, we are gifted with certain abilities that computers can hardly ever master – imagination, creativity, and empathy. Using these gifts, we solve even the most complex problems in the world. Of course, computers cannot replace human decision-making completely. However, they can serve as companions to augment our capabilities and help us make better and faster decisions. We can make our lives much more convenient if we let computers save the time and energy that is otherwise spent on hectic decision-making tasks.

CONCLUSION

There are multiple pieces of research supporting the fact that models perform better than humans in making accurate judgments. Human cognitive abilities are limited and our thinking is flawed due to our inherent biases and noise. Several factors, including emotions, affect our decisions all the time. With information and decision overload, our brains get overwhelmed and tired. Today, we have technologies that can help us reduce our decision-making load. We should focus on tasks that machines cannot perform for us. It is a good idea to channel our resources (time and energy) toward more important and complex tasks and let machines do what they are good at.

As Eric Colson[38] puts it – we need to get us, humans, out of the way and bring AI into our workflows to fully leverage the value in data. We must evolve from data-driven to AI-driven workflows. We must integrate human and machine capabilities if we seek to enhance organizational decision-making. As technology increases, AI models that are superior to traditional models are developed. Modern deep learning and RL technologies are making AI systems much more powerful than ever. These technologies allow us to overcome our inherent limitations as human processors (low throughput, cognitive biases, and noise). Machines can process vast volumes of data. With AI, they can deal with millions of data groupings, work with nonlinear relationships (even if they are exponential), geometric series, and power laws – much more than any single human or team can handle.

It is important to remember that computer systems are not foolproof. Humans design them and human bias can easily creep into the programs that run these systems. However, it is easier to check and resolve these problems in computer programs than in humans. Chapter 8 will discuss how to design DI systems to avoid such flaws. All technology-related ethical concerns can be addressed with the right policies and procedures.

CASE STUDY: JOHNS HOPKINS MANAGES PATIENT FLOW DURING COVID-19 WITH AI-POWERED CAPACITY COMMAND CENTER

In 2020, Johns Hopkins Medicine faced an indefinite surge of highly infectious patients with COVID-19. Major concerns for institutional leaders and clinicians were treatment options, the course of the disease, crucial supply chain shortages, and safety for patients and staff. In addition, they were hearing horror stories from colleagues and news reports about hospital facilities getting overwhelmed with very sick patients. With the help of the Johns Hopkins Capacity Command Center (also known as Judy Reitz Capacity Command Center), Johns Hopkins managed patient overflow successfully while delivering the best services safely to its patients.

The command center incorporates the latest technologies in system engineering, predictive analytics, and innovative problem-solving to effectively manage patient safety, experience, volume, and movement (in and out of the hospital and around the Johns Hopkins Health System). Their partnership with GE Healthcare brought AI advancements that allowed drilling deep into large data streams to predict patient volumes from the next shift to the next day to the following week. During the COVID-19 pandemic, this type of forecasting was crucial to managing operations.

So how does this system work? A dozen extra-large, bright-colored digital screens hang high on the walls of the center. As patients move to and from units and beds throughout the hospital, the AI-powered systems trigger screens to blink and change datasets in real time. The center has separate screens dedicated to:

- Forecast bed occupancy rates in medicine, neurosurgery, surgery, oncology, gynecology, and obstetrics departments. The green light signals open beds, the yellow – capacity is near full, and the red light indicates the unit is full. The screens also show the exact number of beds that need to be cleaned and prepared for new patients.

- Exhibit the number of surgeries in progress in each operating room with their anticipated finish times.

- Show incoming patient transfers from Johns Hopkins member hospitals as well as from outside hospitals and institutions.

- Show a live camera view of people seated, standing, or pacing in the adult emergency department waiting room.

The intelligence generated through the AI system helps the decision-makers at the hospital, including nurses, transport staff, and the admitting team, make better decisions concerning their specific tasks. From March 12, 2020, to March 1, 2021, the Command Center managed 7,529 patient transfers. The Lifeline staff transported 659 patients with COVID-19 to and from Johns Hopkins Health System hospitals. In addition, another 877 COVID-19 patients were transferred internally at the Johns Hopkins Hospital. It was laudable that not a single transmission of the disease from patient to staff is known to have occurred during the transportation process. By March 2021, their bed utilization improved from 85% to about 94%, with the opening of 16 beds on a daily basis without building a new wing or adding new staff. These efficiencies contribute to an estimated $16 million in annual revenue for Johns Hopkins.

While most medical facilities struggled to accommodate patients during the pandemic, Johns Hopkins AI-powered capacity command center saved thousands of lives by augmenting AI into human decision-making.

Since 2016, when the center opened, there has been a 46% improvement in the hospital's ability to accept patients with complex medical conditions from other hospitals around the region and country. The critical care team is dispatched 43 minutes sooner to pick up patients from outside hospitals. Beds are assigned to patients 38% faster (or 3.5 hours faster) after a decision is made to admit them from the emergency department and transfer delays from the operating room (after a procedure) are reduced by 83%. The center, indeed, is a great success.

Source:
Capacity Command Center Celebrates 5 Years of Improving Patient Safety, Access. (2021, April). Retrieved July 27, 2022, from Johns Hopkins Medicine website: https://www.hopkinsmedicine.org/news/articles/capacity-command-center-celebrates-5-years-of-improving-patient-safety-access

QUESTIONS

1. Review information online and discuss the state of capacity management of healthcare institutions, including hospitals in the United States, during the COVID-19 pandemic (focus on years 2020 and 2021).

2. What decision-making challenges do humans face when hit by a sudden, uncertain event such as a pandemic?

3. Discuss how intelligence generated by AI systems helps decisions in admitting patients, transporting patients, nursing, and providing specialized care in healthcare institutions.

4. How did technology and AI help Johns Hopkins deliver excellent outcomes and high-quality service to their patients?

5. How can other similar institutions improve their processes to deliver better outcomes for their patients?

QUESTIONS FOR DISCUSSION

1. Distinguish between normative and descriptive theories of decision-making.

2. Why is it difficult for humans to calculate probabilities or make decisions according to the theory of expected utility maximization?

3. List and briefly define simple heuristics, the rules of thumb that work as quick information shortcuts for human decision-making.

4. Explain a few cultural conditions that prime our brains.

5. Discuss in detail the concept of noise as described by Daniel Kahneman and his fellow researchers.

6. What types of machine models are better than humans in making decisions?

7. Discuss a few examples of situations when system and occasion noise affect human judgment.

8. List instances when you or someone you know made decisions purely based on intuition or emotion. Were those decisions good? Why or why not?

9. Explain the basic decision-making mechanism of computers. What are some physical and non-physical capabilities that computers leverage for decision-making?

10. What are some business use cases where AI is helping us improve the outcomes of our decisions while making the decision-making process more efficient?

11. What do you understand by the term embodied intelligence?

12. How do supervised and unsupervised machine learning algorithms help systems decide?

13. How does an artificial neural network's depth affect its performance in producing accurate results?

14. What is reinforcement learning? How do reinforcement learning systems learn specific behaviors?

15. Discuss the environments or situations in which humans make better decisions than machines.

REFERENCES

1. Briggs, R. A. (2019). Normative Theories of Rational Choice: Expected Utility. In E. N. Zalta (Ed.), *The Stanford Encyclopedia of Philosophy* (Fall 2019). Stanford, CA: Metaphysics Research Lab, Stanford University. Retrieved from https://plato.stanford.edu/archives/fall2019/entries/rationality-normative-utility/

2. The Sveriges Riksbank Prize in Economic Sciences in Memory of Alfred Nobel 2002. (n.d.). Retrieved February 18, 2022, from NobelPrize.org website: https://www.nobelprize.org/prizes/economic-sciences/2002/popular-information/

3. What is Behavioral Economics? | University of Chicago News. (n.d.). Retrieved January 20, 2022, from UChicago News website: https://news.uchicago.edu/explainer/what-is-behavioral-economics

4. Kahneman, D. (2011). *Thinking, Fast and Slow* (1st edition). New York, NY: Farrar, Straus and Giroux.

5. Tversky, A., & Kahneman, D. (1974). Judgment under uncertainty: heuristics and biases. *Science, 185*(4157), 1124–1131.

6. Desjardins, J. (2021, August 26). Every Single Cognitive Bias in One Infographic. Retrieved January 24, 2022, from Visual Capitalist website: https://www.visualcapitalist.com/every-single-cognitive-bias/

7. Kahneman, D., Sibony, O., & Sunstein, C. R. (2021). *Noise: A Flaw in Human Judgment*. New York, NY: Little, Brown Spark.

8. Gutnik, L. A., Hakimzada, A. F., Yoskowitz, N. A., & Patel, V. L. (2006). The role of emotion in decision-making: a cognitive neuroeconomic approach towards understanding sexual risk behavior. *Journal of Biomedical Informatics, 39*(6), 720–736.

9. Gupta, R., Koscik, T. R., Bechara, A., & Tranel, D. (2011). The amygdala and decision making. *Neuropsychologia, 49*(4), 760–766.

10. Bailey, R. (2018, March). The Limbic System and Our Emotions. Retrieved February 25, 2022, from ThoughtCo website: https://www.thoughtco.com/limbic-system-anatomy-373200

11. Camp, J. (n.d.). Decisions Are Largely Emotional, Not Logical. Retrieved March 2, 2022, from Big Think website: https://bigthink.com/personal-growth/decisions-are-emotional-not-logical-the-neuroscience-behind-decision-making/

12. Jarrett, C. (2014). The Neuroscience of Decision Making Explained in 30 Seconds. *Wired*. Retrieved from https://www.wired.com/2014/03/neuroscience-decision-making-explained-30-seconds/

13. He, S., & Shi, S.-H. (2017). Chapter 14 – Lineage-Dependent Electrical Synapse Formation in the Mammalian Neocortex. In J. Jing (Ed.), *Network Functions and Plasticity* (pp. 321–348). Cambridge, MA: Academic Press.

14. Jung, N., Wranke, C., Hamburger, K., & Knauff, M. (2014). How emotions affect logical reasoning: evidence from experiments with mood-manipulated participants, spider phobics, and people with exam anxiety. *Frontiers in Psychology, 5*, 570.

15. Leith, K. P. & Baumeister, R. F. (1996). Why do bad moods increase self-defeating behavior? Emotion, risk taking, and self-regulation. *Journal of Personality and Social Psychology, 71*(6), 1250–1267.

16. Case Western Reserve University. (2012, October 30). Empathy Represses Analytic Thought, and Vice Versa: Brain Physiology Limits Simultaneous Use of both Networks. *ScienceDaily*. Retrieved March 10, 2022 from www.sciencedaily.com/releases/2012/10/121030161416.htm

17. Bossaerts, P. & Murawski, C. (2015). From behavioural economics to neuroeconomics to decision neuroscience: the ascent of biology in research on human decision making. *Current Opinion in Behavioral Sciences, 5*, 37–42.

18. O'Callahan, T. (2010). What Is Neuroeconomics? Retrieved January 20, 2022, from Yale Insights website: https://insights.som.yale.edu/insights/what-is-neuroeconomics

19. Computer Hardware. (n.d.). Retrieved January 30, 2022, from web.stanford.edu website: https://web.stanford.edu/class/cs101/hardware-1.html

20. Reading: Computer Hardware | Introduction to Computer Applications and Concepts. (n.d.). Retrieved January 30, 2022, from https://courses.lumenlearning.com/zeliite115/chapter/reading-hardware-2/

21. Wolfgang, E. (2017). *Introduction to Artificial Intelligence* (2nd edition). Cham, Switzerland: Springer.

22. AlphaFold. (n.d.). Retrieved May 18, 2022, from DeepMind website: https://www.deepmind.com/research/highlighted-research/alphafold

23. Baidu. (2021). These Five AI Developments Will Shape 2021 and Beyond. Retrieved May 18, 2022, from MIT Technology Review website: https://www.technologyreview.com/2021/01/14/1016122/these-five-ai-developments-will-shape-2021-and-beyond/

24. DALL·E: Creating Images from Text. (2021, January 5). Retrieved May 18, 2022, from OpenAI website: https://openai.com/blog/dall-e/

25. Brown, S. (2021). Machine Learning, Explained. Retrieved February 2, 2022, from MIT Sloan website: https://mitsloan.mit.edu/ideas-made-to-matter/machine-learning-explained

26. Springboard, I. (2019, November 5). How Netflix's Recommendation Engine Works? Retrieved February 2, 2022, from Medium website: https://medium.com/@springboard_ind/how-netflixs-recommendation-engine-works-bd1ee381bf81

27. Marr, B. (2017). The Amazing Ways Spotify Uses Big Data, AI and Machine Learning to Drive Business Success. Retrieved February 2, 2022, from Forbes website: https://www.forbes.com/sites/bernardmarr/2017/10/30/the-amazing-ways-spotify-uses-big-data-ai-and-machine-learning-to-drive-business-success/

28. Audience Targeting Made Easier. (n.d.). Retrieved May 18, 2022, from Tellius website: https://www.tellius.com/use-cases/audience-targeting-made-easier/

29. Gupta, S. (n.d.). Customer Segmentation : RFM Clustering. Retrieved January 16, 2021, from Kaggle website: https://kaggle.com/code/shailaja4247/customer-segmentation-rfm-clustering

30. Fuloria, S. (2011) How Advanced Analytics Will Inform and Transform U.S. Retail. Cognizant Reports. Retrieved from http://www.cognizant.com/InsightsWhitepapers/How-Advanced-Analytics-Will-Inform-and-Transform-US-Retail.pdf.

31. Russell, S. & Norvig, P. (2020). *Artificial Intelligence: A Modern Approach* (4th edition). Hoboken, NJ: Pearson.

32. Kochenderfer, M. J., Wheeler, T. A., & Wray, K. (2022). *Algorithms for Decision Making.* London, UK: The MIT Press. https://algorithmsbook.com/

33. Nagabandi, A., Kahn, G., Fearing, R. S., & Levine, S. (2017). Neural Network Dynamics for Model-Based Deep Reinforcement Learning with Model-Free Fine-Tuning. University of California, Berkeley. Retrieved from https://arxiv.org/pdf/1708.02596.pdf

34. Part 2: Kinds of RL Algorithms – Spinning Up documentation. (n.d.). Retrieved July 27, 2022, from OpenAI Spinning Up website: https://spinningup.openai.com/en/latest/spinningup/rl_intro2.html

35. Mnih, V., Kavukcuoglu, K., Silver, D., Graves, A., Antonoglou, I., Wierstra, D., & Riedmiller, M. (n.d.). Playing Atari with Deep Reinforcement Learning. Deep Mind Technologies. Retrieved from https://www.cs.toronto.edu/~vmnih/docs/dqn.pdf

36. Jones, M. T. (2017, July 24). A Neural Networks Deep Dive. Retrieved February 3, 2022, from IBM Developer website: https://developer.ibm.com/articles/cc-cognitive-neural-networks-deep-dive/

37. What Are Neural Networks? (2021, August 3). Retrieved February 3, 2022, from IBM website: https://www.ibm.com/cloud/learn/neural-networks

38. Colson, E. (2019, July 8). What AI-Driven Decision Making Looks Like. *Harvard Business Review.* Retrieved from https://hbr.org/2019/07/what-ai-driven-decision-making-looks-like

CHAPTER 3

Systems and Technologies for Decision-Making

This chapter discusses DI from the system's perspective – how it sits within the organizational system and helps decision-making in various functions. We will discuss decision-making environments and how different subsystems, including humans and technologies, collaborate to support better decisions. Next, we will explore the group dynamics that affect the decision-making potential of human agents, followed by a section covering essential technologies used in AI-powered decision-making systems. Finally, technological systems used for assisting, supporting, augmenting, and automating decisions will be explained in detail.

ORGANIZATION AS A SYSTEM

A system is a mechanism formed by interdependent and interconnected components that create a complex whole. These components work together to achieve the system's overall goal(s). Due to the relationship dynamics, any change in one component affects all other components at different degrees, levels, and scales. The more significant the change, the bigger and more observable the effect would be. Our bodies are the systems, and so are our organizations.

Different organizational functions work together as various system components toward achieving common and shared goals. Think about

DOI: 10.1201/b23322-3

organizational units or departments that execute the functions of strategic planning, research and development, production, technology, operations, marketing, and human resources. Each of these entities is a separate system; some systems are more complex than others. It is just like how human bodies are designed – systems composed of different organs, each organ is a separate system and some are more complex than others. Decision-making is a critical business function and must be seen as an essential component of the organizational system. Nevertheless, decision-making is a system itself.

The open systems model of the firm postulates that any activity in the organization follows the process of taking inputs from the environment, transforming those inputs given the organizational practices and structure, creating outputs to meet stakeholders' needs, and using a feedback mechanism to improve the overall system.[1] All systems work in a similar fashion, including the decision-making system in the organization.

DECISION-MAKING SYSTEM IN THE ORGANIZATION

An organization's decision-making system aims to supply the right decision that helps the organization achieve its goals most effectively while also improving process efficiencies. Figure 3.1 demonstrates an organizational decision-making system with its components.

Before we proceed, it is important to visualize where this system sits in the organizational structure scheme. Organizations typically don't have a separate decision-making unit or department. Instead, each department or management level has its unique mechanism, the decision-making system. In a small, sole proprietary business, this system can be more centralized where a few people make all crucial decisions. Large companies will be decentralized, where each department (such as production, marketing, finance, and human resources) or management level (top, middle, bottom) will make decisions for their specific functional area or strategic focus.

Information, human agents (as decision-makers), and technologies are the key components of any decision-making system. The system takes information from the environment. Humans and technologies then work hand in hand through all the steps in the decision-making process we discussed in the previous chapter. Different decision-driving and restraining factors (environmental factors, capabilities, and constraints) affect different stages in the process. Finally, the decision is made and once implemented, it returns an action (or actions) that initiates specific change(s) in the environment. In Figure 3.1, the small triangles on the far right-hand

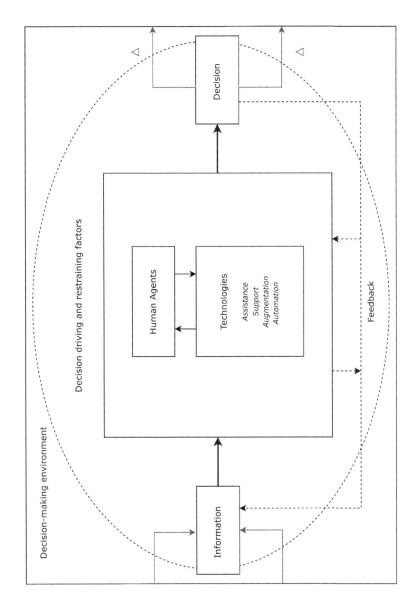

FIGURE 3.1   Organizational decision-making system

side demonstrate the change caused by the implementation of the decision. Decision-makers evaluate and improve the decision's performance using the feedback information.

The quality of the decisions made under the system depends on a few factors. The first and most important factor is data (information). It is necessary to ensure both the quality and quantity of data. If the systems are fed with poor quality data, they will not produce quality results – "garbage in, garbage out." Also, modern systems, especially ones that use machine learning, require lots of data to train models. You need sufficient data to support and justify your decision even if you are not using ML-based systems.

Human agents, including individuals, teams, and groups, make decisions on an organization's behalf. As discussed in the previous chapter, an individual's decisions can often be affected by their inherent biases and cognitive limitations. In addition, teams have their own issues and problems that affect their decision-making. We will discuss team issues in making decisions shortly in this chapter.

Technology, another essential component, includes different capabilities combined to create technological systems for decision assistance, support, augmentation, and automation. Most of these systems run on models that use a set of rules or heuristics to make decisions. As discussed in Chapter 2, these models can process and use much more information and produce more accurate decisions than humans. However, technology is not the answer to all decision problems. For example, our technological systems are far from perfect when it comes to processing information related to subjective experiences such as emotions. Moreover, the algorithm will likely produce faulty conclusions if the programmers' bias has affected its design. You cannot make fair and accurate decisions based on the insights produced by a biased algorithm.

The decisions in an organization are influenced by various factors concerning the business's political, economic, social-cultural, ecological, and legal environments. Given the context, these factors act as driving and restraining forces. For example, great access to market information, open-minded leadership, cutting-edge technology, and availability of resources could be your driving forces for many decisions. Restraining forces, however, constrain our decisions. For example, limited availability of funds for a specific project, time limitations (not having enough time to search for many alternatives), or talent scarcity could constrain many decisions in different ways. All these factors affect a system's decision-making potential.

Feedback is an essential element of the system that helps monitor, evaluate, and improve a decision's performance. Once implemented, a decision initiates a change in the environment. The information related to this change (the consequences of the decision) is fed back into the system through a well-defined feedback loop that is connected with all the important system components. Using information from the feedback loop, you can make changes to the decision right away or plan to implement necessary changes in the future. The feedback mechanism helps immensely in improving the quality of decisions.

In the following few sections, we will explore more details of each component of an organization's decision-making system – decision-making environments, human agents, technological systems, and technologies supporting decision-making systems.

Decision-Making Environments

The nature of decision-making environments and their states significantly impact decision-making systems' functioning. These are a kind of context under which a decision is made. Depending upon the demands and allowances of each environment, we decide what decision-making capabilities (humans and technologies) we should employ in the process of making and implementing decisions. Organizational decisions are usually made in the following types of environments:

- **Fully observable, partially observable, vs. unobservable:** a task or decision environment is fully observable if decision-making agents (humans and machines) are able to detect all the information relevant to the decision alternatives. For example, a situation where human workers can fully observe the process of assembling machine parts on a conveyor belt and decide the next steps accordingly.

    The environment would be partially observable if the information could only be detected partially. For example, you cannot completely observe or sense people's feelings and what they are planning to do next. Several factors, such as the presence of noise, inaccurate sensing, or missing pieces of information, might affect observability, making environments only partially observable.

    If no information relevant to the decision could be observed, it is unobservable. Examples include various events or phenomena from the quantum world, the force of gravity, people's desires, and their motives.

- **Deterministic vs. non-deterministic:** the environment is deterministic if the next state of the environment can be completely determined by the current state. For example, payment (next state) followed by the purchase of the product (current state). Otherwise, it is non-deterministic. Think about the response of an elephant upon its first arrival on Mars. Most real-life decision scenarios are, unfortunately, non-deterministic.

- **Single-agent vs. multiagent:** in a single-agent environment, one agent performs all the actions to maximize the outcome of their decision. Think about being left alone in a maze to find your way out in the best possible manner.

  In a multiagent scenario, more than one agent participates in decision-making. The agents encounter one of the three situations. One, each agent tries to maximize their own performance or outcomes by minimizing others. It is a competitive multiagent environment that can commonly be seen in competitive sports. Two, each agent tries to maximize the performance or outcomes of all agents. It is a cooperative, multiagent environment. For example, driving on the road and ensuring everyone is safe. Three, an agent tries to do both, cooperating while maximizing their own performance or outcomes. This is a partially multiagent environment. Parking a car in the space of your choice while ensuring other cars are not affected is a good example of this situation.

- **Episodic vs. sequential:** the episodic environment is when the agent's next action doesn't depend on the previous actions taken. A decision is one single atomic episode where the agent performs a single action based on specific information received (example: mail sorting). In the case of sequential environments, the previous decisions made by an agent might affect all future decisions, as in a game of chess.

- **Known vs. unknown:** the environment will be known if the decision outcomes or the probabilities of the outcome for all actions are given or known. If the outcomes or their probabilities are not given or are unknown, the environment is unknown.

- **Static vs. dynamic:** in static environments, the environment doesn't change, while the agent is still deliberating. Dynamic environments change with time, making it difficult for an agent to determine their next actions. The change could occur either due to external events outside the agent's control or the agent's previous decisions.

- **Discrete vs. continuous:** this classification relates to the *state* of the environment – its particular condition at a specific time. It is discrete when an environment has a finite number of distinct states or only a finite number of actions that can be performed. For example, in a chess game, you can only have a certain amount of states with limited moves. When the environment has a range of continuous values that change over time, it is continuous. Car driving happens in a continuous environment where drivers can decide to make any number of actions, such as which route to take, which vehicle to overtake, at what speed they should drive, or whether to change their destination.

- **Decision-making under certainty, uncertainty, and risk**[2]**:** when the future state of nature is certain, you are making a decision under certainty. Decision-makers know with certainty the consequence of every decision choice or alternative. So they naturally choose the alternative that results in the best outcome or maximizes their well-being. For example, you want to invest $1,000 for one year and have two alternatives. Alternative 1: open a saving account paying 4% interest. Alternative 2: invest in a government treasury bond paying 6% interest. If both these investments are guaranteed and secure, the treasury bond will certainly pay a higher return, $60, after one year.

 Now, when the future state of nature is unknown, it is decision-making under uncertainty. There are several possible outcomes for each choice or alternative and the probabilities of various outcomes are also unknown. For example, the probability that a republican will be president of the United States 120 years from now is unknown. In the case of decision-making under risk, there are several possible outcomes for each alternative but the probability of occurrence of each outcome is known. For example, the probability of rolling a two on a die is 1/6.

Decision environments significantly affect almost all aspects of organizational decision-making. Today, these environments are much more dynamic and hidden patterns sometimes cannot be observed. Therefore, a proper analysis of the environment is necessary during the early stages of the decision-making process.

Human Agents

As mentioned earlier, decision-makers in an organization could be individuals or groups of the individuals, such as teams. The dynamics of decision-making in groups are quite different from individual decision-making. Chapter 2 has already discussed how humans make decisions but it was mainly in the context of individuals and not groups. Most critical business decisions are made in a group or team environment.

There are various reasons we emphasize keeping humans in the loop when it comes to the crucial, most important business decisions. One of these reasons is that humans' knowledge is quite different and sometimes richer than machines. Our knowledge is everything we sense and learn with every passing moment of time. As a result, we can see a bigger picture and make better sense of things around us. In addition, as groups, we cooperate, coordinate, collaborate, and create *collective intelligence* – the total intelligence of a group that strengthens our decision-making even further.

Collective intelligence has helped manage even the world's most pressing problems, including the COVID-19 pandemic. Thousands of experts in different fields, institutions, and agencies collaborated to find the best ways to handle the challenges posed by COVID-19. Moreover, diversity enhances collective intelligence as people from diverse backgrounds contribute more creative ideas and insights.

Due to its multiple benefits, organizations are going out of their way to get people and groups to collaborate in building collective intelligence. One popular approach to involving outside parties is crowdsourcing – outsourcing the task of building intelligence to large groups of people (crowds). Many organizations, including Airbnb, Lego, Waze, Samsung, NASA, and Starbucks, use crowdsourcing to enhance their decision-making.

Another trend gaining significant attention today is *swarm intelligence* – the collective behavior of self-organized, decentralized, natural, or artificial systems. The colonies of ants and termites, organizational systems consisting of various computer programs, and multi-robot systems generate swarm intelligence that amplifies the decision-making ability of the system at large. AI companies are using swarm intelligence principles to design new AI systems that will revolutionize our decision-making environments in the most unprecedented ways.

Despite all the advantages and opportunities, group decision-making has its challenges. The following group dynamics play a crucial role in how effectively or ineffectively a group makes decisions.

- **Individual differences**: differences in cultural, demographic, and economic backgrounds, age, and race are some observable sources of diversity. What also affects group decision-making are the inherent and acquired individual differences such as personalities, attitudes, beliefs, values, experiences, qualifications, and skills. People face different types of conflicts due to these differences, which sometimes cannot be noticed but affect decision-making at the most granular level. For example, think about people who demonstrate incivility by being overly critical of others, ignoring others, or using flames in communication. Such behaviors block the team's ability to collaborate effectively and work cooperatively.

- **Leadership:** with the creation of a group, leadership emerges. People lose confidence in the group when they see poor leadership and a lack of direction. Although there are many skills that leaders must develop, creating an environment where people feel psychologically safe is paramount for successful leadership. Group members feel discouraged, hesitate in giving feedback, or avoid sharing ideas when leaders fail to ensure psychological safety.

- **Power and influence:** people gain power through different sources. Some people have a position advantage (legitimate power), some are experts, and some have more influence over others since they are more charismatic. Power affects group dynamics. People with more power influence team decisions more often and more significantly.

- **Groupthink:** in a group setting, people tend to agree with each other more quickly without exploring different alternatives. This tendency is called groupthink. There could be many reasons for groupthink but it happens largely due to group members' tendency to conform, bystander effect, fear of being laughed at, or feeling discouraged by others.

Today, we have new platforms that empower groups with cutting-edge solutions for group decision-making. Different types of AI-powered digital assistants, group support systems, online brainstorming, and several groupware tools are available in the market to augment human agents' capacity to make crucial business decisions.

SUPPORTING TECHNOLOGIES FOR MODERN DI SYSTEMS

In the previous chapter, we discussed the basic design of computer decision-making and explored AI, ML, and RL – the key enabling technologies that power various DI forms and systems. However, there are other technologies that are combined with the enabling technologies to create DI systems that help us make the most optimal decisions. These technologies can be called supporting technologies for modern DI systems and they are as follows:

AutoML

Manually deploying ML models into production is a resource-intensive and time-consuming task. AutoML solves this problem by automatically training models, making predictions, and generating insights for users to help them make better decisions. Most of the DI solutions available today use AutoML capabilities to generate automated insights for decision-making. AutoML, thus, is one of the most crucial technologies that powers key DI platforms.

The technology was developed to democratize AI and ML and allow businesses to gain better agility without the need for experts with extensive data science knowledge and programming skills. It makes ML available for all users while accelerating the decision-making process. AutoML also helps businesses avoid potential errors caused by manual work. We can build highly effective ML models using state-of-the-art technologies and advanced user interfaces in a few clicks.

Several AutoML solutions are available designed for self-service analytics, building, training, and deploying predictive models. Some solutions are focused on a specific industry area, such as the analysis of biomedical data, whereas others offer help in completing particular tasks such as hyperparameter optimization, algorithm configuration, architecture search, and automated deep learning. Some popular AutoML providers include DataRobot, Dataiku, Google Cloud AutoML, Enhencer, H2O, JADBio AutoML, and Akkio. AutoML will play a crucial role in shaping the future of DI. The application case in the Natural Language Processing (NLP) section is a good example of how integrated AutoML and NLP capabilities can enable businesses to solve critical problems.

Computer Vision

Intelligence in humans is generated through processing multiple inputs and one of the most fundamental inputs is visual information. Our brains receive visual input from our eyes which is processed in the brain to create knowledge albeit intelligence. Machines or computers needed similar capabilities to process visual information to make meaning of visual data. Therefore, computer vision technologies were developed to train computers on how to interpret and understand different types of visual information. It was in 1970 when a commercial computer used computer vision to interpret text using optical recognition. It is a field of AI that uses digital images and applies deep learning models to accurately identify and classify objects or features in those images.

A large volume of image data, computing capabilities, hardware design, and deep neural networks such as CNN enable computer vision to accurately detect and react to different visual inputs. The key computer vision techniques include image segmentation, object detection, facial recognition, edge detection, pattern detection, image classification, and feature matching. The models are mainly built to identify patterns, cues, or anomalies in data. In some automated DI systems, such patterns, anomalies, defects, or hazard cues generate automated responses prompting immediate action.

Google Cloud's Cloud AutoML Vision helps in creating custom ML models for image recognition with increased accuracy and faster turnaround time to production-ready models. Its drag-and-drop interface allows users to upload images, train models, and deploy them directly on the Google cloud.[3] The interface is designed to accelerate the pace of decision-making. It is way faster and easier to use than other similar technologies.

Computer vision technologies are used in a large number of applications today, including recommendation systems, autonomous vehicles, and robots, tracking wildlife populations, diagnosing disease, detecting parking occupancy, detecting pedestrian activity, monitoring road conditions, and analyzing X-Ray data. Computer vision helps systems expand their knowledge and use it to enhance a business's decision-making ability.

Audio Processing

Audio input is another important component of machine intelligence. It is quite common to see machines interacting and talking to us these days. For example, think about our interactions with digital assistants such as Siri and Alexa. So what is happening behind the scenes? It is the AI-enabled audio processing technology at work that processes audio signals or data extracted through digital devices. Different models are used to classify sounds, segment audio clips based on classes, and collect sound files related to similar content. Once the audio data is prepared for analysis, it goes through the annotation step, where it is segmented into layers, timestamps, and speakers. Specific methods such as audio transcription, also known as automatic speech recognition (ASR) or audio classification, are applied for analysis. ASR facilitates interactions between humans and technology by transcribing spoken audio into text.

Audio classification algorithms train models to learn to classify data under different labels. Therefore, data needs to be prepared with labels that can be differentiated. These technologies leverage NLP and deep neural network technologies to produce accurate outputs.[4] The common applications of audio analysis can be seen in virtual assistants, chatbots, voice-activated search functions, in-car command prompts, text-to-speech engines, meeting or call transcripts, enhanced security with voice recognition, phone directories, and translation services. They are also used in designing DI solutions that combine NLP with audio processing enabling users to ask ad hoc questions using their natural voice. Companies like Tellius are already incorporating these capabilities to make their platforms more user-friendly and responsive.

Natural Language Processing (NLP)

NLP processes human language expressed through text and spoken words to understand its meaning. Human language enters the system in the form of data (text or voice data) where computer algorithms, ML, and deep learning models automatically extract, classify, and label features of the data. A statistical likelihood is then assigned to each possible meaning of those elements. Deep learning models, including CNN, and RNN empower NLP models to learn more effectively and extract more accurate meanings from the massive volumes of data inserted in the system in all different formats. Some of the critical tasks that NLP performs are as follows[5]:

- **Speech recognition:** humans talk with varying emphasis and notations, quickly, slurring words together, using different accents, and with many more differences and imperfections. Speech recognition, also called speech-to-text, helps convert voice data into text data for applications that use voice commands or answer spoken questions.

- **Word sense disambiguation:** the process of selecting the meaning of a word that has multiple meanings, given a particular context. Through the process of semantic analysis, the model chooses the most suitable meaning of the word that fits the present situation or the context.

- **Corpus analysis:** understanding corpus, document structure, and preparing data as input for further analysis and model building.

- **Part of speech tagging:** determining the part of speech of a piece of text or a word in a given context. The process is also known as grammatical tagging.

- **Named entity recognition:** identifying words or phrases as useful entities.

- **Sentiment analysis:** extracting subjective qualities from text, including emotions, attitudes, sarcasm, suspicion, confusion, and more.

- **Co-reference resolution:** identifying when or if two words refer to the same entity.

- **Natural language generation:** producing natural language output by putting structured information into human language.

Today, NLP is used in a wide range of business applications. DI platforms use it to create functionalities that help users to ask questions using natural human language. NLP processes the words or voice data and provides the system with the most accurate meaning. The system then uses the information to output the most accurate and suitable solution or recommendation. Using natural language generation, DI platforms produce responses to users' queries in natural human language.

NLP is also used in spam detection to scan emails for language that indicates phishing or spam. Apple's Siri, Amazon's Alexa, and all similar voice assistants, chatbots, and virtual agents use speech recognition technology to recognize patterns in the human voice. These technologies have also revolutionized academic and business research in multiple areas. Text summarization uses huge volumes of text data to create summaries and synopses for research databases and indexes. Many businesses use social media sentiment analysis today to uncover hidden sentiments of their customers or stakeholders expressed on different social media platforms.

**APPLICATION CASE 3.1: CLOUD NATURAL LANGUAGE AND
CLOUD AUTOML TO AUTOMATE CONTENT CLASSIFICATION –
DATA-DRIVEN PUBLISHING AT MEREDITH DIGITAL[6]**

Meredith Corporation, one of the largest brand-powered media companies, owns some renowned brands, including PEOPLE, InStyle, Allrecipes,
Better Homes & Gardens, Martha Stewart Living, and Food & Wine. It is
known for service journalism and uses multiple platforms, including broad-
cast television, digital, print, mobile, and video, to provide trusted content
around a wide range of interest areas such as entertainment, food, home,
lifestyle, health, wellness, travel, and luxury. The company has successfully
grown its reputation and portfolio during more than a decade of digital
transformation. The company uses business intelligence technologies to
identify and respond to emerging content trends to create more relevant,
high-impact audience experiences.

It took them years to reach the unique level of content classification
maturity for Allrecipes with a manual content review process. Their teams
manually classified recipes and reviews to determine how the content would
appear in the navigation and search results and how it would help make
recommendations based on customers' choices and preferences. It was
manually cumbersome and not scalable to apply to all Meredith's brands.
Using Google Cloud's *AutoML Natural Language* solution, Meredith was
able to use ML to make content classification more repeatable and scalable
throughout its multiple businesses.

Meredith used entity detection and sentiment analysis to extract actionable insights on social media about user experience to identify new topics
of interest. AutoML Natural Language helped them monitor conversations
and discover topics that they were not aware of. The Natural Language
API helps in discovering syntax, entities, and sentiment in text. It classi-
fies text into a predefined set of categories. Meredith no more required
in-house ML expertise to train custom ML models to automatically predict
text categories. Content classification enabled advanced personalization
by allowing the connection of relevant terms and topics. For the Allrecipes
brand, they were able to develop and maintain a robust custom taxonomy
for content classification that used a controlled vocabulary of standardized
terms to monitor food trends.

AutoML Natural Language helped Meredith build readership and loyalty
by creating more relevant and engaging customer experiences. They were
able to classify text content across the entire portfolio of media properties
in months vs. years. By gaining greater awareness of new trends and customer interests, Meredith was able to stay on top of trends. The technology
has shortened their time to insight with automated content classification
based on specific business needs, their custom taxonomy, and custom
models. The speed at which Meredith is moving now is phenomenal.

TECHNOLOGICAL SYSTEMS FOR DECISION-MAKING

Technologies we discussed so far work through different types of technological systems designed for specific purposes. For example, an industrial robot designed as an intelligent agent uses reinforcement learning combined with other technologies to learn from its environment and execute its actions. The robot itself is a technological system, an integrated whole made of various physical and non-physical components that can be employed to automate decisions.

In this section, we will learn about decision support systems (DSSs) and intelligent agents as technological systems that aid decision-making in different contexts. Where DSSs are mainly used for decision support (although more advanced DSSs can even augment decisions), intelligent systems are designed with capabilities that support all forms of DI – decision assistance, support, augmentation, and automation.

Decision Support Systems

DSSs are considered an important component of the decision-making system in any organization. They are one of the most common DI tools used to support decisions of specific types. DSS is a type of information system that helps decision-makers make more informed decisions. These systems have been around for a long time. One of the very first practical DSSs was designed in the late 1960s. As technology advanced, so did DSSs.

The capabilities embedded in DSS help the system gather and analyze volumes of data to compile comprehensive information that serves as the basis of decision-making. Some of the key applications of DSSs can be seen in medical diagnosis, revenue projections, crop planning, inventory management, and digital marketing. In fact, DSS can be tailored for any industry or type of business.

Businesses use different types of DSSs based on the kind of support they want. For example, if your company wants human decision-makers to analyze every piece of information themselves, you might consider using a manual DSS. However, if they seek to optimize their inventory decisions that require the deployment of highly accurate computer models, they might select using an intelligent DSS. Let's discuss different types of DSSs designed to serve different purposes.[7]

- **Manual DSS:** often, managers need to get involved in the analysis that requires the human eye at every step. A manual approach to decision support or manual DSS is used in such cases. For example, think about managers performing a SWOT analysis, cost-benefit analysis, or creating decision matrixes for strategic decisions. The manual DSS could be an individual or a team responsible for collecting, analyzing, assessing, synthesizing, and compiling information to support decisions.

- **Hybrid DSS:** it uses a combination of different approaches and technologies to produce the information sought. Depending upon the need, they can integrate technologies as simple as spreadsheets to the most complex forecasting models. The term *hybrid* is quite broad and so are hybrid DSSs. They could be a hybrid form of any two or more forms of other DSSs. Many organizations, including healthcare institutions today, are using hybrid DSSs for various decisions.

- **Data-driven DSS:** it allows organizations to use current and historical, internal, and external data to provide information on important decisions. As a user inputs a query, information is processed with data mining techniques to generate answers for specific questions or queries.

- **Document-driven DSS:** it retrieves unstructured information from different sources, including webpages, search engines, and documents in databases. In fact, whenever we use an internet search engine, we use a document-driven DSS that is designed to find documents based on a specific search term or a set of keywords.

- **Model-driven DSS:** it uses information (data and parameters) provided by the users to run models that help generate effective insights for decision-making. They use complex, quantitative models to analyze the information and provide comprehensive results that humans can understand and use conveniently. These DSSs are most suitable for tasks that require the application of sophisticated mathematical models such as scheduling, decision analysis, financial modeling, and optimization.

- **Knowledge-driven DSS:** designed for specialized tasks, these DSSs generally provide suggestions and recommendations for decisions. They use an organization's knowledge management system and data mining techniques such as diagnosis, predictions, and classification to produce results for decision-makers. A product selection software is a good example of knowledge-driven DSS.

- **Communication-driven DSS:** it supports communication and collaboration across various units of the organization. Different types of collaboration software, chats, instant messaging, and even email systems come under this category. They are mostly targeted at internal teams that need collaboration to perform different tasks and make decisions as a group. Team members can share tools that allow multiple people to communicate digitally and work together cohesively on a project.

- **Intelligent Decision Support System (IDSS):** one of the most conspicuous examples of intelligent agents, IDSSs use AI capabilities for data mining to identify patterns and trends, analyze problems, and sometimes even make recommendations (the following section discusses the concept of intelligent agents in detail). Mimicking human capabilities as close as possible, IDSSs can produce effective results even in the most complex and uncertain environments. Advanced ML algorithms combined with many other tools such as case-based reasoning, adaptive reasoning, fuzzy logic, multiattribute decision-making (MADM), multiattribute utility theory (MAUT), and sensitivity analysis allow IDSSs to process large amounts of data to solve various problems in real-time. As a result, many industries are using IDSSs for many applications. Some of these applications and use cases include:

  - Predictive maintenance: factories run more efficiently as they identify supply shortages, eliminate unnecessary maintenance, increase capacity, and prevent potential dysfunction.

  - Image processing: the system pre-selects the images so radiologists can detect cancer faster and more accurately.

  - Optimization: mathematical models help factory managers optimize inventory to avoid issues such as stockouts, backorders, and overstocking, allowing managing costs and meeting demand simultaneously.

  - Simulation: models imitating real-world scenarios such as virtual patient simulators that mimic real medical cases on virtual patients help decision-makers enhance their reasoning and decision-making. A variety of augmented reality simulators are being developed to simulate medical learning practices in safe environments.

- Anomaly detection: detect fraud with credit cards, insurance, and bank accounts. Behavioral biometrics powered by ML detects anomalies in consumer spending in real-time, triggering warnings and blocking suspicious action in many situations.

- Facial recognition: cameras and sensors installed in some vehicles help the system identify driver fatigue or distraction signs. The system then sends a warning signal to drivers so they can make decisions instantly to protect themselves and others on the road.

- Forecasting: weather forecasting systems and apps help policymakers create better disaster prevention and recovery plans.

- Recommender systems: streaming services, social media, and e-commerce websites use these systems to help users make faster decisions about their purchases and entertainment choices.

Intelligent Agents

As explained in Chapter 1, intelligent agents mimic human decision-making and action-taking mechanisms. An intelligent agent is a system of integrated subsystems that enable these agents to work autonomously with little or no human intervention. These subsystems are also called sub-agents since they perform specific tasks to ensure that the system as a whole achieves its goals successfully. Think about the human body as an intelligent agent made of subsystems, each responsible for a specific task – the nervous system, muscular system, endocrine system, cardiovascular system, digestive system, lymphatic system, and more. Each subsystem works in coordination with others to ensure that the body keeps functioning healthily. AI-powered intelligent agents make decisions just like humans. They perceive their environment with incoming data, process (analyze, compare, synthesize, and evaluate) the information using different mechanisms, make decisions, and take actions autonomously. Many of these systems are designed to improve their performance through learning and experience.

Intelligent agents could be physical systems, including industrial robots, autonomous vehicles, and IoT devices such as thermostat systems installed in our houses. They could also be non-physical systems built into computer programs or software, such as IDSSs, chatbots, digital game players, and virtual assistants. Some of the cutting-edge DI platforms and solutions discussed in Chapter 6 are non-physical intelligent agents designed to perform different decision-making tasks autonomously.

AI-driven robo-advisors are another excellent example of intelligent agents. As PWC[8] informs AI is primarily taking the shape of support systems for investment decisions. Trained with thousands of priorly given advice, robo-advisors make highly effective recommendations with options adjusted to a user's goals. At the retail level, they are the "outsourcees" of investment advice. These robo-advisors are nothing but software running economic models in the application's background. Using trading algorithms, they provide online portfolio management with minimal human intervention.

In the following subsections, we will discuss different kinds of intelligent agents and explore recommender systems, one of the most popular DI tools and AI agents used by modern companies today. Intelligent agents will be addressed as agents from here on.

KINDS OF INTELLIGENT AGENTS

An agent's decision-making ability is affected by the type of percepts it receives. Russel and Norvig[9] define percept as the content an agent's sensors perceive. The percept sequence in an agent's design is the complete history of everything that an agent has ever perceived. Agent's decision in any given situation is determined by their percept sequence and all the knowledge the agents possess. Two essential components for these agents to function are the agent's architecture and the agent program. Agent architecture includes onboard computers, sensors, processors, circuits, etc. The architecture makes the percepts (information) received from sensors available to the program, runs the program, and then feeds the action choices of the program to the actuators that finally execute the decision or action. Agent programs implement the agent's function: an action the agent is supposed to take. The design of the agent is highly affected by the nature of the task environment – the problem scenarios where decision agents are used as solutions: decision environments discussed earlier in this chapter could be considered different types of task environments. According to Russel and Norvig,[9] the four basic kinds of agent programs that represent the principles underlying most of (almost all) the agents are as follows:

1. **Simple reflex agents:** the simplest of all, these agents ignore all the percept history and select actions based on current percept only. A good example of a simple reflex agent would be a robot that is

programmed to pick up and remove defective machine parts from the conveyor belt in a machine manufacturing factory. It doesn't matter how many parts it picked before (percept history). When its sensors see the defective part, they initiate the action to remove that part from the belt. Simple reflex agents are mostly designed on if-then or if-then-else heuristics. However, it is also possible to add different conditions depending upon the purpose the agent is built to accomplish. For these agents to function successfully, the environment must be fully observable. In our example, the robot's sensors register all the parts that pass through the conveyor belt. Therefore, the environment is fully observable.

2. **Model-based reflex agents:** these agents base their decisions on an internal model created through percept history. Model-based reflex agents are designed to work in partially observable environments. The agent maintains an internal state, the part of the world it cannot see now or the information that is not evident in the current percept. They keep track of the current state and then use an internal model (*"how the world works"*) to choose the action the same way as a simple reflex agent.

   A good example of a model-based reflex agent would be a car driving agent or an autonomous car. Imagine a few cars stopping simultaneously as the traffic light turns red. How would an agent decide at what distance it needs to start braking? The current percepts might inform the system what other cars on the road are doing. Still, they might not provide information on many other aspects that are not observable at present. Think about suddenly appearing puddles on the road, a rash driver changing lanes, or a teenager jaywalking. In cases like these, internal models come handy to inform an agent's decision. The agent will use both current percepts and the model based on percept history to make the braking decision.

3. **Goal-based agents:** goal-based agents use a similar programming structure as model-based reflex agents. The decisions of these agents, however, are based on goal information that describes the desired outcome the agent should achieve. It is not always enough to know the current state and even the model of the world. If an agent is expected to achieve a particular goal, it needs that information coded in its program. Let's get back to the example of an autonomous car. If the car stops at a junction, how will it decide whether to turn left,

right, or move straight on? The correct decision will depend on where the car is desired or expected to get to – its goal.

It is easy to program these agents when action selection is straightforward. It can be trickier when the agent must make multiple decisions in a long sequence, where each current decision affects the next decision. To help agents make decisions in such complex situations, search and planning algorithms are used.[10]

4. **Utility-based agents:** utility-based agents use utility measurement, a measure of success at a given state. They can choose the best alternative when there are multiple alternatives available. Goals direct an agent's behavior but it doesn't ensure the agent demonstrates the best behavior possible. For example, many action sequences in the agent's program will get the autonomous car to its destination. A simple goal-based agent will guarantee the arrival at the destination but it might not ensure that the car arrives quickly and safely and takes the most cost-effective route. Arriving quicker, safer, and in the most cost-efficient manner could be considered the desirable way (measures of success) since it results in a happy state. In economics, this happy state is called utility. In our example, the agent's utility function will explain all the desirable ways of getting to the destination.

The utility function essentially internalizes the agent's performance measures. Since utility-based agents are flexible and adaptive to changing environments, they could be both model-based and model-free. They can make rational decisions even when goals are inadequate. In the real world, decision-making under uncertainty is ubiquitous since environments are not completely observable and are non-deterministic. In such scenarios, utility-based agents choose the action that maximizes the expected utility of the action outcomes.

When the learning element is introduced to the agent's design, it can learn from its experiences, analyze performance, and even improve its own performance. The intelligence of the agent is mainly embodied in its ability to make decisions. Building the right action-selection function, therefore, is a crucial task in designing agent programs. In the next chapter, we will discuss how an agent can maximize its expected utility by following the basic principles of decision theory.

Recommender Systems

Most big companies today use recommendation systems to enhance customer experience. Amazon, Netflix, YouTube, Google Play Store, and Spotify are just a few examples of such companies. Every time you go on these platforms, you see some specific content or product suggestions. It makes your browsing easier and helps you find the content you wouldn't have thought to look for on your own. Their recommendation systems are working in the background generating these recommendations for you. These systems are intelligent agents that use ML technologies to help users decide, helping companies grow their revenue through enhanced customer experience.

In technological terms, a recommender system is an information filtering system designed to predict user preferences based on past information and make recommendations. These systems use different methods to filter the information and generate the most suitable recommendations. *Content-based filtering* uses the content of the previously searched items by the user. When you search for particular content, it is tagged by the system using certain keywords based on which the system makes predictions. *Collaborative filtering* uses the preferences of a group of users to make predictions and recommendations on unknown preferences of other users. This means that the system is predicting your preferences based on the interests and preferences of other similar users to make recommendations.

Item-based collaborative filtering (item-to-item) uses user ratings or information about the positive interaction of the user with a particular item to make recommendations for similar items. For example, the system will suggest you buy an item similar to that you have previously purchased. The system calculates the similarity scores based on which it makes predictions and recommendations on the user's preference for a specific item. In comparison, *user-based collaborative filtering* predicts whether the target user will prefer the item based on the ratings given to that item by other similar users. For example, the system will find users with similar tastes as yours and then use their preferences and ratings to make recommendations for you.

The case study at the end of this chapter informs how recommendation systems can be created using innovative filtering techniques with deep learning algorithms. It is important to note that a simple recommendation system can be built using classical ML tools. However, deep learning is the most suitable for creating models that use large volumes of unstructured data and must run at scale.

CONCLUSION

In order to understand decision-making in the organizational context, it is essential to see it from the system's perspective. An organization is a system where decision-making works as a subsystem responsible for ensuring that decisions are made most effectively and efficiently. In addition to other components, human agents and technologies are two key components of an organization's decision-making system. Human agents make decisions individually and in groups; various dynamics affect their decisions' quality. Similarly, different technological capabilities are combined to assist, support, augment, and automate decision-making. Decision environments today are very different from the environment of the past. Today, we make decisions under a high level of complexity and uncertainty. As technology advanced, we moved from Boolean logic to probabilistic reasoning. With big data innovations, we could use insurmountable amounts of data that made machine learning possible and more effective.

Due to the requirements of new decision environments and the technological capabilities available, we created more advanced technological systems capable of performing multiple tasks that help us make better decisions. Among other capabilities, these systems include DSSs and intelligent agents that enhance an organization's decision-making by producing valuable information, generating insights and recommendations, making decisions, and acting on behalf of human agents. Most of the commercial decision intelligence solutions available today can be considered intelligent agents.

It is important to understand that a system cannot function well in the absence of the right management and leadership. Decision-making systems require managers and leaders who are able to orchestrate different components and organize decision-making resources effectively. The system needs to be monitored regularly for feedback so the right action can be taken at the right time to avoid failures or improvise. The managers must know and understand the system, its components, and the processes that affect the system's functioning. In addition, they also require social-emotional skills to collaborate with others while making decisions in groups and teams. DI is the very foundation of this system, and when managed successfully, it can become a great source of competitive advantage for businesses.

CASE STUDY: RECOMMENDER SYSTEM FOR COVID-19 RESEARCH – INNOVATIVE DEEP NEURAL NETWORK MODELS

The COVID-19 pandemic will be marked as one of history's deadliest events. By August 2022, more than 6.41 million people had died of COVID-19 worldwide. To manage the spread of such disease, its complications, consequences, and future prevention, we need a better understanding of all the aspects related to the disease. This calls for deeper and wider academic research performed by researchers with different expertise and in multiple contexts at various institutions.

In March 2020, CORD-19 Research Dataset was launched in response to a request from the White House's Office of Science and Technology Policy to promote COVID-19 research. CORD-19 is a collection of over 45,000 scholarly articles (over 33,000 full-text) on a wide range of COVID-19-related topics. This free resource has already been downloaded over 200,000 times and serves as the basis of many COVID-19-related analyses.[11]

Microsoft collaborated with AI2, the NLM at the NIH, and other prestigious research institutions to empower AI researchers worldwide with text and data mining tools to accelerate and support COVID-19 research. Microsoft's research team developed a use case project to help researchers in the healthcare domain find relevant articles related to COVID-19. Among other important information, the project informs researchers on how to create an effective recommendation system using the knowledge graph, classify topics of a publication, use relevant APIs to understand topics of academic text, recommend related papers for researchers based on their citation history, and operationalize knowledge graph-based recommender system with right tools and platforms. The step-by-step process of developing a recommender system is as follows:

First, data is prepared for two tasks – user-to-paper recommendations and item-to-item recommendations. Then, pre-train the embeddings, the process of training word embeddings, and entity embeddings for deep knowledge-aware network (*DKN*) initializations. DKN, a content-based deep recommendation framework, is used for click-through rate (CTR) prediction that substitutes traditional ID-based collaborative filtering. It incorporates knowledge graph representation into content recommendations and uses an attention module to dynamically calculate a user's aggregated historical representations. DKN's main component is knowledge-aware convolutional neural network (*KCNN*), a multi-channel and word-entity-aligned network that fuses semantic and knowledge-level representations of content. KCNN helps in treating words and entities as multiple channels. It explicitly keeps and maintains their alignment relationship during convolution. To encode entities into embedding vectors, a graph embedding model is then used. DKN will use both entity embeddings and context embeddings.

In the next step, hyperparameters are created and the DKN model is trained and tested. Knowledge-aware, item-to-item recommendations using DKN with organized training and validation instances are then executed. After the model is trained, we can get document embeddings through the document embedding inference API. Next, user-to-item recommendations will run. For this execution, you use *LightGCN*, a simple, linear, and neat graph convolution network (GCN) model for recommendations. In this simplified convolution, only the normalized sum of neighbor embeddings is performed toward the next layer removing other operations like self-connection, feature transformation, and non-linear activation. In *Layer Combination* at each layer, we sum over the embeddings to obtain the final representations. After we run the model, its performance is compared against the performance of the DKN model by making predictions on the same test set. To do so, we infer the user/item embeddings and then compute the similarity scores between each pair of user-item in the test set.

The system will now need to be operationalized. It is when you deploy the whole pipeline into the infrastructure to make sure that it is ready to use and serve its purpose. Today, there are a variety of platform services available to help businesses operationalize these systems. Depending upon their needs, businesses can choose from a wide variety of products and platforms available in the market. Pinterest uses PinSage, their highly scalable graph convolutional network for GCN-based recommendation system that is capable of learning embeddings for nodes in web-scale graphs with millions of objects. Microsoft Azure can be used to build, deploy, and test recommender systems conveniently. Among other features, it offers hyperparameter tuning, tracking, and monitoring metrics, scaling up and out, deploying web service to Azure Kubernetes Service, and submitting pipelines.

The knowledge-graph-based models can be applied to multiple industrial applications. Retail companies such as eBay, Alibaba, and Amazon are using them to enhance customer experience, create more targeted marketing campaigns, and for digital assistance. Finance companies such as Bloomberg and MIT-IBM Watson AI Lab use these models for anti-money laundering, fraud detection, and "Know-Your-Client" applications. They are also popular among public goods and internet-based companies such as Microsoft, Pinterest, Facebook, LinkedIn, Google, Airbnb, and Uber.

Using knowledge-graph-based recommendation systems, we can change revolutionize academic research in multiple domains. New knowledge must be developed to devise preventative and curative strategies for catastrophic events such as COVID-19, based on numerous pieces of scholarly research. In today's world of information overload, it is difficult for researchers to decide which scholarly publications, papers, and articles they should select to support their studies.

According to the latest research performed by Microsoft Academic Graph (MAG) team, there are more than one million papers published every month, equivalent to a new paper published every 2.6 seconds. It is beyond the human cognitive capability to read all the research papers relevant to a specific topic such as COVID-19. Deep learning technologies, including neural networks, can help in creating intelligent recommendation systems that will allow researchers to make quick and effective decisions on the most suitable reading materials for their work. It will not only accelerate the pace of their research but will also help in reducing their cognitive load, enabling them to utilize their cognitive resources to perform tasks that are more significant and valuable for research.

Sources:
Wang, H., Zhang, F., Xie, X., & Guo, M. (2018). DKN: Deep Knowledge-Aware Network for News Recommendation. *Proceedings of the 2018 World Wide Web Conference on World Wide Web – WWW '18*, 1835–1844. https://doi.org/10.1145/3178876.3186175

Fierro, M. (2022, April). Recommenders. Retrieved from GitHub website: https://github.com/microsoft/recommenders

Association for Computing Machinery (ACM). (2020, December 18). *KDD 2020: Hands-On Tutorials:* In Search for a Cure Recommendation with Knowledge Graph on CORD-19. Retrieved from https://www.youtube.com/watch?v=4IXgVsDXPDA

QUESTIONS

1. Search the internet to learn more about the knowledge graphs introduced by Microsoft. How does a knowledge graph help communicate and codify knowledge in the organizational system?

2. Summarize the step-by-step process of building a recommender system as directed by this project.

3. Explain in detail five use cases of knowledge graph-based recommendation systems. Discuss the benefits and drawbacks (or limitations) of these systems for each use case.

QUESTIONS FOR DISCUSSION

1. Explain the concept of organization as a system.

2. How do you see decision-making as one of the essential systems in an organization?

3. What is the open systems model of the firm?

4. Discuss all the components of a decision-making system in a typical organization.

5. List the factors that affect the quality of decisions in different organizational contexts.

6. Explain how human agents and technologies complement each other within the system of decision-making and how they collaborate to enhance the organization's decision-making potential.

7. What is the role of feedback in improving the quality of decisions?

8. List five technologies, solutions, or applications that help at each decision assistance, support, augmentation, and automation level of DI.

9. Do some research to familiarize yourself with Microsoft Sharepoint. At what level of DI (assisting, support, augmentation, automation) does Microsoft Sharepoint help?

10. Discuss some common decision-driving and restraining factors for financial investment decisions.

11. Explain the concept of an agent in AI.

12. Describe different types of decision-making environments with the help of suitable examples.

13. What are the challenges for decision-makers in a group setting?

14. How do AutoML, computer vision, audio processing, and NLP technologies help create better DI systems?

15. Compare IDSSs against the traditional DSSs.

16. What do you understand by the term intelligent agent? Discuss different kinds of intelligent agents.

17. Give examples of at least five large companies that use recommender systems for different purposes. Try using examples that are not already used in this chapter.

18. How do you see the future of decision-making as more innovative and advanced technological systems are introduced for DI?

REFERENCES

1. Luhman, J. T. & Cunliffe, A. L. (2013). Systems Theory. In *Key Concepts in Organization Theory* (pp. 167–170). London, UK: SAGE Publications Ltd.
2. Render, B., Stair Jr., Ralph. M., Hanna, M. E., & Hale, T. S. (2018). *Quantitative Analysis for Management, 13th Edition*. New York, NY: Pearson.
3. Li, F.-F., & Li, J. (2018, January 17). Cloud AutoML: Making AI Accessible to Every Business. Retrieved May 23, 2022, from Google website: https://blog.google/products/google-cloud/cloud-automl-making-ai-accessible-every-business/
4. An Introduction to Audio, Speech, and Language Processing. (2021, April 22). Retrieved May 24, 2022, from Appen website: https://appen.com/blog/an-introduction-to-audio-speech-and-language-processing/
5. What is Natural Language Processing? (2021, August 16). Retrieved May 24, 2022, from IBM website: https://www.ibm.com/cloud/learn/natural-language-processing
6. Meredith Corporation Case Study. (n.d.). Retrieved May 24, 2022, from Google Cloud website: https://cloud.google.com/customers/meredith
7. Decision Support System Examples to Guide Decision-Making. (n.d.). Retrieved July 31, 2022, from Indeed Career Guide website: https://www.indeed.com/career-advice/career-development/decision-support-system-examples
8. AI-Powered Decision Support Systems, What Are They? (2020, September 18). Retrieved March 10, 2022, from THE BLOG pwc website: https://blog.pwc.lu/ai-powered-decision-support-systems-what-are-they/
9. Russell, S. & Norvig, P. (2020). *Artificial Intelligence: A Modern Approach, 4th Edition*. Hoboken, NJ: Pearson.
10. Dragoni, M. (2020, 2021). Fundamentals of Artificial Intelligence. Retrieved from http://www.maurodragoni.com/teaching/fai/material/2020-2021/LAB-01-02-Intro-IntelligentAgents.pdf
11. Zhang, L., Shen, I., Lian, J., Wu, C.-H., Gonzales, M., & Argyriou, A. (2018). In Search For A Cure: Recommendation with Knowledge Graph on CORD-19. Retrieved May 19, 2022, from GitHub website: https://kdd2020tutorial.github.io/cord19recommender/

CHAPTER 4

Intelligent Agents

Theoretical Foundations

So far, we have been focusing on fundamental concepts of DI with great emphasis on DI technologies. One of the most promising technological systems for DI is intelligent agents. An agent's decision-making potential depends on its architecture. This chapter unveils how AI agents are designed to make simple and complex decisions in different environments. Since we have already covered technologies running these agents in the previous chapters, we will now focus on the theoretical foundations that inspire intelligent agents' architecture. Several concepts from economics and mathematics will be discussed that serve as the foundation element of any agent's program. We will also cover multiagent decision-making and how intelligent agents make decisions with and in the presence of other agents. Knowing the intricacies of intelligent agents' makeup will help you better understand how they make rational decisions autonomously.

MULTIDISCIPLINARITY OF INTELLIGENT AGENTS

Intelligent agents are designed with a multidisciplinary approach. A program sits at the core of an agent's design and helps the agent implement its function through instructions. These instructions use theoretical concepts from multiple disciplines (mainly economics, mathematics, and psychology), enabling the agent to make optimal decisions.

Decision theory is used to build rational agents that make decisions considering all possible actions and choosing the one that leads to the best-expected outcome. According to Russel and Norvig,[1] decision theory combines probability theory (that describes what an agent should believe based on some evidence) and utility theory (that describes what an agent wants) together to describe what an agent should do. Two key branches of decision theory are descriptive and normative theories, which we discussed briefly in Chapter 2.

Where descriptive theories (including the famous prospect theory) explain how people *do* make decisions, normative theories tell us how people *should* make decisions. Human agents make decisions as explained in descriptive theories in behavioral economics. However (as discussed before), their decisions are often affected by heuristics, biases, and noise. To avoid the pitfalls of human decision-making, we use normative theories to design intelligent agents that make decisions faster, more accurately, rationally, and effectively.

Normative theories use concepts of the utility function extensively. Utility can be explained as satisfaction or happiness we derive from owning, doing, or using something. It can be considered the numeric representation of our preferences. The utility function is a mathematical notation using which we can rank-order our preferences where larger numbers indicate preferred choices. In general, the utility function is expressed as a function of quantities. The function is denoted differently in different situations. For example, if an agent prefers one action (a1) vs. another (a2), the utility function will be U (a1, a2). If two actions (a3 and a4) are perfect substitutes for each other, the utility function would be U (a3, a4) = a3 + a4.[2]

Expected utility theory is a predominant normative theory of rational choice that provides a way of ranking the actions based on how choice-worthy each action is. The higher the expected utility of the action, the better it is to choose that action. Expected utility theory principles are incorporated in the design of various decision-making agents today.

The expected utility concept represents the agent's preference over risky actions where the outcome is uncertain. The agent's preferences can be explained by a utility function that assigns a single number expressing the desirability of a state. The expected utility of an action (given the evidence) is the average utility value of the outcomes that are weighted by the probability that the outcome occurs. In the following sections, we will discuss these concepts with the help of different examples. Let's first explore how to use normative theory principles to design agents for simple and complex decisions.

AGENTS FOR SIMPLE DECISIONS

Simple decisions in this context are rational choices that an agent makes in an uncertain, episodic environment (the next episode doesn't depend on the actions taken in previous episodes) that maximizes the expected utility. Let us discuss this with the help of an example.[3]

A university's decision support system (agent) is facing a simple decision-making situation: the agent needs to decide the best course option a student should enroll in from a range of alternative courses in order to make a suitable recommendation. The agent's goal is to seek maximum happiness (expected utility). The expected utility will be determined based on the student's success in the recommended course.

This decision-making situation comprises:

- A set of possible actions Val(A) = {a¹,...,aᴷ}

- A set of states of the world Val(S) = {s¹,...,sᴺ}

- A distribution P(S|A)

- A utility function U(S|A)

In this situation, the agent is expected to choose an *action* from different course alternatives {a¹,...,aᴷ}. There is a set of *states of the world* {s¹,...,sᴺ} (all the possible states that might come about). Then, we have the probability of state *s* conditional on action *a* – P(S|A). The probability will be affected by many factors, some of which are possibly out of the agent's control (such as the student not submitting assignments or doesn't have the aptitude required for the course).

Finally, we have the equation that defines the agent's preferences: U(S|A). For example, the utility (U) could be – very happy, moderately happy, or not happy. The agent evaluates the merits of different actions by assigning a numerical utility to each action. The equation tells if an agent takes action A and has a particular state of the world (S), how happy the agent will become (the higher the number of utility, the happier the agent).

The happiness here is related to the student's success in the course (they pass the course with good grades). The notion of expected utility for this decision problem can be explained as follows:

$$\text{EU}\left[a\right] = \sum_s P\!\left(s|a\right) \text{U}\!\left(s,a\right)$$

The expected utility of this decision problem, given the action a, can be calculated by summing up all possible states of the world, the probability of the state, given the action multiplied by the utility of the state-action pair. The expected utility will represent the overall happiness that the agent gets on average in this decision-making situation.

According to the principle of maximum expected utility (MEU), the rational choice for the agent is to choose an action that maximizes the agent's expected utility:

$$a^* = \operatorname*{argmax}_a EU[a]$$

The agent's purpose here is to calculate various quantities and choose the action (a^*) that maximizes the expected utility. We will discuss MEU further with an example in the next section.

We can design decision-theoretic agents to help humans solve simple problems by figuring out their utility functions. This process is called preference elicitation and involves presenting choices to humans and using the observed preferences to determine underlying utility functions. In the real world, there is no absolute scale for such utilities. However, as explained by Russel and Norvig,[1] we can still establish a reasonable scale on which utilities can be recorded and compared.

Decision Networks

Also called influential diagrams, decision networks extend the Bayesian network by adding utility nodes and decision nodes, allowing for reasoning about the agent's actions and utility. They are the graphic representation of decision problems that require decision-making under uncertainty. Decision networks are most appropriate for finite sequential problems in a deterministic environment. Through the decision networks, you can get information on the agent's current state, its possible actions, the possible outcomes of the actions, and the utility of the actions.

Decision networks use three types of nodes.

1. Chance nodes: Represented as oval-shaped nodes, these nodes contain conditional probabilities included in the problem's conditional probability tables (CPT). The probabilities depend on the state of the parent nodes.

2. Decision nodes: These square-shaped nodes represent alternatives or options available to the agent.

3. Utility nodes: These nodes are diamond-shaped and represent the overall utility based on the states of the parent nodes.

Decision networks are built on the assumption that the agent remembers all past observations and decisions. The *value of the information* that the agent has (or what it remembers) plays a crucial role in the creation of decision networks. Let's discuss how to create decision networks with the following example:

You run a travel agency and your business is planning to launch a new vacation package. Imagine this is the year 2021 and if the COVID-19 pandemic continues, your proposition will not receive a positive response from the market. Due to the pandemic, people avoid going on vacations. If the pandemic ends, your proposition will succeed. For about two years, travel has been restricted and it will pick up very quickly as the pandemic ends and travel restrictions are lifted. With the help of the following decision network (and calculations), you can determine which decision will maximize your expected utility.

Figure 4.1 shows the decision network for this problem. The decision alternative is whether or not to launch the package. The decision node in the rectangle represents this variable. The oval-shaped node is a chance

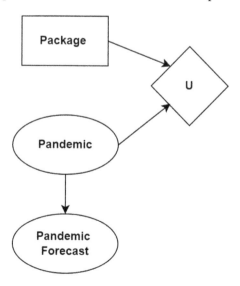

FIGURE 4.1   Travel package decision network

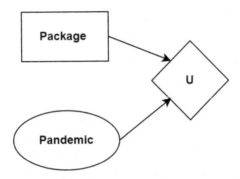

FIGURE 4.2   Travel package decision network – forecast not available

node that represents the chance of the pandemic ending or continuing. The pandemic forecast (if available) will help calculate this node's probabilities. Finally, the diamond shape node represents the overall utility of this decision.

Calculating Utilities to Determine the Optimal Decision
The problem is based on two variables: the action (whether or not to launch the package) and the chance (the pandemic will end or continue). First, we will work on the problem where the information on the pandemic forecast is not available. Figure 4.2 represents a decision network for the travel package decision when the forecast is not available.

Distribution of pandemic variable: The probability that the pandemic will end before the launch is 70% and the probability that it will continue is 30% (Table 4.1).

Utilities of all the actions (Table 4.2):

- We launch and pandemic ends: 100

- We launch and pandemic continues: 0

- We hold and pandemic ends: 20

- We hold and pandemic continues: 70

TABLE 4.1   Distribution of Pandemic Variable

P	P(p)
Ends	0.7
Continues	0.3

TABLE 4.2   Utility Table

A	P	U(A,p)
launch	Ends	100
launch	continues	0
hold	Ends	20
hold	continues	70

Expected Utilities of the Two Decisions and MEU
Expected utility of launching the package:

$$EU\left(launch\right)=\sum_{p}P\left(p\right)U\left(launch,\ p\right)$$

$$EU\left(launch\right)=0.7*100+0.3*0$$

$$EU\left(launch\right)=70$$

Expected utility of holding the package:

$$EU\left(hold\right)=\sum_{p}P\left(p\right)U\left(hold,\ p\right)$$

$$EU\left(hold\right)=0.7*20+0.3*70$$

$$EU\left(hold\right)=35$$

The optimal decision should result in the MEU, and therefore, it can be represented as follows:

$$MEU(o)=\max_{a} EU\left[a\right]$$

Or, as informed in the previous section:

$$a^{*=}\ \underset{a}{argmax}\ EU\left[a\right]$$

Optimal decision = launch
The decision to launch the package seems more optimal in this case since it results in a higher expected utility (70 compared to 35).

The Value of Information
As we discussed above, the value of information counts when making the right decisions using decision networks. We will now work on the problem

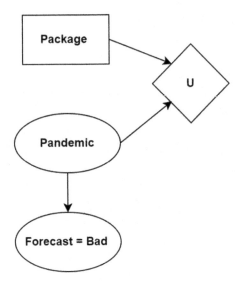

FIGURE 4.3   Travel package decision network – forecast available

where information on the pandemic variable is available. As shown in Figure 4.3, the pandemic forecast says the pandemic will not end anytime soon and will only spread faster. The forecast is bad!

The calculations get a little complex in this case. Since the information is available, instead of using simple probabilities, we will use the Bayes theorem to calculate posterior probabilities, a type of conditional probabilities in Bayesian statistics:

$$P(A|B) = \frac{P(B|A)P(A)}{P(B)}$$

The utilities, in this case, remain the same. The new probability distribution, given the condition that the forecast is bad (posterior probabilities), is shown in Table 4.3.

TABLE 4.3   Distribution of Pandemic
Variable – Posterior Probabilities

p	P(p | F=bad)
ends	0.34
continues	0.66

Expected Utilities of the Two Decisions and MEU
Expected utility of launching the package:

$$EU\left(\text{launch}\,|\,\text{bad}\right) = \sum_p P\left(p\,|\,bad\right)U\left(\text{launch},\,p\right)$$

$$EU\left(\text{launch}\right) = 0.34*100 + 0.66*0$$

$$EU\left(\text{launch}\right) = 34$$

Expected utility of holding the package:

$$EU\left(\text{hold}\,|\,\text{bad}\right) = \sum_p P\left(p\,|\,bad\right)U\left(\text{hold},\,p\right)$$

$$EU\left(\text{hold}\right) = 0.34*20 + 0.66*70$$

$$EU\left(\text{hold}\right) = 53$$

The optimal decision (information is available):

$$MEU(F = bad) = \max_a EU\left[a\,|\,bad\right] = 53$$

Optimal decision = hold
In this case, the decision to hold the launch of the travel package seems optimal (the expected utility of 53 is higher than 34).

AGENTS FOR COMPLEX DECISIONS

Designing agents for complex decisions can be an extremely exhaustive process. A large number of complex decisions are made in sequential environments where the current action of an agent affects all the following decisions. Think about the game of chess, where each move the player makes affects the game's final outcome. One wrong move and you might lose the entire game. Such problems are also called sequential decision problems. Dynamic programming focused on solving Markov Decision Process, or MDP, is used to build agents that can deal with complex decisions in uncertain, sequential environments. It allows recursively breaking down a problem into sub-problems, remembering the optimal solution of one sub-problem, and using it to solve similar sub-problems, helping to solve the overall problem more effectively.

MDP provides a mathematical framework to model decisions under fully observable, discrete, and stochastic environments. It is used widely in AI, operations research, robotics, economics, behavioral economics, and many more applications. MDPs are applied in different variations to a large number of decision problems. It is beyond the scope of this book to cover all those scenarios. Therefore, we will cover only the fundamental concept of MDP to give you an idea of how they can be used to build agents that can make decisions under complexity. Professors Dan Klein and Pieter Abbeel from UC Berkeley have created some great resources on MDPs that are available online.

The MDP aims to determine the policy – the most optimal decision that an agent should make at each step to ensure that it accomplishes the final goal. MDP focuses on making long-term plans of action.

- A typical MDP model contains:
- A set of possible *states of the world* represented by S.
- A set of possible *actions* represented by A.
- A real value *reward function* represented by R(s, a, s').
- A *transition function* defined as a probability distribution over the states represented as T(s, a, s'). In some cases, it is also written as P($s'|s, a$).

The MDP solution must direct the agent on what action to take for any state the agent might reach. This solution is called a policy, represented by the symbol π in the MDP framework.

The goal is to find the optimal policy that yields the highest expected utility represented. The π^* symbol represents the optimal policy (the symbol * represents optimality). This policy seeks to maximize the cumulative function of the random rewards.

The key assumptions of MDP include:

- There is a finite number of actions or states.
- The environment is fully observable, where the new state resulting from the agent's action will be known to the system.
- The successor state or the cost depends only on the current state, not on the prior history (Markovian transitions).

Some of these assumptions might not apply to real-life situations but they are useful for creating a model that produces the best possible decision or policy. While working with MDP problems, it is also essential to consider a few other important factors. Think about the *time horizon* that represents utilities over time. When the agent has limited time to solve the problem, the optimal action may depend upon how much time is left to solve the entire problem. Limited time means we have a finite horizon for decision-making and therefore we use a nonstationary policy. It can change given the fact that the agent is expected to achieve its goal, given the time limitations. In the case of the infinite horizon, where the agent doesn't have a fixed deadline to solve the problem, it can conveniently use a stationary policy that is much simpler.

Another important factor is calculating the utility of state sequences. In the infinite horizon case, the environment doesn't contain a terminal state. The environment histories and sequences, therefore, can get infinitely long, with infinite utilities with additive undiscounted rewards. There are multiple ways to address this issue but the most common and effective method is to use additive or cumulative discounted rewards. The reward function is a mechanism to reinforce optimal decisions. When an agent receives a positive reward, it learns that it has made the right decision. When it receives a negative reward, it learns that the decision was wrong. The utility of an infinite sequence becomes finite with discounted rewards.[1] The discounted sum of rewards or the discounted return along any trajectory is bounded (always) in a range. Considering this, we have[4]:

$$0 \le \sum_{t=1}^{\infty} \gamma^{t-1} r_t \le \sum_{t=1}^{\infty} \gamma^{t-1} R_{max} = \frac{R_{max}}{1-\gamma}$$

It is reasonable in MDP problems to maximize the sum of rewards and prefer rewards now to rewards later. Rewards that are taken sooner usually have higher utility. The value of a reward is considered 1 if the agent prefers to take the reward now (no discounting). This doesn't work for infinite horizon problems. Summing an infinite rewards series yields infinite rewards and this can make equations unsolvable. The reward is denoted as γ if it is preferred to be taken in the next step and γ^2 if it is preferred in two steps (discounted rewards). Discount factor γ is a number between 0 and 1. Discounting rewards helps find the optimal policy by helping the algorithm converge more efficiently.

The goal of any agent is to choose a policy that maximizes the expected discounted sum of rewards, also called *value*. Algorithms designed to solve MDPs use the *state value function*, which consists of the expected reward for some state, given the agent is following some policy. It can be explained as follows[5]:

$$V^{\pi}(s) = E\left\{\sum_{k=0}^{\infty} \gamma^k r_{t+k+1} \mid s_t = s, \pi\right\}$$

The solution of an MDP can also be called a policy that specifies what an agent should do for any state it might arrive at or reach. A policy is denoted by π. All MDP problems aim at finding a policy that guarantees the maximum reward, given some reward criterion. Obviously, this is the policy that yields the MEU for the agent. We call it the optimal policy, one which is undominated. No other policy in any state can expect to do better than this policy. The optimal policy denoted by π* dominates π if and only if for every s *(state)*:

$$V^{\pi^*}(s) > V^{\pi}(s)$$

Q-function, also called an action-utility function, is another important quantity to consider. It can be expressed as Q(s, a), the expected utility of taking action *a*, given it was taken in state *s*.

The Bellman equation (after Richard Bellman, 1957) provides the framework for determining the maximum reward an agent can receive if they make the optimal decision now and for all future decisions. Bellman equations characterize optimal values. Here are some important Bellman equations:

Bellman equation for state values:

$$V^*(s) = \max_a \sum_{s'} T(s, a, s')\left[R(s, a, s') + \gamma V^*(s')\right]$$

Bellman equation for Q-values:

$$Q^*(s, a) = \sum_{s'} T(s, a, s')\left[R(s, a, s') + \gamma \max_{a'} Q(s', a')\right]$$

Maximization over the action space:

$$V^*(s) = \max_a Q^*(s, a)$$

As mentioned before, the agent aims to find the optimal policy that yields maximum reward. The optimal policy with Q-function could be explained as follows:

$$\pi^*(s) = \underset{a}{\operatorname{argmax}} Q(s, a)$$

MDP lays the foundations of reinforcement learning (RL). RL is used to create agents that are able to make decisions about their actions and determine the optimal policy by computing the value of each action. MDPs describe the environment for RL and you can formalize almost all RL problems as MDPs.

MDPs can be solved using offline and online algorithms. Offline algorithms use the history of the problem from the beginning in the form of problem data. The algorithm knows all the input based on which it outputs the result. Online algorithms, however, do not know the whole input or the past data about the problem. They process input piece by piece, serially, in the order in which the input is fed to the system. Online algorithms are becoming more popular as the volume, velocity, and variety of data increase. These algorithms require smaller data storage and limited memory applications. As they process only a small chunk of data at a time, they keep the complexity of each update limited and small.

Dynamic Decision Networks

Dynamic decision networks, or DDNs, are a compact, factored representation of MDPs that extend dynamic Bayesian networks to allow a repeated structure for indefinite or infinite horizon problems. They form the basis of decision-theoretic planning by allowing better visualization of the decision context. They are very similar to the decision networks discussed in the previous section. However, in the real world, many problems involve high levels of complexity and the decision networks become more dynamic as more complexity is added to the environment. DDNs use decision nodes, reward nodes, and utility nodes to model substantial real-world problems.

The conditional probability distribution associated with each node represents the relationship between the variables. MDPs represent nodes in multiple time slices that store the information on the agent's current beliefs about the world. These time slices allow nodes to be partitioned into sets. The system can determine which decision yields the MEU by calculating the expected utility of performing each possible action. This might need updating the MDP several times.

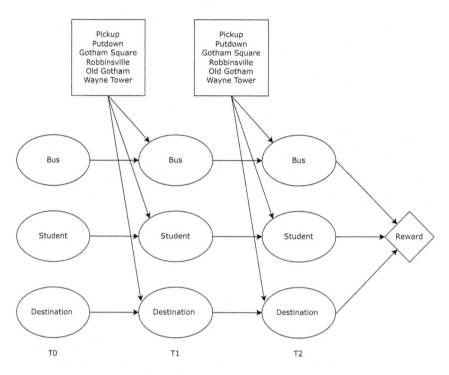

FIGURE 4.4 Dynamic decision network – school bus problem (Credit: Turkett and Rose, Planning With Agents: An Efficient Approach Using Hierarchical Dynamic Decision Networks)

DDNs can be explained with a school bus agent example. As shown in Figure 4.4, the agent is an autonomous school bus running in Gotham City. It serves Gotham Square, Robbinsville, Old Gotham, and Wayne Tower areas. In a DDN, the agent can perform six primitive actions that are represented in decision nodes: Pickup (picking up a student), Putdown (letting a student out), Gotham Square (heading to Gotham Square), Robbinsville (heading to Robbinsville), Old Gotham (heading to Old Gotham), and Wayne Tower (heading to Wayne Tower). There are three random variables: Bus, Student, and Destination.

The DDN represents T0, the current time step, T1 and T2, two-time steps in the future with an action taking place between each time step. The agent receives a reward at the end of all actions based on the final location of the student. When the student and destination locations are the same, the reward would have the maximum value. Rewards will be progressively lower when the student is further away from the destination.[6] The case study provided at the end of this chapter shows how agent design incorporates several time slices to devise models that help agents determine the most optimal actions.

While DDNs can be solved using decision tree algorithms, variable elimination algorithms are more suitable for increased efficiency in finding optimal solutions. Variable elimination algorithm aims at finding out a function for the last decision, which determines the action with MEU, given any past.

To begin planning with DDN, the agent first enters its evidence (about the world) into the initial time slice of the network. An optimal ordering of actions that provide maximal utility for the agent is then returned based on the policy functions calculated by the variable elimination algorithm. The variable elimination technique is very similar to the value iteration covered in the next section. Both techniques are applied to find out the best policy for an agent.

Solving MDPs with Value Iteration and Policy Iteration

As discussed earlier, MDP aims to find out the optimal policy (π^*) that maximizes the utility of the state sequence. This section will discuss how optimal policies can be determined using value iteration and policy iteration. They are both offline algorithms. Remember, the optimal policies can also be obtained using other methods such as linear programming and Monte Carlo planning. Where linear programming (discussed later in Chapter 5) is another offline algorithm, Monte Carlo planning (methods discussed later in this chapter) belongs in the family of online approximate algorithms.

Value Iteration

Using *value iteration*, we can compute an optimal MDP policy with its value. The *utility of a state* (value) can be considered as the expected sum of rewards when an optimal policy is executed in that state. The value iteration process starts at the end and works backward iteratively, solving a set of equations on each state's utility to those of its neighbors. Only one iteration is performed at each step. The optimal policy is obtained once all the state values are successfully converged to the optimal state values.

As demonstrated by Kleinn and Abbeel,[7] grid world problems can explain how MDP algorithms are used to build agents that make optimal decisions in a maze-like environment. Imagine you are a robot that is trying to find an optimal policy. You are instructed to move under a 4 × 3 grid

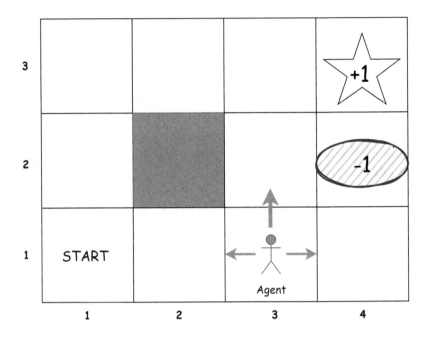

FIGURE 4.5   The grid world

world representing a factory floor (Figure 4.5). You will earn the reward of +1 if you arrive at your expected location (4,3). This is the area where you will sort the finished products. You must not enter (4,2) a fire pit location where all the harmful materials are disposed of and destroyed. If you enter this area, your reward will be −1. There is a wall located at (2,2) and this location is inaccessible. Locations (4,3) and (4,2) are the terminal states. Once you arrive at any of these locations, you exit.

Although big rewards (+1 and −1) come at the end, you also earn small rewards at each step just for moving inside the grid. These rewards can be positive or negative and usually have small values, something like 0.02 or 0.04. These so-called *living rewards* encourage the agent to keep moving until it reaches its final destination and exits the environment.

You can only move in one of four adjacent states at a time – North (N), East (E), South (S), or West (W). Your actions are non-deterministic since this is a stochastic environment. There can be a high probability of you moving in one direction but it is not always certain that you will move in that direction. If you take action N, you will move to North 80% of the time. However, 10% of the time, taking action N will take you to the West, and 10% of the time, to the East (probabilities: N=.80, W=.10, E=.10). If you move off the grid, you remain in the same state.

We calculate the utility of each state and then use the state utilities for optimal policy selection. The following equation, a value update or Bellman update, can be used to compute the optimal values:

$$V_{i+1}^{*}(s) \leftarrow \max_{a} \sum_{s'} T(s,a,s') \left[R(s,a,s') + V_{i}^{*}(s') \right]$$

When starting from state s and acting optimally for a horizon of i steps, $V^{*}i(s)$ represents the expected sum of rewards accumulated.[8] There will be n Bellman equations for n possible states (one equation for each state). We start with utilities of all states initialized to 0. The right-hand side of the equation is calculated first and the calculated values are then plugged into the left-hand side. This way, you update the utilities of each state from the utilities of its neighbors. The process is repeated until you reach equilibrium. At each iteration, the update is applied simultaneously to all the states. You are guaranteed to reach equilibrium if you apply the Bellman update infinitely often. In this case, according to Russel and Norvig, the final utility values will be the solutions to the Bellman equations and the corresponding policy will be considered optimal.[1]

The values for our grid world problem after 100 iterations can be seen in Figure 4.6. The calculations can go exceptionally longer and therefore, specialized software is used to perform all these calculations. The arrows in each box (on the left-hand side) directing in a specific direction represent the optimal policy. Q-values shown in the right side grid include the probabilities of all four actions in each state. Since it is a stochastic environment, Q-values help us determine which direction we should move in and which actions will yield the highest utility value.

The optimal value function V^{*} for the discounted infinite horizon problem is found at convergence. This answers the question – how long should we keep iterating? Run value iteration till convergence. Value iteration after it runs for a certain number of times always converges. At that point, the following Bellman equation is satisfied:

$$V^{*}(s) = \max_{A} \sum_{s'} T(s,a,s') \left[R(s,a,s') + \gamma V^{*}(s') \right]$$

Pay attention to the arrows in Figure 4.7 (values after 9, 10, and 11 iterations). You will notice that after ten iterations, the optimal policy is already

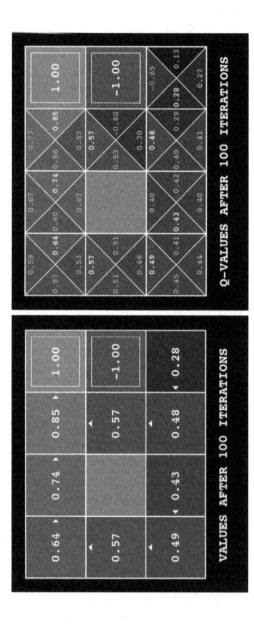

FIGURE 4.6   Values and Q-values after 100 iterations (Credit: Klein and Abbeel, Artificial Intelligence Markov Decision Process II)

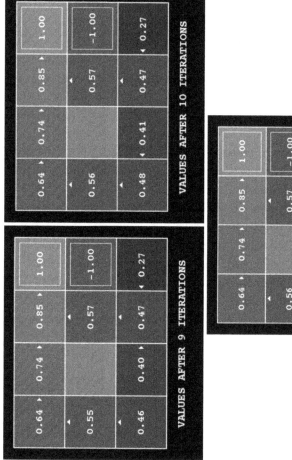

FIGURE 4.7   Values after 9, 10, and 11 iterations (Credit: Klein and Abbeel, Artificial Intelligence Markov Decision Process II)

found since the direction of the arrows in the boxes is no longer changing. This is the same policy shown in Figure 4.6 (values after 100 iterations). Even though the values are changing (slightly) after ten iterations, the policy (direction of arrows) is not. The 10th and 100th iterations suggest the same policy. Therefore, there is no reason why we should keep running iterations indefinitely. The values have converged after ten iterations, and congratulations – you have found your optimal policy.

Policy Iteration
Policy iteration, the alternative approach to finding the optimal policy, can converge much faster under some conditions than value iteration. *Policy iteration algorithms* are used for improving and updating the current policy by calculating the utilities of states (values) under the current policy. It helps the agent learn the optimal policy that maximizes its long-term discounted reward. A finite MDP has only a finite number of policies. Therefore, policy iteration must converge to an optimal policy in a finite number of iterations. Policy iteration is done in two steps: policy evaluation and policy improvement.

Policy evaluation is similar to value iteration, where the value of each state is determined after performing a series of calculations. In fact, policy evaluation is simpler than value iteration since the action in each state is already fixed by the policy. We use a more simplified version of the Bellman equation that relates the utility of s under πi to the utilities of its neighbors. Similar to value iteration, the state values corresponding to the starting policy are computed based on an iterative expression. The expression again is taken from the Bellman equation:

$$V_{i+1}^{\pi}(s) \leftarrow \sum_{s'} T(s, \pi(s), s')\left[R(s, \pi(s), s') + \gamma V_i^{\pi}(s')\right]$$

It starts with calculating utilities for some fixed policy and continues until convergence. Notice that we are not considering the number of actions here. It is because the action in each state is fixed by the policy. Hence, we have a fixed policy: $\pi(s)$.

In our grid world solution, the recommended action for (1,1) is to go up. According to Russell and Norvig, the calculation for the simplified Bellman equation in this case will be:

$$Vi(1,1) = 0.8\left[-0.04 + Vi(1,2)\right] + 0.1\left[-0.04 + Vi(2,1)\right] + 0.1\left[-0.04 + Vi(1,1)\right]$$

Remember, there is an 80% chance that it will go in the recommended direction. Ten percent of the time, it can go West, and 10% to East. Since West is not available, it will stay at (1,1). The value of the discounted reward is −0.4. Since there is no "max" operator, the equations throughout the process are linear. This means that for *n* states, we have *n* linear equations.[1] The process of iteration goes on until values converge.

Policy improvement is step 2, which helps extract the policy that is better than the initial policy. To update the policy, we use one step look ahead with resulting converged utilities as future values. One step look ahead uses:

$$\pi_{i+1}(s) = \operatorname*{argmax}_{a} \sum_{s'} T(s, a, s')\Big[R(s, a, s') + \gamma V^{\pi_i}(s') \Big]$$

The process is repeated until the policy converges. At convergence, the final policy and its value function are optimal policy and the optimal value function.

Monte Carlo Methods

It is difficult to find an optimal or near-optimal solution in large spaces with multiple states and non-deterministic, stochastic scenarios using MDPs. This is where approaches like Monte Carlo methods come in handy. Monte Carlo methods are a group of online algorithms that are widely used in planning and designing agents based on the principles of inferential statistics. It is an experimental technique that uses random sampling methods to obtain a range of possible outcomes for a real-life scenario. Monte Carlo algorithms simulate the behavior of a complex system to model a probabilistic real-world process.

Imagine you want to calculate the average height of the adult population of your country. How much work would it take? Calculations and other administrative work aside, you will need to collect data from hundreds of millions of people. We all know that it is neither viable nor a smart thing to do. We can instead use a sample of the same population and compute the average height of people in that sample. The result will not be the same as the true average but it will surely be a good approximation of the true average. A simple yet effective statistical technique called sampling can be used to solve a wide variety of similar problems. But does sampling provide a great degree of accuracy?

Due to the limitation of resources, we trade off accuracy for speed. The law of large numbers comes into play here. If you increase your sample size and keep increasing it, the approximation converges to the true average. As you increase your sample size, the error between the approximation and the true average gets smaller. If you have studied statistics, this might sound quite familiar. Approximation based upon the sample is the basic idea behind all Monte Carlo methods – it is called Monte Carlo approximation. These methods are mostly used as simulations and share a common three-step framework:

1. Model the process representing a probabilistic system.

2. Define inputs (they can be either continuous or discrete inputs).

3. Run the experiment with multiple simulations and aggregate results with the goal of having an aggregated output that explains the modeled phenomenon.

The bigger the number of simulations, the more accurate your result will be (the law of large numbers). Different sampling algorithms are used for specific distributions. Monte Carlo algorithms are tedious since they require cumbersome mathematical calculations and are difficult to perform manually. Therefore, we use computers to perform these calculations, producing highly accurate results at a significantly high speed.

Monte Carlo methods are an effective tool for online planning. They provide exceptional performance in large, fully, and partially observable domains. They can also be applied to solve large partially observable Markov decision problems (POMDP) successfully. Table 4.4 exhibits different application areas of Monte Carlo-based agents.

Several Monte Carlo methods are used in designing autonomous agents that make decisions in highly complex environments. Autonomous vehicles are a notable example of intelligent agents that operate in large spaces, multi-lane roads, and unsignalized intersections with dense traffic.

Monte Carlo tree search can be combined with RL and other technologies to create a simulator that helps in motion planning for autonomous vehicles.

Weingertner et al.[9] published a study proposing a motion planning system that uses Monte Carlo tree search with deep learning heuristics and deep RL. The task of the motion planner is to reach an objective or destination safely, comfortably, and efficiently while dealing with multiple crossing points and overcoming all the obstacles. Real-time computations,

TABLE 4.4   Monte Carlo Application Areas

Field	Application Example(s)
Finance and Insurance	Estimating mortgage payment rates, testing stock market efficiency, projecting cash flows, analyzing portfolios and investments
Healthcare	Estimating hospital costs, assessing healthcare claim risk, evaluating medical technology
Manufacturing	Optimizing production and manufacturing, estimating capabilities, scheduling production, improving job-shop scheduling decisions
Marketing	Sizing markets, determining customer lifetime value, determining prices, maximizing profits, improving customer service management, simulating campaigns, predicting sales,
Retail	Managing inventory, determining the optimal price point for products, estimating sales
Logistics	Estimating reliability of supply chain networks, estimating logistics costs
Pharmaceuticals	Simulating drug development, determining drug prices, designing and managing clinical trials, modeling diseases

scalability to more complex scenarios, and different road geometries are some other challenges that the agent might have to encounter. The approach proposed by this research reduced the complexity of the search model.

The agent designed based on their study outperformed other agents in various challenging scenarios where they benchmarked safety, comfort, and efficiency metrics. To see the actual simulator with agents in motion, visit their GitHub repository *Monte Carlo Tree Search with Reinforcement Learning for Motion Planning*. As of August 2022, this repository is available at https://github.com/PhilippeW83440/MCTS-NNET.

APPLICATION CASE 4.1: AIRLINE PRICE OPTIMIZATION WITH MONTE CARLO SIMULATION[10]

One of the important applications of Monte Carlo is in optimizing prices. Optimization problems use certain inputs, objectives, and rules or constraints. This example aims to determine optimal ticket prices to maximize the airline's cumulative revenue.

For any given airline and a particular flight, the booking starts days in advance. The number of seats available for booking is usually capped.

Like any pricing model, there is an inverse relationship between price and quantity sold. When price increases, demand decreases. Airlines use these dynamics to their advantage. When there is a strong demand, the airlines increase their revenue by quoting higher prices, and when it is low, they reduce the price to increase sales and ensure better flight occupancy. Let's create simulations with two different strategies:

1. Sell an equal number of tickets each day irrespective of the demand (linear pricing function).
2. Sell more tickets when demand is higher (adaptive pricing function).

First, we create a recursive aggregating function that exits (or terminates) only when there are no days left for the flight or all the seats are sold. It calls the pricing function with three inputs:

1. Days left until the flight.
2. Seats left on the flight for booking (quantity).
3. Market demand – the quantity to be sold at a given price.

A helper function then calculates the cumulative revenue, given a specific pricing function as an argument. Finally, the recursive call takes care of revising the seats and days left, adding the daily revenue to a variable that is returned as the cumulative revenue. We experiment with the pricing function and simulate the cumulative revenue, repeatedly feeding a probabilistic daily demand. The revenue will be calculated iteratively for each day.

MONTE CARLO SIMULATION WITH LINEAR PRICING FUNCTION

In a first heuristic approach and setting a baseline, let's assume that the airline sells an equal number of tickets each day, irrespective of the demand. The equation for the price is as follows:

$$Price = Demand - \frac{Tickets\ left}{Days\ left}$$

After running the Monte Carlo simulation code 10,000 times, a histogram for the cumulative revenue shown in Figure 4.8 is generated. The mean revenue is $14,900, with a standard deviation of 292. The experiment also shows that the airline can earn $15,271 in revenue by charging $152.7 for each ticket.

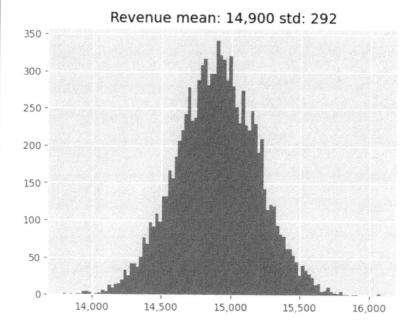

FIGURE 4.8   Cumulative revenue histogram using a linear price function

MONTE CARLO SIMULATION WITH ADAPTIVE PRICING FUNCTION

Let us try a different approach by factoring in demand to sell more tickets on the days when demand is higher than the average of 150 seats. Considering the relationship between price and demand, we will try to keep prices low. We are trading off the price for increased ticket sales when demand increases.

The pricing equation in this case is as follows:

$$\text{Price} = \text{Demand} - \left(1 + \text{Adaptive factor}\left(\frac{\text{Demand}}{150}\right)\right) * \frac{\text{Tickets left}}{\text{Days left}}$$

An adaptive factor in the price equation is used to allow selling more tickets for the same demand we used for the linear pricing function. Setting the adaptive factor to 0 will work the same as the linear pricing function.

Upon running the Monte Carlo simulation 10,000 times with the adaptive factor set to 2, we saw a significant increase in mean revenue to $15,591 with a standard deviation of 358. Figure 4.9 shows the result of this simulation.

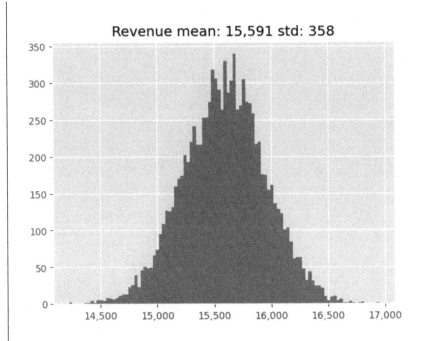

FIGURE 4.9 Cumulative revenue histogram using adaptive pricing function

At adaptive factor 3, revenue increased further and reached above $15,600. The experiment informed that the airline could earn $15,628 by charging $156.3 for each ticket.

This example of Monte Carlo simulation showed how an airline could earn higher revenue by reducing ticket prices when the demand is higher. Conversely, maintaining the same price and not considering demand fluctuations might hurt their overall revenue and profit potential.

Monte Carlo methods open possibilities of testing out many other strategies, such as maximizing profit and optimizing prices and resources. As discussed above, several Monte Carlo methods are used today across different industries and for various purposes.

MULTIAGENT DECISION-MAKING

As discussed earlier, the idea of intelligent agents is based on the principles of the biological design of humans and how we make decisions. Therefore, the behavior of these agents is quite similar to ours, and so are their environments. Like humans, agents also function in multiple environments.

Systems in which multiple agents interact in a shared environment to achieve conflicting or common goals are called multiagent systems.

Agents designed for multiagent systems use distinctive design principles and different algorithms. As the power of our devices and connectivity grows, multiagent systems become increasingly relevant. The agents in a multiagent system learn from each other and from the environment using RL algorithms. They are learning agents aiming to maximize their reward by cooperating or competing with other agents in the system. Although many of the actions of these agents are based on the actions of other agents in the system, we can preprogram them with some desired behaviors.

In previous sections, we discussed how decision theory is used to design agents that aim at identifying the best course of action to reach the optimal outcome. Game theory, a branch of economics, can be considered a close relative of decision theory that explains the interactions between self-interested agents in conditions of uncertainty. Multiagent decision-making in the context of designing AI agents is the subject of game theory.

You can see game theory in action through strategic games such as checkers and chess, where each player tries to optimize their outcome with a series of strategic actions. In most multiagent scenarios, the outcome of the game depends upon the choices made by all agents. For each choice, therefore, an agent must take into account the decisions that other agents may make. It should also consider the fact that each agent will try to optimize their own outcome since they all aim to serve their individual self-interests.

Although there are multiple approaches to explain multiagent decision-making, here we will stay focused on Markov games, which can be called the multiagent extension of an MDP. Also known as stochastic games, Markov games are a collection of coupled strategic games, one per state. Like how an agent seeks to find the most optimal policy in an MDP, each agent in a Markov game aims to use a strategy that maximizes their individual welfare. Agents for multiagent environments are designed with algorithms that use a variety of strategies, some of which we will discuss in this section. Often, designers or developers use a combination of different strategies depending on the need of the situation.

Pure Strategy and Saddle Point Equilibrium

A deterministic plan dictating the agent's action in every information set is similar to a policy in an MDP problem and is called a *pure* strategy. In cases where the players have perfect information about the outcomes and the payoff matrix has a saddle point or an equilibrium point, the players

TABLE 4.5   Pure Strategy Payoff Matrix

		Clyde		
		A	**B**	**C**
	1	3	−2	−6
Zoe	**2**	2	−5	7
	3	6	3	8

use a pure strategy. Pure strategy is mostly used in competitive, zero-sum games. Zero-sum means what is good for one agent is bad for the other (if one wins, the other loses). They are called zero-sum, as if you add all the players' winnings, accounting for losses counted as negative winnings, the net result of the game is zero.

Let's discuss this with an example. Zoe and Clyde are playing a game where each of them can take three possible actions. Zoe can take actions 1, 2, and 3, and Clyde can take actions A, B, and C. The payoff matrix of this game can be seen in Table 4.5. The player we are rooting for is Zoe. Let's see how she finds her strategy in this case.

The matrix in Table 4.5 only shows Zoe's payoffs. Clyde's payoff in each cell is just the opposite of Zoe's payoff. This is the basic assumption in this game – every dollar that Zoe wins comes out of Clyde's pocket.

Both players in the game are rational and use *maxmin* and *minmax* strategies. While applying maxmin, Zoe would seek to maximize her worst-case minimum payoff. Clyde will use minmax strategy to minimize Zoe's best-case, maximum payoff. Remember, it is a zero-sum game where each player chooses a strategy that enables them to win.

In a two-player game, the maxmin strategy for player *I* can be denoted as follows:

$$arg\ max_{s_i}\ min_{s_{-i}} u_i\left(s_1, s_2\right)$$

The minmax strategy for player *I* would be:

$$arg\ min_{s_i}\ max_{s_{-i}} u_{-i}\left(s_1, s_2\right)$$

where

- *i*: the index of the player of interest.
- *-i*: the other player (or players except for player *i*).
- s_i: the strategy used by player *i*.
- s_{-i} : the strategy used by the other player (or all other players).

- u_i: the value function of player i.

- u_{-i}: the value function of the other player (or all other players).

- s_1, s_2: the strategy profiles of both the players.

Table 4.6 shows the calculations of the players' strategies. For Zoe's strategy, we will pick the minimum value in each row (Row Min), and from all the picked values, we will choose the maximum of the minimum values. Clyde's options are placed vertically and we will select the maximum value in each column to determine his minmax strategy.

All finite two-player zero-sum games have a *value* that constitutes an equilibrium point of the game. No player can do any better than the value by deviating from their strategies. The maxmin value for one player is equal to the minmax value for the other player. Conventionally, the maxmin value for player 1 is considered the value of the game. In our example, this value is 3. Zoe is clearly maximizing her minimum payoff. The maximum value out of all her losses (row minimum) is 3. Clyde's minmax strategy results in the same value. At 3, he is minimizing Zoe's maximum payoff. Therefore, the value in this game is 3, which can also be called this game's *saddle point*.

Zoe and Clyde used pure strategy in this zero-sum game. In many real-world two-player cases, agents are not aware of their opponent's responses and hence the exact outcome. Using a pure strategy in such cases might not work. Instead, the agent uses a *mixed or randomized* strategy, a combination of strategies with some fixed probabilities. Mixed strategies are mostly used in games with no saddle points.

Mixed Strategy and Nash Equilibrium

In certain situations, the agents seek stability. This means that all the agents sharing the environment prefer to follow a joint policy if no agent receives any incentive to unilaterally change their policy. At a particular state, no agent would take an action that is not equal to the joint policy, assuming

TABLE 4.6   Saddle Point Equilibrium

		Clyde			
		A	B	C	Row Min
	1	3	−2	−6	−6
Zoe	2	2	−5	7	−5
	3	6	3	8	3 (Maxmin)
	Col Max	6	3 (Minmax)	8	

that all other agents will stick with their equilibrium (stable) policies.[11] This is called *Nash equilibrium*. The payoff function of the player can be defined as u_i that represents player i's preferences. It can be denoted as follows[12]:

$$u_i(a^*) \geq u_i(a_i, a^*_{-i}) \text{ for every action } a_i \text{ of player } i$$

Nash equilibrium can be explained with the help of the prisoner's dilemma, a popular concept in economics. It explains a situation where two selfish agents choose a suboptimal choice that is good for both agents instead of choosing the most optimal option for their individual benefit. The prisoner's dilemma is a matrix, a *general sum* game. In general sum games, instead of following a rational or pure strategy, players use a mixed, randomized strategy.

Sam and Lisa are arrested together on a bank robbery case. Unfortunately, police don't have sufficient evidence to get a jury to convict. As their investigation proceeded, police found strong evidence of Sam's and Lisa's involvement in the theft of a truck in Kansas City last month. A clever prosecutor makes each of them the offer – "you might choose to confess or deny the bank robbery." The conditions of the offer are as follows:

1. If you both deny bank robbery, you will each do three years in prison for auto theft.

2. If you confess, but your accomplice denies, you will do only one year and your accomplice will do ten years in prison.

3. If you deny and your accomplice confesses, you will do ten years, while your accomplice will only do one year in prison.

4. If you and your accomplice confess, each of you will spend five years in prison.

The payoff matrix of this example can be seen in Table 4.7. The players' outcomes are represented as a pair of payoffs (Rij, Cij), where Rij is the outcome that the row player (Sam) receives and Cij is the outcome that the

TABLE 4.7   Prisoners' Dilemma Payoff Matrix

		Lisa	
		Confess	**Deny**
Sam	**Confess**	(5, 5)	(1, 10)
	Deny	(10, 1)	(3, 3)

column player (Lisa) receives. It seems that the most optimal choice for each of them is to deny the bank robbery charges and only do three years in prison. Both Sam and Lisa are criminals, selfish people who only care about their own welfare. However, according to game theory principles, they are more likely to choose option 4. Both will confess and do five years in prison. Their "dilemma" is that whatever their accomplice does, each is better off maintaining stability which in this case is confessing.[13]

There are multiple views on justifying this behavior. It seems obvious that the cost of lying is terrible. If they lie and their accomplice confesses, they might have to do ten years in prison. If they confess, the best case is one year, and the worse is five, much better than ten years.

The more famous interpretation of this behavior is players choose socially desirable altruism over selfish behavior. It is believed that individuals who pursue self-interest over the interest of their group end up being worse off compared to those who pursue the interest of their groups over their individual interests. In the prisoner's dilemma game, both the agents make the decision with the altruistic move. They choose stability, the right thing to do. Nash equilibrium can be applied to a variety of situations, including coordination games, network traffic, and even some competition-based games.

Dominant Strategy Equilibrium

Sometimes, an agent decides to take an optimal action regardless of how other agents or players act. It is because the situation allows the agent to take an action that maximizes their overall satisfaction. The situation where an agent chooses the action best for them without considering other agents' actions is called *dominant strategy equilibrium*. This states that the agent has a strategy that always yields the best outcome regardless of what the other players do.

For example, Arron and Alicia are colleagues working at the same office. They both like each other's company. Their workplace has announced a flexible work policy according to which every employee can choose to work from home or to come to the office. Arron doesn't like where he lives: a tiny apartment where he cannot even set up a decent workspace. Alicia lives alone and she doesn't like staying at home by herself. Their relationship is still new and they are both too shy to communicate whether to stay home or come to work. Staying home definitely yields less reward for both since they cannot see each other. They prefer to go to the office where they can enjoy each other's company. Table 4.8 shows Arron and Alicia's payoff matrix.

TABLE 4.8   Dominant Strategy Payoff Matrix

		Alicia	
		Home	Office
Arron	Home	(0, 0)	(0, 1)
	Office	(1, 0)	(2, 2)

Credit: Davies, Game Theory through Examples.

Both Arron and Alicia have a set of strategies that are represented as a pair of payoffs (Rij, Cij), where Rij is the utility that the row player (Arron) receives and Cij is the utility that the column player (Alicia) receives. If Arron goes to the office and Alicia stays home, Arron derives a utility of 1, whereas Alicia derives 0 units of utility (1,0). Similar utilities will be seen if Alicia goes to the office and Arron stays home (0,1). They would both choose to come to the office as their strictly dominating strategy. It is a dominating choice since it will yield the optimal outcome no matter what the other person does. It is better than staying at home, which yields 0 utility for each player. Therefore, Office-Office (2,2) is the dominant strategy equilibrium for this game. Since Arron and Alicia are rational agents, they don't need to cooperate to plan or execute their actions ahead of time. They can each pursue their dominant strategy and receive the maximum reward for their actions.[14]

Pareto-Optimal Outcome

The game's outcome will be called Pareto-efficient if no agent can be made better off without making at least one other agent (or another agent) worse off. Let's continue with the example we shared in the previous section (dominant strategy equilibrium). The context remains the same (workplace announcement of a flexible work policy) but we change the players. Jeff is Emily's boss and Emily hates him. Jeff, however, likes Emily. They are both aware of their relationship and how they feel about each other. As a result, both of them prefer not to communicate whether to go to the office or not. Their payoff matrix can be seen in Table 4.9. Again, players' strategies are represented as a pair of payoffs (Rij, Cij), where Rij is the row player's (Emily's) utility and Cij is the utility that the column player (Jeff) receives.

TABLE 4.9   Pareto's Outcome Payoff Matrix

		Jeff	
		Home	Office
Emily	Home	(2, 0)	(2, 1)
	Office	(3, 0)	(1, 2)

Credit: Davies, Game Theory through Examples.

Office-Home (3,0), Home-Office (2,1), and Office-Office (1,2) are all Pareto-optimal (or efficient) outcomes in this case. The total combined utility of both players in these scenarios is 3 (3+0=3, 2+1=3, 1+2=3). This is better than the total combined utility of Home-Home (2+0=2), which is the only outcome that is not Pareto-efficient. If no agent can do better than that outcome, without making another worse, the outcome will be Pareto-optimal or efficient.

Another thing to consider: Emily's strategy depends on what Jeff decides to do. Since she is a rational agent, she might assume that Jeff will come to the office because coming to the office is his dominant strategy. In this case, she might decide to stay at home because the utility of 2 is higher than 1. We call it *iterative dominance* since Emily gets higher utility than Jeff because of their relative preferences. Jeff gets less utility than he would have if Emily wanted to come to the office and be with him.[14]

The strategies and equilibrium concepts discussed here lay the theoretical foundations for designing agents for multiagent scenarios. With technology and our knowledge of multiagent systems increasing, we are creating systems capable of performing highly complex tasks with much greater efficiency. We live in a world where multiagent systems can be seen everywhere. Think about your family, workplace, markets, economies, traffic, sports, and even nature. We can see multiple agents at work to run and manage these systems. As they interact, they choose specific behaviors depending on the demands of the situation. For example, some situations demand agents to compete (sports and games), whereas others demand them to cooperate (traffic), coordinate (workplace) negotiate (family), communicate (market), learn and predict other agents' behavior (economy), and sometimes just maintain the balance and equilibrium (nature). Agents designed for such multiagent systems have these behaviors incorporated into their algorithms. In the future (very near!), we will see more of these agents around us. Home assistance robots, drone delivery agents, autonomous cars, and smart energy grids will soon be commonplace.

CONCLUSION

Intelligent agents are designed with theoretical foundations based on concepts taken from different disciplines. Their design is multidisciplinary. Intelligent agents are mostly built for automated sequential decision-making and require planning under uncertainty. These plannings can be modeled using MDPs and other decision theory techniques.

Agents for simple, non-complex decisions can be built using decision networks and the concept of MEU to determine the most optimal decision.

However, agents built to make decisions in complex environments require more sophisticated approaches such as MDPs, DDNs, and algorithms, including policy iteration, value iteration, and Monte Carlo methods. Using specific theoretical principles, intelligent agents are also designed to function in multiagent environments. One commonality between all (or most) types of intelligent agents is that they all seek to determine the most optimal decision while maximizing the overall expected utility of their actions. It makes sense. As humans, we do the same.

With advancements in research on the human brain and how our bodies work, we are learning more about our natural design. As more knowledge of human design is created, better AI technologies will be developed. Indeed, AI has been created to mimic human intelligence. RL, the key technology behind intelligent agent design, is getting more advanced as it integrates other technologies making models learn faster than ever before. These advancements will pave the way for the development of more effective and autonomous intelligent agents that will help us make better decisions in the future. In the next chapter, we will discuss some key tools and techniques used for decision-making in different contexts.

CASE STUDY: DESIGNING AGENT FOR COMPLEX ENVIRONMENT – MULTIAGENT PATH PLANNING WITH NONLINEAR MODEL PREDICTIVE CONTROL

In research supported by the European Union's Horizon 2020 Research and Innovation Programme, researchers designed and tested a model-based controller to address the multirotor Micro Aerial Vehicles (multi-MAVs) reactive collision avoidance problem. Multi-MAVs are a type of drone, flying robot flying autonomously or controlled remotely with software-controlled flight plans embedded in its system. The plan is executed in conjunction with sensors, global positioning system (GPS), and other physical parts of the drone. As technologies advance, these systems are becoming cheaper and more reliable. Today, the use of drones can be seen in inspection and exploration, mapping, crop monitoring, surveillance, and security applications.

Multi-MAVs operate in a multiagent environment where multiple MAVs share the same airspace. This poses the risk of mid-air collisions. So far, this problem is being handled by using a centralized, collision-free trajectory for each agent. This limits MAV's adaptivity and binds it to the preplanned trajectory. If any change happens to the task, the whole trajectory needs to be re-planned.

The research introduces a unified framework for multiagent control and collision avoidance. Their approach exploits the full MAV dynamics considering physical platform limitations to achieve agile and natural avoidance maneuvers. They used nonlinear model predictive control (NMPC) framework to create a decentralized mechanism that helps control multi-MAVs in a complex environment. Trajectory tracking and collision avoidance were unified into a single optimization problem to enable decentralized control. MAV model was employed in the controller formulation based on the dynamics of the system and attitude models. The multiagent collision avoidance NMPC controller and the unified trajectory tracking were designed with clearly defined optimal control problem (OCP), cost function, constraints, agent's motion prediction, uncertainty propagation, implementation, and priority.

The OCP sits at the core of the design. The system state vector x and control input u were defined as follows:

$$x = [p^T \ v^T \ \phi \ \theta \ \psi]^T$$

$$u = [\phi_{cmd} \ \theta_{cmd} \ T_{cmd}]^T$$

The following OCP is solved online at every time step:

$$\min_{U,X} \int_{t=0}^{T} \left\{ J_x\left(x(t), x_{ref}(t)\right) + J_u\left(u(t), u_{ref}(t)\right) + J_c\left(x(t)\right) \right\} dt + J_T\left(x(T)\right)$$

Subject to:

$$\dot{x} = f\left(x, u\right)$$

$$u(t) \in \mathbb{U}$$

$$G\left(x(t)\right) \leq 0$$

$$x(0) = x(t_0)$$

where f is composed of equations that describe the motion of the vehicle, J_x, J_u, J_c, representing the cost function for reference trajectory x_{ref} tracking, control input penalty and collision cost function; J_T is the terminal cost function. The set of admissible control inputs is represented by $\mathbb{U}$ and G represents a function for the state constraint. To achieve better tracking performance based on desired trajectory acceleration, the control input reference u_{ref} is chosen.

For implementation, they discretized the system dynamics and constraints over a coarse discrete time grid $t_0, \ldots, t_N$ within the time interval $[t_k, t_{k+1}]$. The model was evaluated with simulation and experimentation. The resulting performance can be seen in the video available at https://www.youtube.com/watch?v=Ot76i9p2ZZo&t=40s.

The experiments showed that the approach suggested by this research could be used as an agent design component that ensures agile and dynamic collision avoidance maneuvers. It helps maintain system stability at a reasonable computational cost while making it possible to assign priority to certain agents with regard to following their reference trajectories. As the approach accounts for state estimator uncertainty by propagating the uncertainty along the prediction horizon, it helps increase the minimum acceptable distance between flying agents, ensuring robust collision avoidance.

Source:
Kamel, M., Alonso-Mora, J., Siegwart, R., & Nieto, J. (2017, March 3). *Nonlinear Model Predictive Control for Multi-Micro Aerial Vehicle Robust Collision Avoidance.* arXiv. https://doi.org/10.48550/arXiv.1703.01164

QUESTIONS

1. Explain different use cases and applications of MAVs in real-world scenarios.

2. Discuss why MAVs are considered agents involved in complex decision-making.

3. Summarize the NMPC framework suggested by the research in this case.

4. How does this approach relate to the contents discussed in this chapter?

5. What are the other areas where this approach (or similar approaches) can be used to design intelligent agents that effectively augment human decision-making?

QUESTIONS FOR DISCUSSION

1. What are the two key branches of decision theory? Explain in detail.

2. Explain the concept of expected utility with reference to the normative theory.

3. Search online and list five examples of agents that are designed to make rational choices in an uncertain, episodic environment (agents making simple decisions).

4. With the help of an example, discuss the equation that describes how an agent chooses the action that maximizes its expected utility.

5. While using a decision network, how do you calculate utilities to determine the optimal decision?

6. Why is the game of chess considered a complex environment?

7. What is dynamic programming?

8. Describe the concept of MDP and list at least five areas where it is applied.

9. What are the key assumptions of MDP problems?

10. Discuss how MDP concepts are related to reinforcement learning.

11. What is the relevance of the time horizon in MDP problems?

12. How do discounting rewards help the agent find an optimal policy?

13. Discuss how different nodes work in a dynamic decision network.

14. How are the time steps used in designing dynamic decision networks? What do the arrows represent in a typical dynamic decision network diagram?

15. Distinguish between value iteration and policy iteration.

16. Search online and discuss the history of Monte Carlo methods.

17. With the help of an example, discuss how you can design a simulator using Monte Carlo algorithms.

18. What challenges do the agents in a multiagent environment face compared to those in single-agent environments?

19. Discuss the strategies used in designing agents for multiagent environments.

20. List five examples of agents designed as multiagent systems. Describe their design principles and applications in detail.

REFERENCES

1. Russell, S. & Norvig, P. (2020). *Artificial Intelligence: A Modern Approach, 4th* Edition. Hoboken, NJ: Pearson.
2. Emerson, P. M. (2019). Module 2: Utility. Retrieved from https://open.oregonstate.education/intermediatemicroeconomics/chapter/module-2/
3. Machine Learning TV. (2017, February 7). Decision Theory: Maximum Expected Utility - Stanford University. Retrieved from https://www.youtube.com/watch?v=JtF5-Ji8JrQ
4. Jiang, N. (2020). MDP Preliminaries. Retrieved from https://nanjiang.cs.illinois.edu/files/cs598/note1.pdf
5. Neto, G. (2005). *From Single-Agent to Multi-Agent Reinforcement Learning: Foundational Concepts and Methods.* Lisbon, Portugal: Institute for Systems and Robotics. Retrieved from http://users.isr.ist.utl.pt/~mtjspaan/readingGroup/learningNeto05.pdf
6. Turkett, W. H. & Rose, J. R. (n.d.). Planning with Agents: An Efficient Approach Using Hierarchical Dynamic Decision Networks. Department of Computer Science and Engineering, University of South Carolina. Retrieved from https://jmvidal.cse.sc.edu/library/turkett03a.pdf
7. Adapted from: Kleinn, D. & Abbeel, P. (n.d.). CS 188: Artificial Intelligence Markov Decision Processes II. Retrieved from https://inst.eecs.berkeley.edu/~cs188/fa18/assets/slides/lec9/FA18_cs188_lecture9_MDPs_II_6pp.pdf
8. Abbeel, P. (n.d.). Markov Decision Processes and Exact Solution Methods: Value Iteration, Policy Iteration, Linear Programming. Presented at the UC Berkeley EECS. UC Berkeley EECS. Retrieved from https://people.eecs.berkeley.edu/~pabbeel/cs287-fa12/slides/mdps-exact-methods.pdf
9. Weingertner, P. (2022). PhilippeW83440/MCTS-NNET. Retrieved from GitHub website: https://github.com/PhilippeW83440/MCTS-NNET (Original work published 2020).
10. Zoto, G. (2020, December 16). Kaggle Mini Courses - Airline Price Optimization Microchallenge. Retrieved from https://www.youtube.com/watch?v=irjpteecxdg
11. Vlassis, N. (2007). *A Concise Introduction to Multiagent Systems and Distributed Artificial Intelligence.* San Rafael, CA: Morgan & Claypool. Retrieved from https://jmvidal.cse.sc.edu/library/vlassis07a.pdf
12. Osborne, M. J. (2002). *An Introduction to Game Theory.* Oxford, UK: Oxford University Press.
13. Ross, D. (2021). Game Theory. In E. N. Zalta (Ed.), *The Stanford Encyclopedia of Philosophy* (Fall 2021). Stanford, CA: Metaphysics Research Lab, Stanford University. Retrieved from https://plato.stanford.edu/archives/fall2021/entries/game-theory/
14. The examples discussed in Dominant Strategy Equilibrium and Pareto-Optimal Outcome sections are adapted from: Davies, T. (2004). *Game Theory through Examples.* Stanford, CA: Stanford.Edu. Retrieved from https://web.stanford.edu/class/symsys202/Game_Theory_Through_Examples.html

CHAPTER 5

Decision-Making Building Blocks, Tools, and Techniques

In order to perform any task effectively and efficiently, we need certain requirements fulfilled and resources available. For example, to cook a nice stew, apart from a good recipe (method or technique) and basic ingredients, you also need tools such as utensils (pots, dishes, spoons) and a cooktop. Similarly, effective decision-making requires information: good quality data as a primary building block or a basic ingredient. Furthermore, it is essential to have the right tools and techniques. Decision analysis, for example, is a technique that can be performed using decision trees and decision table tools. An analysis correctly done strengthens the chances of success of your decision. Suitable tools and techniques make all analyses possible.

MDPs are powerful tools that help us design intelligent agents to augment and automate our decisions. However, there are many other tools and techniques that are used to assist and support our decisions in multiple contexts. This chapter will discuss important decision-making building blocks, tools, and techniques. Depending upon how we integrate these building blocks with technologies discussed in the previous chapters, we can purpose-build the systems to assist, support, augment, and automate decisions. For example, advanced technologies such as deep neural networks and reinforcement learning can use optimization tools and techniques to create systems that can automate our decisions. When you

DOI: 10.1201/b23322-5

perform a predictive analysis using classical ML, it helps with decision support. As it is combined with more advanced AI technologies, it can become a tool for decision augmentation and even automation.

In this chapter, we will explore why data is one of the most important building blocks of effective decision-making. The concept of decision analysis will be discussed, followed by decision modeling. Finally, we will see how text analytics concepts can be applied to make critical business decisions.

DATA FOR DECISION-MAKING

It is data that turns decision-making from an art to a science. With the right data, we can apply mathematical and scientific methods to solve decision problems and improve the quality of decision-making. Today, more and more businesses are using data to empower decision-makers at strategic, tactical, and operational levels. Most large companies, such as Facebook, Apple, Netflix, Airbnb, and YouTube, harness the power of data to expand their businesses beyond boundaries. Also, many medium- and even small-scale companies are now moving to more data-driven decision-making.

This is the age of big data – datasets that are too large and too complex to be handled by traditional data processing applications. Annual revenue from the global big data analytics market is expected to reach $68.09 billion by 2025 (from around $15 billion in 2019). By 2025, we will be creating 181 zettabytes of data worldwide.[1] The moment you click a web link on the internet, you create a footprint – a new data record. Think how many people are engaged in the same activity round the clock, across different time zones worldwide. The data we generate is the foundation of business intelligence and becomes the basis of decision-making when analyzed. Enterprises are accumulating and sourcing data in volumes bigger than ever before. Data becomes more powerful as it increases in:

- Volume: the amount of data both in data points and in the number of variables per data point.

- Velocity: the speed at which data is accumulated. Due to several technologies and devices such as sensors, we are collecting vast amounts of data at an incredible speed.

- Variety: data forms and formats. Today, we can access data in multiple formats, such as structured data in spreadsheets and tables; semi-structured and unstructured data in text, images, videos, and audio.

Despite its various benefits, big data also presents a number of challenges for enterprises. In order to manage and handle data at a massive scale, you require the right resources and infrastructure. In addition, given the speed of change today, data management technologies quickly get obsolete. With the adoption of new technology comes the challenge of training people. Finally, data quality is another major issue in managing data. More data doesn't mean quality data. Remember: *"garbage in – garbage out."* You cannot expect good results from your analysis if the quality of your data is poor. In a survey of more than 2,000 BI practitioners, the researchers found that poor data quality was the most commonly identified reason for business intelligence problems; the most important trend was master data/ data quality.[2]

In order to ensure the quality of data, Rick Sherman[3] recommends following the five Cs of the data framework. The five Cs in this framework include the following:

1. Clean: one of the most tedious tasks recognized by data analysts and scientists is data cleaning. Unclean or dirty data might have several possible problems, such as invalid entries, missing items, incomplete records, duplicated records, and incorrect entries. These problems can cause considerable damage if not fixed before putting the data to use. To some degree, most of the data that we source from different platforms is dirty. Therefore, it is essential to perform data profiling and cleansing before storing or using it.

2. Consistent: many decisions are made at a team level and sometimes many teams can be involved in one decision. Data used for decision-making should be consistent throughout the teams and decision-makers. Different versions of data or information might cause a lot of confusion. If possible, avoid keeping too many versions or copies of data. Once you update a dataset, consider removing the outdated copies from your records. All the individuals and teams involved in decision-making should use the same version of data to produce consistent and accurate results.

3. Conformed: data must be categorized and described in the same way across multiple facts and/or records. Moreover, it should be analyzed across common, shareable dimensions if multiple decision-makers are using the same information.

4. Current: it is obvious but using obsolete data is not a good idea. It is necessary to base your decisions on whatever level of currency is necessary for the decision problem. In some cases, you need data to be up to the minute.

5. Comprehensive: in order to make an effective decision, you need enough data. Regardless of where it comes from or its granularity level, data must be comprehensive and sufficient to support the decision under context.

In addition to ensuring the quality of data, businesses also need to adopt suitable strategies for data architecture, management, and governance. As discussed in Chapter 1, well-designed *data architecture* is essential for all data-driven enterprises. It enables decision-makers to access the information and make use of it.

Businesses using data in massive amounts need robust *data management* systems that ingest, store, organize, and maintain data sourced and accumulated by the enterprise. Establishing such systems requires resources and a good strategy. One good thing about using big data is that it is deployed in the cloud. Commercial object storage services such as Amazon Simple Storage Service (S3) can handle data more conveniently and effectively.

Data governance is another key concern for data management. With data becoming extremely powerful, companies must turn to making data governance one of their strategic priorities. In addition to ensuring data integrity, consistency, and security, it also helps manage the availability and usability of data in the enterprise system. Using data governance, you can establish necessary policies, processes, and standards on approved methods and accountability for data usage.

DECISION ANALYSIS

Let's start this section with a bit of exercise. Make a list of ten of the worst decisions you have ever made. It could be a marriage, a relationship, buying the wrong car, investing in a bad property, or anything else. Reflect on each decision now and think about the reasons why those decisions didn't work out. It is highly likely that you did not spend enough time analyzing your choices while you were making those decisions. You were either not considering all the alternatives available to you or basing your decisions on emotion or intuition instead of logic. This is the premise of this section: decision analysis, a systematic approach to decision-making that includes analyzing all the essential decision variables, all the possible alternatives available to us, and the consequences of our choices.

The concept of decision analysis is centuries old. However, it was first popularized by Professor Ronald Howard[4] of Stanford University in 1988. Initially, professionals in management sciences were engaged in decision analysis research but soon it gained significant attention from scholars, researchers, and decision-makers in a wide variety of disciplines. Today, decision analysis is used in many professions and critical corporate and public applications. Some of the examples of decision analysis applications are as follows:

- Investment and portfolio analysis
- Determining how to help patients improve their health and quality of life (pharmaceuticals)
- Hiring defense contractors and other officials for military operations
- Manufacturing and production decisions
- Risk assessment
- Strategic planning
- Social services
- Real estate decision-making.

Although decision analysis can be applied to any level of decision-making, it is mostly used for strategic decision-making in organizations. Analyzing decisions takes resources, including time and effort. Spending critical resources on day-to-day operational decisions is not a good idea. Decision analysis is therefore considered for critical (highly important) decisions that are complex in nature and are made under uncertainty and risk.

Decision analysis is usually considered a quantitative and visual approach to decision-making. Under uncertainty, when a decision-maker doesn't know the probabilities of different outcomes, they use one of the following five criteria (examples of some of these criteria will be discussed in the next section):

1. **Maximax criterion:** while using this criterion, the decision-maker lists all the alternatives with their payoffs and then selects the alternative that maximizes the maximum payoff of the decision over

all available alternatives (example: Table 5.2). Since this criterion is based on a highly optimistic approach, it is also known as the *optimistic* criterion.

2. **Maximin criterion:** this is opposite to the Maximax approach. While using maximin, the decision-maker takes an extremely conservative view of the future. It is, therefore, also called the *pessimistic* criterion. The decision-maker chooses the alternative that maximizes the decision's minimum payoff over all the available alternatives (example: Table 5.3).

3. **Minimax regret criterion:** while using this criterion, a decision-maker minimizes their highest regret while choosing one alternative over the others. This criterion is based on the concept of *opportunity loss* or *regret*. The difference between the optimal and actual payoffs received is the opportunity loss for any decision. It can be considered as the payoff lost by not choosing the best alternative. Decision-makers first develop the opportunity loss table with opportunity loss values (the difference between the actual and the best payoffs) and then select the alternative representing the minimum of the maximum regrets (example: Tables 5.4 and 5.5).

4. **Hurwicz criterion or criterion of realism:** in reality, most of us fall between the two extremes of optimism and pessimism. This means that an average decision-maker is never too optimistic or too pessimistic. The criterion of realism (Hurwicz) allows a decision-maker to use the *coefficient or realism* called alpha (α) to help them measure their level of optimism regarding future outcomes.

   The value of α is between 0 and 1. α provides the information on the optimistic view, whereas $1-\alpha$ represents the pessimistic view of the outcomes. The value of α equal to 0.5 would represent a neutral decision-maker. The realism payoff is nothing but a weighted average for maximum and minimum payoffs. This criterion, therefore, is also called the weighted average criterion, where α and $1-\alpha$ are the weights assigned to each payoff. The decision-maker first calculates realism payoffs for all the alternatives and then chooses the alternative with the highest realism payoff.

5. **Laplace criterion or equally likely criterion:** this criterion assumes that any state of nature can occur or all the outcomes are equally

likely to occur. The average payoff is calculated for each alternative and the decision-maker chooses the alternative with the maximum average payoff.

For decision-making under risk, we can perform decision analysis by assigning probabilities to possible events, choices, or actions based on historical information or our understanding of the problem in context. The probabilities can be used only when the decision-maker has some idea about the probabilities of occurrences of different outcomes.

Decision analysis can be seen as a five-step process:

1. Define the decision problem.

2. List all the possible alternatives (solutions) and states of nature (possible states in the decision environment).

3. Identify a suitable tool for decision analysis.

4. List/calculate all the payoffs (outcomes) for each alternative and state of nature.

5. Using an appropriate technique or model, choose the best alternative.

Unlike some other techniques (such as optimization), decision analysis doesn't produce an optimal solution to the problem. Instead, it helps decision-makers take the 10,000-foot view of the problem by breaking it down into small, manageable decision alternatives and analyzing each alternative separately in detail. As discussed in the previous chapters, human decision-making is highly affected by the constraints of the human mind. Decision analysis helps us overcome such limitations and provides better tools to analyze decisions in a more structured way, more logically, and systematically. Now, we will discuss two important decision analysis tools – decision tables and decision trees.[5]

Decision Tables

A decision table is a tabular, visual representation of a decision problem consisting of possible actions an agent can take for each alternative available, given specific conditions, and under different circumstances. Decision tables consist of payoffs or outcomes of decision variables or alternatives. In addition, they might also include information on other aspects such as uncontrollable variables (for example, market conditions) and result variables such as return on investment or profit. This tabular structure allows you to apply a suitable mathematical model or decision criteria to solve a decision problem. Most of the data analytics are performed on datasets that are organized in spreadsheets. Major spreadsheet applications such as MS Excel are designed to include this tabular format. Tables provide a structure to the complex information allowing human brains to process information faster and more conveniently.

The following example shows us how to use the five-step decision analysis process and apply different decision criteria using decision tables.

Step 1 – Identifying the decision problem: you have saved some money from your income over the past few years and want to make an investment that gives you the highest return.

Step 2 – List all the possible alternatives and states: the three investment alternatives available to you are treasury bonds, stocks of company A (stocks A), and stocks of company B (stocks B). The market environment is uncertain and the economy constantly fluctuates with growth, stability, and decline periods (states of nature).

Step 3 – Identify a suitable tool for decision analysis: decision tables are chosen to perform this analysis. The columns in the table represent different states of the market and the rows represent the payoffs from different investment alternatives. When a decision table includes values representing payoffs, it is called a payoff table.

Step 4 – List/calculate all the payoffs (outcomes) for each alternative and state: the calculated payoffs for each alternative (investment choices) and states of nature (market states) are shown in Table 5.1. The value in each box represents the payoffs or dollar value return on your investment.

TABLE 5.1   Investment Decision Table

Alternatives	Market		
	Growth	Stability	Decline
Treasury Bonds	38	47	8
Stocks A	72	34	−10
Stocks B	45	38	−3

TABLE 5.2 Investment Decision Payoffs – Maximax (Optimistic) Criterion

Alternatives	Market			Best
	Growth	Stability	Decline	
Treasury Bonds	38	47	8	47
Stocks A	72	34	−10	**72**
Stocks B	45	38	−3	45

Step 5 – Using an appropriate technique or model, choosing the best alternative: let's use the maximax criterion first. As shown in Table 5.2, we will pick the maximum (best) payoff values from each row and put them next to the payoff table. Since it is the optimistic criterion, we will choose the maximum value from all the values we picked. It seems the best decision will be to invest in stocks A as they offer the maximum return of $72.

Let us see what happens when we adopt the conservative, maximin approach. From each row, we will pick the minimum or worst value. Since we are trying to maximize our minimum payoff, we will focus on the best of worst payoffs. As shown in Table 5.3, we will choose to invest in treasury bonds since they return $8, which is the maximum of all minimum payoffs listed.

TABLE 5.3 Investment Decision Payoffs – Maximin (Pessimistic) Criterion

Alternatives	Market			Worst
	Growth	Stability	Decline	
Treasury Bonds	38	47	8	**8**
Stocks A	72	34	−10	−10
Stocks B	45	38	−3	−3

Last, what if we choose to use the minimax regret criterion? Since it is based on the concept of opportunity loss or regret, we will need to calculate the value of regret for each alternative in each given state. The regret values are calculated by subtracting the payoff received from the best payoff in each state of nature (column).

The regret values for our example are calculated as shown in Table 5.4. First, we take the maximum value from each column (the best payoff) and then subtract the actual payoff received in each cell from the maximum value in its respective column.

TABLE 5.4 Investment Decision Payoffs – Minimax Regret Calculation

Alternatives	Market		
	Growth	Stability	Decline
Treasury Bonds	72 – 38 = 34	47 – 47 = 0	8 – 8 = 0
	38	47	8
Stocks A	72 – 72 = 0	47 – 34 = 13	8 – (–10) = 18
	72	34	–10
Stocks B	72 – 45 = 27	47 – 38 = 9	8 – (–3) = 11
	45	38	–3

TABLE 5.5 Investment Decision Payoffs – Minimax Regret Decision

Alternatives	Market			Maximum
	Growth	Stability	Decline	
Treasury Bonds	34	0	0	34
Stocks A	0	13	18	**18**
Stocks B	27	9	11	27

We now pick the maximum value from each row and put it under the maximum (regret) list on the right-hand side, as shown in Table 5.5. As a decision-maker using this criterion, you will choose the decision with a minimum of all the maximum regrets. The minimum value of all maximum regrets is $18. Therefore, we will choose to invest in the stocks of company A. It is interesting to note how the decision changes as we change our decision-making criteria.

Decision Trees

Decision trees can be used as an alternative to decision tables. They allow a convenient way to analyze the decision scenario with different variables involved in the decision problem. Before we go further, it is important to note that the term decision tree can have different connotations. A predictive analytics algorithm named the *decision tree* is used for classification purposes. In this section, we are not talking about the algorithm but the decision tree as a tool for decision analysis.

A typical decision tree looks like a network diagram with nodes and arcs. There are usually two types of nodes in a decision tree: decision nodes and the outcomes nodes. A square represents a decision node and the arcs or lines originating from this node show the options or alternatives available for the decision. A circle represents an outcome node. The arcs or lines originating from this node show the possible outcomes that could occur at

TABLE 5.6   Investment Decision Payoffs
with Probability Values

	Market	
Alternatives	Growth	Decline
Treasury Bonds	40	12
Stocks A	72	−10
Stocks B	18	18
Probabilities	*0.4*	*0.6*

this node. When the problem includes probabilities of outcomes, this node is also called a chance node. When we use chance nodes, we assume that the decision-maker doesn't have full control over the outcomes.

Some decision trees might also use terminal nodes represented by small circles that show the end of the paths or the analysis process. To discuss decision tree analysis in detail, we will continue our previous example of analyzing three different investment options. Let's consider that this is another year and the situation is slightly different.

In this situation, we are dealing with the problem of decision-making under risk. The decision-maker is now aware of the probabilities of the occurrence of different outcomes. Table 5.6 shows this new scenario. There are only two possible states of nature (market): growth and decline. To start a decision tree, we will first take a decision node (square) that represents the decision. As shown in Figure 5.1, we will then create three different

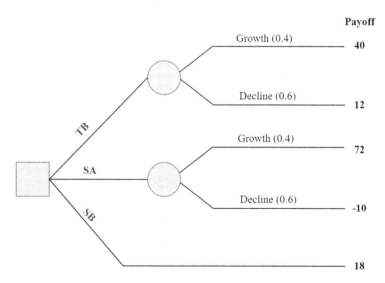

FIGURE 5.1   Decision tree problem scenario

arcs showing three investment decisions: TB (treasury bonds), SA (stocks of company A), and SB (stocks of company B).

The next step is to add chance nodes and create arcs further originating from these chance nodes denoting the probability of occurrence of each state of nature. We will then write down the payoffs or outcomes of each node in each state. Since the outcome of SB is the same in each state, we do not create two separate arcs for it.

Let's go ahead and analyze this scenario with some calculations. This decision tree can be solved by calculating the *expected value* of each outcome in all the possible states. The expected value in cases involving multiple events or probabilities is calculated as the probability-weighted average of all possible events. It can be denoted as follows:

$$EV = \sum P\left(X_{i)} \times X_i\right.$$

where

$$EV = \text{Expected Value}$$

$$PX_i = \text{the probability of the outcome}$$

$$X_i = \text{the outcome}$$

The process of analyzing a decision tree to determine the optimal decision is called folding back the decision tree: we start calculating expected values from the payoffs and work our way back to the decision node (the first node starting from the left).

Expected values for each alternative are calculated as follows:

$$EV \text{ for TB}\left(\text{Treasury Bonds}\right) = 0.4(40) + 0.6(12) = 23.2$$

$$EV \text{ for SA}\left(\text{Stocks A}\right) = 0.4(72) + 0.6(-10) = 22.8$$

$$EV \text{ for SB}\left(\text{Stocks B}\right) = 0.4(18) + 0.6(18) = 18$$

Figure 5.2 shows how we find the optimal solution for this problem. The calculated expected values are placed above each respective chance node. The maximum expected value is $23.2, which is also placed next to the decision node that represents the final, optimal decision – we will invest in treasury bonds.

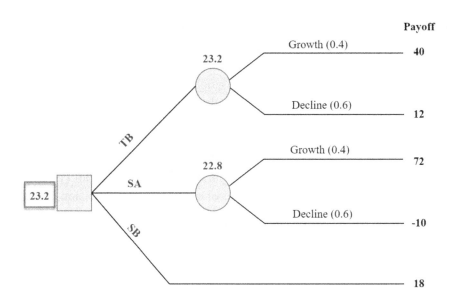

FIGURE 5.2   Decision tree – finding optimal solution

This is a simple example of a decision tree. Although decision trees can solve a variety of complex problems, it is recommended not to use them for problems that are too complex and where the tree is likely to get too large. Since it is a graphical representation of the decision, your audience should be able to see all the layers of the tree clearly. Adding too many layers to your tree will affect the visual quality of your decision tree graphic. You can find several online applications and add-ins, such as TreePlan add-in for MS Excel, to create and solve decision trees.

DECISION MODELING

Decision modeling helps us define a problem mathematically, so it can be solved with a well-structured, sequential process. A model is a representation of a subject (process, person, phenomenon, event, system, or object), telling us how it works or should work. It provides a framework that serves as an example that can be followed or imitated to produce better and more effective outcomes. When you model a decision, you try to create a framework to describe and solve a decision problem using proven techniques such as predictive and prescriptive modeling, which we will discuss shortly.

Decision modeling is a structured approach that starts with listing essential questions concerning the problem. It focuses on using all the necessary information to determine the relationships and dependencies between different variables. The more complex the decision, the more detailed information you will need. A model of a decision may include business logic that helps communicate business rules more clearly to the decision-makers. Although there are several ways to model decisions, we mostly use a standard notation or algorithm embedded in decision-making systems.

Decision modeling works best for decisions that are valuable for business, measurable, applied consistently, and expensive to make, including ones that need to be made repeatedly and quickly, reviewed and audited, changed frequently, and have a high cost or risk of error.[6] Decision modeling has been proven extremely valuable in the following areas:

- Improving customer service

- Managing high-value operations

- Optimizing production and resources

- Managing risk

- Managing high transaction volume and high-scale operations

- Detecting and preventing fraud

- Responding to stakeholders in real time

- Handling cross-channel (mobile, web, in-person) interactions with stakeholders.

When the same model is used multiple times, it improves decision-making quality over time. In addition, models that are successfully used for a reasonable period and are proven highly effective at testing and verification can be used to automate decisions enabling organizations to achieve greater levels of efficiency. As discussed in Chapter 2, models work much better than human decision-making since they base their judgment on a well-defined logic to analyze all the important decision variables. In the upcoming sections, we will discuss the most commonly used decision-making models by enterprises today.

Predictive Modeling

Predictive modeling is a statistical technique used to make predictions and projections for the future. It uses historical data and a model incorporated as an algorithm to predict future outcomes. Using several data mining technologies, companies are deploying various predictive models to support a wide range of business decisions. As they analyze massive amounts of historical data, predictive models identify common patterns in data and make predictions based on the knowledge gained from the analysis.

The mathematical approach of predictive modeling is different from the computational approach that allows us to use highly advanced and sophisticated predictive modeling algorithms. The mathematical approach requires a series of tedious calculations that consume a lot of time and energy. Also, it is not easy to guarantee the accuracy of the results since human agents perform the calculations. Today, most of the predictive modeling is done using the computational approach. ML approaches have been proven highly effective for predictive modeling due to their capabilities that help us save resources (such as time, energy, and money) and produce highly accurate results even in real time. In this section, we will only focus on ML-based predictive models.

Predictive models can be created with both supervised and unsupervised ML. A quick review of what we learned in Chapter 2: supervised learning is suitable when your decision problem has a labeled dependent variable (one that needs to be predicted). It is therefore used mostly for regression and classification models. Unsupervised learning, in comparison, is more suitable for problems with several underlying patterns or hidden relationships between the variables. Clustering is a popular unsupervised learning model that we will discuss shortly.

Today, predictive models are widely used in fraud identification, designing new products, segmenting customers, quality assurance, predictive maintenance, content recommendation, healthcare diagnosis, and many other enterprise applications. Remember, we discussed recommender systems in Chapter 3? Those recommendation systems use predictive models to generate recommendations and insights for the business and its stakeholders.

The process of predictive modeling starts with collecting data that is cleaned and transformed into a usable form. This data is then used to create a model that includes decision variables to make desired predictions accurately. The predictive modeling process involves three important steps: training, testing, and validating the model. You should use three different subsets of data for each of these three steps. Make sure to have a sufficient number of observations for each subset. ML models need lots and lots of data to function effectively.

The suitable proportion at which your main dataset should be divided is arbitrary. Some modelers use 60/20/20 (60% for training, 20% for testing, and 20% for validating), whereas others use 60/30/20 proportions. You can also choose to go through only training and validation steps while avoiding testing. While this approach requires only two subsets and lesser amounts of data, it might negatively affect the quality of your model's overall performance in the absence of testing.

Building predictive models involve trying several models to determine which model performs the best on a given dataset. The model is created on the training dataset (or subset). The performance of the model is then tested using a different dataset called the test set. If the performance is not satisfactory, we retrain the model (again with the training dataset) using different combinations of settings, parameters, or sometimes a different algorithm. The model is iterated multiple times to make sure it produces predictions accurately. The predictive validity of a model is then determined using specific model validation techniques on the validation set that also helps in fine-tuning the model's parameters. However, validation is not required for all types of models.

We can choose the most suitable modeling technique depending on the nature of the variables and the expected outcome (what is being predicted) for the decision problem. If the outcome is a class label (for example, sick or not sick), the prediction problem will be called a classification problem and will use classification algorithms to make predictions. However, if the outcome is a numeric value (for example, a person's body mass index [BMI]), the prediction problem will be called regression, and a suitable regression algorithm will be used to predict the outcomes. Some of the most common and widely used predictive models and techniques are as follows:

Regression Models
One of the primary techniques in predictive modeling is regression analysis. Companies use regression analysis for many purposes. These models inform how dependent and independent variables are related while also focusing on the level and strength of the association between different variables under study. The dependent variable is the factor you try to predict and the independent variable(s) would be the factor(s) you suspect impact your dependent variable. Regression analysis can help you determine which independent variables impact the dependent variable, which ones are most or least significant, and how strong the relationship is between the variables.

Let's discuss the application of regression models with the help of an example. A health insurance company seeks to determine the most suitable insurance premium for each customer. It is not in favor of the company if a customer is charged a low premium and the company has to pay more for their medical treatment. However, it is not fair to charge them a higher premium without any justifiable reason. Therefore, to determine the right premium amount, they must analyze each customer's health history with due caution.

Their team of analysts created a multiple linear regression (MLR) model that can help determine a suitable premium amount for each customer. MLR was chosen since multiple variables were involved in this problem. They predicted each customer's health expenses based on their age, gender, BMI, number of children, and smoking habits. The standard notation for an MLR model can be written as follows:

$$y = \beta_0 + \beta_1 x_1 + \beta_2 x_2 + \cdots + \beta_k x_k + \epsilon$$

The model in this study was explained as follows:

$$Health\ expenses = (-2285) + (266.7)age + (6.9)bmi + (-2.01e + 04)smoker + (1431)bmi : smoker + \epsilon$$

To select the most significant variables, they used the backward elimination method, where you start with the maximal model with all the variables included and then delete variables one by one until all the remaining variables make significant contributions to the response (dependent) variable. At each step, the variable that shows the smallest contribution to the model is removed. It is also important to check the interactions between key independent variables. Why? The probability of a person dying of obesity increases if the person is also elderly (this shows the impact of the interaction between obesity and old age on death). The team analyzed and tested three different interactions (using p values) to determine if they were significant to be included in the model.

According to the final model, 83.6% variation in a customer's health expenses could be explained by the combination of age, BMI, smoker (whether or not a person smokes), and bmi:smoker (interaction between BMI and smoking). They started with seven variables, and the final model concluded only three variables and an interaction between two variables significantly impact the health expenses of the customers. Q plots and diagnostic plots were used to ensure the model's quality while ensuring the model fulfills the fundamental requirements (or assumptions) of linear regression. With hypothesis testing, the team concluded that their MLR model explains a linear relationship between the dependent variable and at least one of the independent variables.

Classification Models

Classification models place new inputs into respective classes or groups based on the patterns they learn from historical data. What happens when a computer is asked to identify whether or not the recently received email is *spam*? This is a case of binary classification. The problems that have only two class labels are called binary classification problems. So, the computer will go ahead and analyze each email. If the attributes of an email match spam (repetitive, unsolicited, sent in bulk), it will be marked as *spam*. Otherwise, *not spam*. Commonly, we use logistic regression and support vector machines for binary classification.

Now think about this situation: your computer (or system) has information on seven different classes of plant species. This information is fed to the system via a training dataset that informs the model about the different characteristics of each species. You then present 50 images of different plants to the computer and ask it to identify the class of the plant shown in each picture. How will the computer do this? This is where multi-class classification models are applied. They handle tasks that include more than two class labels. The model will draw conclusions from the observed images using the information it already has. Decision trees, K-nearest neighbors, Naïve Bayes, gradient boosting, and random forests algorithms are used for multi-class classification predictions. In addition to binary and multi-class models, multi-label classification and imbalanced classification models are also used for different purposes.

Remember, regression and classification are supervisory learning methods discussed in Chapter 2. They both require labeled datasets to predict outcomes accurately.

Time Series Models

Time series models are primarily used for forecasting purposes. Many important business decisions are based on forecasts. For example, a real estate business forecasts housing prices for the next few years for property investment decisions and a manufacturing business forecasts demand before determining the quantity that needs to be produced. Nevertheless, many forecasting models are running in the background of applications we use for daily decision-making. For example, weather forecasting applications help us decide what to wear, when we should leave or not leave home, and whether or not to use the bike to commute to work.

Time series models use data with sequential data points that are mapped at a certain successive time duration. The model forecasts future outcomes or conclusions on the basis of historical data. Time series data can be modeled with three different techniques:

1. *Moving average:* most basic of all, this method is used for the univariate (one-variable) analysis. Moving average models can help in identifying and highlighting trends and their cycles. The model's output is assumed to have a linear dependence on the values included in the time series data.

2. *Exponential smoothing:* this method is also used to analyze univariate data. However, future forecasts are made on the basis of the weighted average of past values. The weights are assigned on the recency of each value, where the weights of older observations decrease exponentially.

3. *Autoregressive Integrated Moving Average (ARIMA):* this model is suitable for multivariate non-stationary data and involves the combination of three time series models. The algorithms for ARIMA are usually based on the principles of autoregression, autocorrelation, and moving average.

Exponential smoothing and ARIMA models are the most widely used time series forecasting models. They can be applied to many industrial scenarios to generate accurate forecasts. While ARIMA models mainly describe the autocorrelations in data, exponential smoothing aims to describe the trend and seasonality in the data.

Outliers Models

An outlier can be considered as an individual data point that is distant from other points in a given dataset. Have you ever experienced a situation when your bank refused your transaction as it was marketed as an unusual or suspicious activity? Unfortunately, it happens quite often to a lot of people these days. The outlier detection models (aka outliers models) running in the bank's system mark your transactions as suspicious or not suspicious (depending on the label assigned). They analyze the information to identify abnormal, unusual, or outlying data points.

From the training dataset, ML models learn trends in data. This learning enables them to spot unusual patterns that do not match the common patterns or what the model has already learned to be normal. An outliers model usually triggers an account or activity freeze, or it escalates the issue for human intervention. Most of the time, it does both.

Anomaly detection is one of the most successful applications of outliers models that help solve multiple problems in today's big data context. Anomaly detection combines multiple algorithms such as regression, classification, and clustering to find outliers in the given dataset. Outliers, as explained before, are the observations that stand out among other observations. They differ from the so-called normal observations significantly.

Today, anomaly detection is critical in many areas, including fraud detection (finance), fault detection (manufacturing), intrusion detection (computer networking), and detecting health risks in health data (healthcare), to name a few. Nevertheless, these models are critical in keeping our systems and lives safe. The case study provided at the end of this chapter illustrates a successful application of anomaly detection in real time.

Clustering Models

Clustering models make use of unsupervised learning to analyze and create clusters in datasets that do not have labels or variables that can be clearly identified. They help identify underlying patterns or uncover hidden relationships between variables. Clustering models are widely used in applications such as image recognition, anomaly detection, recommendation engines, customer segmentation, and medical diagnoses of different types.

Clustering algorithms such as k-means clustering, hierarchical clustering, probabilistic clustering, and principal component analysis process raw and unclassified data objects into groups that represent specific structures or patterns in the information. When compared to manual observation, results generated by clustering allow businesses to identify patterns more quickly and accurately in large volumes of data.[7]

Many retail companies use clustering models for market segmentation – identifying groups of households that demonstrate significant similarities, such as similar characteristics and behaviors. This information helps them target the right market segment for various marketing initiatives such as marketing campaigns.

For example, a retail company collects data on customers' spending patterns, household income, household size, and residential location. Then, they use this information to create four customer clusters: *large family-high spending; large family-low spending; small family-high spending; small family-low spending.*

Using these clusters, the company can create marketing campaigns targeted to specific market segments (clusters). They can send personalized direct emails to individual customers and display company ads on every customer's individual Facebook page. Large family-low spending customers can be attracted by promotions, ads, and emails regarding value packs of products and quantity discounts.

The cluster dendrogram in Figure 5.3 shows clusters (rectangles) representing the four different market segments. This dendrogram was created using hierarchical clustering, where each cluster includes information from customers who demonstrated similar behaviors or preferences. The second cluster (rectangle) from the left is the largest and the third is the smallest. As a rational decision-maker, the marketing manager of this company will target most of its marketing initiatives toward the largest cluster. Moreover, product managers can use this information to design products with features preferred by this largest market segment.

Prescriptive Modeling

Prescriptive models help prescribe the future course of action based on analytics performed with sophisticated algorithms. Where predictive models inform what is happening or what will happen, prescriptive models suggest what should be done.

Several prescriptive analytics packages available in the market today are built to solve common industry or business problems. Usually available through the cloud (such as Software as a Service [SaaS] and Platform as a Service [PaaS]) solutions, these packages are available as specialized solutions or different optimization platforms. Most DI platforms use recommendation engines powered by prescriptive analytics to help clients find the most suitable solutions for their queries or questions.

Prescriptive models are built on predefined criteria such as expected profit, cost, and time constraints. They are tested and validated on historical and current data to ensure that they solve business problems effectively. While some models, such as optimization models, make direct recommendations on the most optimal decision, others (for example, simulation) help you take a bigger picture that helps in formulating the most

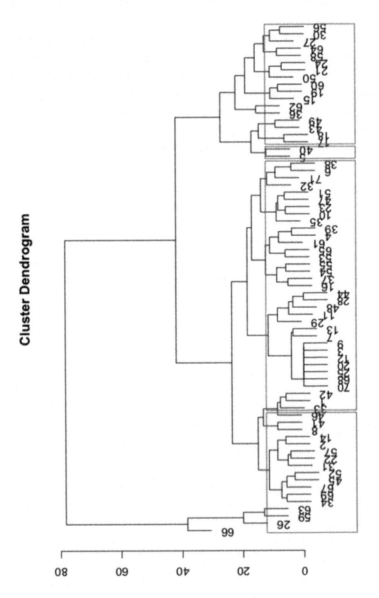

FIGURE 5.3   Hierarchical clustering for market segmentation

optimal strategy to solve the problem under context. In short, prescriptive modeling is a technique to optimize your decisions or find the most optimal solution to your decision problem. The most commonly used prescriptive models are discussed as follows:

Heuristics Models

Heuristics models use a rule-based approach and are suitable for decisions that are repeated multiple times and can be automated. Compared to optimization, heuristic models are easier to create and faster to implement. They are not ideal for complex strategic and tactical decisions that require decision-makers to apply several levels of analysis. One of the commonly used techniques of heuristics modeling is heuristic programming.

In Chapter 2, we discussed how humans make decisions using mental shortcuts. Heuristics programming work in a similar way: instead of focusing on finding an optimal or perfect solution, the model employs a method to find a solution that is sufficient to reach an immediate goal (we trade off outcome for efficiency). Heuristics are based on past experiences with similar problems. These experiences are simple to be programmed as strategies that can produce a good enough solution in a reasonable time frame. Many heuristic programming techniques are used to automate decisions.

Since the models are based on specific rules, they get obsolete as the decision environment or variables change significantly. Heuristics-based models are widely used in making different types of business decisions. Some of the applications of heuristic programming are as follows:

- Allocation: allocating resources such as how much raw material should be sent to each mixer/machine in the factory daily.

- Purchase: deciding when to purchase the raw materials, selecting the suppliers that are located closest to the factory.

- Demand Fulfillment: making decisions on the order of fulfillment of demand, for example, deciding to meet the demands of those who have families while single customers wait.

- Marketing: based on the behavior people demonstrate on social media, placing advertisements that match their preferences, likes, and life choices.

- Business Process Automation: based on the rules defined by the business, automating the business processes such as approving health insurance claims, credit card applications, and loan applications.

Optimization Models

Where heuristics models use a rule-based approach to making decisions, optimization models are based on mathematical algorithms to find the most optimal or feasible solution to a decision problem. Optimization can be considered a mathematical framework used to optimize a business objective based on constraints and the data available on different decision variables.

Optimization models use several calculations through different levels of analysis and can handle higher-level complexity. Thankfully, today we have technological capabilities that can accurately perform many complicated and cumbersome mathematical calculations in a fraction of time (compared to humans). Optimization models are used when a decision-maker has an objective to achieve (maximize or minimize); they have multiple alternatives and resource constraints that force the decision-maker to trade off among alternatives. Optimization models are widely used across different industrial applications today. Some of the examples include[8]:

- Financial Services: loan pooling, product/price recommendations, trade crossing, portfolio optimization, and rebalancing.

- Manufacturing: supply chain network design, inventory optimization, production planning, shipment planning, truck loading, detailed scheduling, and maintenance scheduling.

- Transportation and Logistics: fleet assignment, network design, depot or warehouse location, vehicle and container loading, vehicle routing and delivery scheduling, yard/crew/driver/maintenance scheduling, and inventory optimization.

- Utilities, Energy, and Natural Resources: power generation scheduling, supply portfolio planning, distribution planning, water reservoir management, mine operations, and timber harvesting.

- Telecom: routing, adaptive network configuration, network capacity planning, antenna and concentrator location, equipment, and service configuration.

- Other applications include revenue and yield management, workforce scheduling, advertising scheduling, marketing campaign optimization, appointment and field service scheduling, and combinatorial auctions for procurement.

It is appropriate to say that the concept of optimization is the very foundation of most of the AI-driven decision-making agents surrounding us today. Think about your Alexa or Siri, autonomous cars, gaming bots, and other robots. In the previous chapter, you must have noticed that most intelligent agents seek one thing in common – an optimal solution to a problem. DI is about finding the optimal solutions to all decision problems. Optimization models make it happen.

Different optimization problems require different mathematical techniques depending upon the nature of the problem and certain environmental characteristics. The most common techniques include linear programming, mixed integer programming (MIP), nonlinear programming, and constraint programming. Since linear programming is one of the most frequently used techniques, we will discuss it in detail following brief descriptions of other techniques.

LINEAR PROGRAMMING OPTIMIZATION

Linear programming is a mathematical modeling-based optimization technique that primarily applies to situations where repeatable, programmed decisions are made. All linear programming problems have the following properties and assumptions in common:

- **Maximize or minimize an objective:** this could be any business objective that needs to be either maximized or minimized. It is essential that this objective can be defined mathematically. In general, businesses seek to maximize profits and minimize costs. This property is known as the objective function.

- **Constraints limitations:** often, there are restrictions limiting our ability to achieve the objective. For example, scarce resources such as time and money can prevent us from achieving the results and hence our objective. Such limitations are called constraints.

- **Availability of alternatives:** we wouldn't need optimization if we have one clear choice – the final decision. LP and other optimization techniques work when you have several courses of action or alternatives to choose from. For example, you can either produce 1,000 units of a product, 5,000 units, or 50,000 units. Which quantity should you produce to maximize your revenue? LP helps solve problems with alternative courses of action.

- **Linear mathematical relationships:** linear equations or inequalities must be used to express the objective and the constraints of an LP problem (all terms not squared or to the higher power or appear more than once).

- **Proportionality:** any change in the constraint inequality will result in a proportional change in the objective. For example, a 1% increase in the cost of raw materials will result in a 10% decrease in profit.

- **Additivity:** this property asserts that the total of all activities equals the sum of the individual activities. For example, the total amount of resources used will be determined by the sum of resources used by each product separately.

- **Certainty:** an important property that states the parameters, quantities, or numbers in the objective and constraints is known with certainty. It is also important that these numbers do not change during the period being studied.

- **Divisibility:** it deals with the fact that the solutions don't have to be in whole numbers. The decision variables can take on any fractional or non-integer values.

- **Nonnegative values:** another critical property that asserts the values of all variables are nonnegative. This makes sense because it is impossible to have negative values for most of the physical quantities. You cannot produce negative quantities of products. In some cases (for example, profits), the values can be negative, indicating a loss. In such situations, we use specific mathematical operations to transform negative values into positive ones.

There are a variety of commercial solutions available today that are used for different types of LP problems. Based on the nature of the problem, we choose the most suitable algorithms. LP algorithms can be used with commercial packages or solutions such as MS Excel Solver or you can train a neural network with these algorithms using ML capabilities. One of the most popular LP algorithms is called Simplex.

Simplex operations start with converting the problem into standard form and then into slack form. To do this, we insert some slack variables into inequalities and turn them into equations. The next step is to perform operations to find the pivot position that helps compute the equation's coefficients for the new basic variable(s) and constraints. Finally, you compute the objective function and new sets of basic and non-basic variables.[9]

The following example shows how we can use the Simplex algorithm with MS Excel Solver to find the optimal solution without using any codes or programming language.

Your company manufactures two different types of laptops – gold and platinum. According to the long-term projections, the expected demand for gold laptops is 100, and for platinum, it is 85. The production capacity at your factory is limited. You cannot produce more than 200 gold and 175 platinum laptops. To satisfy the contract with the distributor, you must ship at least 250 laptops each day. Each gold laptop yields a profit of $950, and platinum yields a profit of $1,175. How many gold and platinum laptops should you produce daily to maximize your company's profits?

Our objective is to maximize the profit by optimizing the quantities of two products. The objective function for this problem will look like this:

$$z = 950A + 1175B$$

The constraints that must be satisfied are the demand, production capacity, shipping quantity, and nonnegativity – you cannot produce anything below zero quantities.

Mathematically, we can express this LP problem as follows:

$$\text{Maximize } 950A + 1175B$$

Subject to:

Demand: $A \geq 100$; $B \geq 85$

Production capacity: $A \leq 200$; $B \leq 175$

Shipping requirement: $A + B \geq 250$

Negativity constraint: $A, B \geq 0$

We used the MS Excel Solver add-in and applied the Simplex algorithm to solve this problem (Figure 5.4). Initially, the values were set to 0. These values were the variables that needed to be determined (production

		A (Gold)	B (Platinum)	Total
Quantity to produce		200	175	375
Profit		950	1175	395,625

Constraints			
Demand A	200	≥	100
Production Capacity A	200	≤	200
Demand B	175	≥	85
Production Capacity B	175	≤	175
Shipping Requirement	375	≥	250
Negativity A	200	≥	0
Negativity B	175	≥	0

Determine
Maximize

FIGURE 5.4   LP solution maximizing profits

quantity required – light gray cells) and maximized (profit – dark gray cells). As we inserted the objective function mentioning the value we seek to maximize, the quantities we need to determine, and the constraints, the Solver, produced the output that suggests we should produce 200 units of gold and 175 units of platinum laptops. These quantities will maximize our profits to $395,625. This seems like an optimal solution to our problem since it satisfies all the constraints while resulting in the maximum profit. To perform a check, let us plug the resulting values into the objective function:

$$395,625 = 950 * 200 + 1175 * 175$$

It works!

Even though Solver is not an AI technology, it is still a powerful computational tool that can help solve various complicated problems. It is a great tool for optimization that doesn't require writing complicated codes.

Nevertheless, you will need to use ML capabilities if you want to create optimization systems that need to be scaled and integrated with other systems. LP algorithms can be used to train neural networks for different types of optimizations. Python and its various packages (such as SciPy, NumPy, and PuLP) facilitate solving different LP problems and the models can be deployed using Amazon AWS, Microsoft Azure, or Google Cloud platforms.

Mixed Integer Programming (MIP), as the name suggests, involves problems where at least one of the decision variables is constrained by integer values. However, not all the variables are restricted to be integers. These problems can be quite difficult to solve. The use of integers in the problem expression makes the optimization problem non-convex and more complicated to solve. MIP is more suitable when you are seeking to automate your decision-making process.

The classic knapsack problem is a good example where we can use MIP. Knapsack means a backpack. Imagine there is a thief with an old knapsack that has a limited capacity. He gets into a home with the intention of robbing. The house has a fixed number of items, each with its own weight and value. He cannot split these items into pieces, and he must decide which item to take and which to leave. How will he decide which item to take and which to leave? You cannot apply linear programming to such decision problems. You need either MIP or dynamic programming algorithms to make decisions when the problem involves multiple subproblems or layers of analysis. MLP, a type of combinatorial optimization technique, works quite well at solving such problems.

Nonlinear programming uses the same fundamentals as linear programming. It aims at optimizing (maximizing or minimizing) an objective function given certain constraints. However, it is suitable to use if your objective and/or constraints do not fulfill the assumption of linearity. Often, the feasible solution is determined by the use of nonlinear constraints. In the real world, we face many problems that cannot be explained as linear problems. Nonlinear programming, therefore, is used in many large-scale systems. One drawback of nonlinear programming is that, except in very special circumstances, you cannot guarantee a globally optimal solution to your problem.

Constraint programming is similar to MIP as it uses variables defined as integers that make problems non-convex. This technique is quite new and is appropriate for combinatorial optimization problems characterized by non-convexity. It is designed for optimization problems that aim to reach the optimal solution by satisfying certain constraints by assigning symbolic values to variables. A great advantage of constraint programming is that you can determine a globally optimal solution, even if your problem is nonlinear and highly complex.

Simulation Models

Simulation imitates a real-world process to help optimize decisions. At its core, it is more descriptive than prescriptive. The simulation uses real-world models to create imitation scenarios; therefore, the models used for simulation must be accurate and credible. Today, simulations are used for many industrial applications. They can be applied to:

- Explore how the unexpected event will affect the company's investments in different assets.
- Test the safety of equipment or infrastructure.
- Simulate production plants.
- Model and analyze supply chains with the help of supply chain simulation.
- Choose drilling projects for oil or natural gas.
- Crash test a new line of vehicles for automobiles.
- Make decisions on reservation policies for airlines.
- Evaluate the environmental impact of a new project, such as building an industrial plant or a new bridge.

Simulation helps decision-makers to step into the actual world of the decision scenario. They can explore how the systems within that scenario operate and how things will change if we introduce changes to the existing scenario. It helps in making predictions about how the systems will behave in the future in response to changes or uncertainties. It is a faster, cheaper, and safer way to test whether a decision will work in a real-world setting. Simulations unravel several hidden patterns in a complex system. They can be incorporated into physical devices such as an airplane model or used purely as computer simulation applications.

Simulation models are based on equations that mimic the functional relationships in a decision environment. Each variable and the relationships between the variables are defined as mathematical expressions and in a programmable instruction format. The resulting model presents the dynamics of the behavior of the real-world scenario. In situations where high levels of uncertainty are involved, Monte Carlo simulations are mostly used. Monte Carlo techniques based on game theory and decision theory principles can test multiple what-if scenarios quite rapidly. The Monte Carlo simulation was discussed in the previous chapter. Today, even small businesses can purchase personalized simulation software. Some of the major vendors include Siemens AG, IBM, MathWorks, Autodesk,

Honeywell, AnyLogic, FlexSim, Ansys, Microsoft, AWS, SAP, Huawei, and Adobe.

TEXT ANALYTICS TECHNIQUES FOR DECISION-MAKING

The changing nature of data streaming in all formats allows companies to harness the power of text-based analytics, including web and social media analytics. Text analytics, also known as text mining, is a technique to extract patterns from large amounts of unstructured text data sources, including excerpts, PDF files, XML files, word documents, websites, and social media pages. It is usually considered a predictive analytics technique. However, the scope of text analytics goes beyond predictive analytics. Many scientific discoveries are made using text analytics, where researchers use deep analysis of text-based information to discover how past events unfolded. Nevertheless, text analytics provides valuable insights that support predictive analysis. Some major text analytics applications can be seen in improving customer service, managing risk, filtering spam, and managing healthcare services and maintenance.

The first two steps in text analysis are gathering and preparing data for analysis. We then create models, train and test them to ensure the model's quality. Text analytics uses NLP to understand human language and convert human expressions into structured representations that computer programs can process easily. We discussed NLP technologies in detail in the previous chapter. NLP also enables the organizing and structuring of complex text and turns it into meaningful data for *text classification*: the process of assigning categories to unstructured text data.

Text classification is used widely for topic analysis, sentiment analysis, language detection, and intent detection. Another method, *text extraction*, helps companies save time by avoiding sorting data manually to pull out desired pieces of information. Using text extraction algorithms, you can perform a variety of tasks, such as keyword extraction, named entity recognition, and feature extraction.

Sentiment analysis is one of the most popular methods of text analysis. It helps understand the sentiments people demonstrate on social media related to a particular product, brand, or service. Businesses monitor online conversations on social media platforms such as Facebook and Twitter using text mining algorithms and extract subjective information on people's sentiments. This information is then processed and used to make decisions such as which product features need improvement or what additional services people expect the business to offer. Similarly, companies can use web analytics to gather insights regarding many different aspects of their business. The following example covers both sentiment analysis and web analytics techniques of text mining.

Let's explore this topic further with the help of an example. A small college learns that its enrollment numbers are declining and they assume that it is possibly due to increasing student complaints. To test this assumption, they are interested in analyzing the sentiments of their students expressed through college reviews that students posted on different websites. Their analytics team selected five websites where students frequently post their reviews: cappex.com, niche.com, collegesimply.com, unigo.com, and gradreports.com. In total, they collected 441 reviews through data scraping and stored all these reviews in an MS Excel file. The dataset consisted of some unwanted symbols that were removed during the data cleaning step.

Using R programming, the team performed sentiment analysis and found that students expressed more positive emotions than negative emotions about their college experience in their reviews. However, the number of negative emotions (anger, disgust, fear, and sadness combined) is not insignificant. Sentiments were measured as eight different emotions and their frequency can be seen in Figure 5.5.

Decision-makers were interested in knowing more about how students explain their experiences, especially their pain points. The analytics team presented this information in two forms: a horizontal bar chart (Figure 5.6)

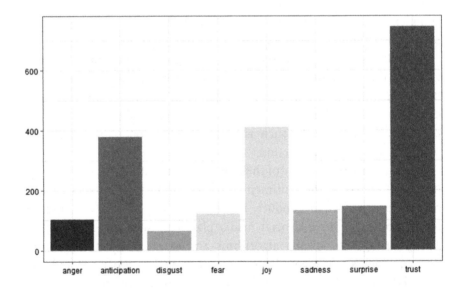

FIGURE 5.5   Sentiment analysis – bar chart

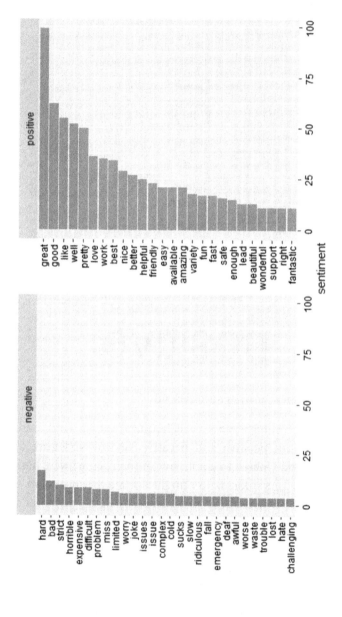

FIGURE 5.6   Sentiment analysis – horizontal bar chart

FIGURE 5.7 Sentiment analysis – word cloud

showing the exact frequency for each frequently used word; and a word cloud showing both positive and negative keywords (Figure 5.7). The words that the team wanted to emphasize in their report were highlighted under rectangles. This information might not make sense to an outsider, but if you know your institution, you can easily figure out what students are talking about. For example, when they say cold and freezing, they are talking about their dorm rooms. The college buildings and equipment are old and the heating systems don't work quite effectively.

This analysis helped the college administration to analyze and understand the actual problem. They tested their assumption and found it was quite close to the actual truth. Students do have pains and issues that must be addressed on an urgent basis. It was a great revelation for the decision-making team.

CONCLUSION

The first few chapters of this book emphasized fundamental concepts of decision-making, technologies, and agents that can augment and automate human decision-making. This chapter discussed some classical and advanced decision-making tools and techniques that can help with all forms of DI. Some of these tools, such as decision tables and trees, are ages-old. In contrast, others, including advanced prescriptive analysis models, are modern techniques that use sophisticated algorithms to find optimal solutions to highly complex business problems.

AI is powerful but many businesses cannot use AI capabilities due to several limitations. One of the main limitations is the availability of data. AI-ML models need massive amounts of data. If you are a company seeking to adopt AI for decision-making, you should consider working on data-related requirements first. You will also need people to be trained on how to use data for different types of analyses. Classical techniques are easy to learn, but when it comes to using advanced techniques and tools, such as predictive and prescriptive analyses and text analysis, you need highly skilled people.

Analyses become more complicated as the forms of data change from structured to semi-structured and then unstructured, and decision contexts get more complex. To address this complexity in both data and decision contexts, AI-powered DI solutions are created. We will discuss some of these cutting-edge DI solutions in the next chapter.

CASE STUDY: DETECTING ANOMALIES AND PREVENTING EQUIPMENT FAILURES IN STEEL WITH NOODLE.AI ASSET FLOW

Noodle.ai provides professional Enterprise Artificial Intelligence solutions for supply chain management to help companies reduce waste of all types, optimize business processes via customer data analytics, and improve decision-making. It was approached by a multi-billion-dollar multinational steel-producing company that sells made-to-order goods to large and small businesses in automotive, home appliances, construction, capital goods, container, and other industries. They produce more than ten million tons of finished products every year through their vast network of steelmaking facilities, finishing facilities, and service centers.

With this partnership, the company wanted to reduce operating expenses for unnecessary preventative maintenance, maximize revenue by increasing uptime for plants in operation, and manage capital expenditure by extending the life of factory equipment so the expenses of replacing equipment could be reduced. To detect anomalies and predict time-to-failure for production equipment across the majority of its mill processes, they implemented Noodle.ai's Vulcan Manufacturing Suite's Asset Flow application.

The application comprises the following two powerful AI inference engines that run on supercomputers:

Asset Sentinel – Anomaly: it ingests datasets from about 40,000 sensors and transforms the information into trillions of data points. This data is then fed to the system to train sophisticated algorithms using recurrent neural networks with unsupervised ML. Next, the engine performs a deeper analysis to find hidden complex patterns and creates clusters (or categories) of the patterns as normal operating conditions or specific failure modes. This approach correctly identifies anomalies that other systems would miss while significantly reducing the chances of false negatives and positives.

Asset Precog: this module is built on the foundation of Asset Sentinel to predict the time of future asset failure. Trillions of sensor data points and failure windows are used to train algorithms that use neural networks and supervised learning techniques. Digital simulations are used to predict when components will fail. Using Bayesian logic engines, this module also explains why the algorithms believe the failure will occur. As the engine receives more data and keeps performing, it learns and improves using reinforcement learning techniques.

Through this application, Noodle.ai addressed 140 failure modes for their client. To populate the AI inference engines, they established data pipelines from continuous casting to hot rolling, cold rolling, and to galvanized lines. The AI inference engine helped in:

- Detecting complex anomalies from real-time sensor data by showing warnings based on abnormal multivariate sensor patterns to the maintenance/operations team and providing underlying sensor contributions to support inspection and diagnosis.

- Predicting equipment failure days in advance with associated probability by showing the time frame in which the equipment is predicted to fail and providing a confidence interval with the prediction.

Each of the 140 failure modes contained tens to hundreds of models within them, which were increasing exponentially. Such complexity can only be handled with the computational capabilities of AI and an enterprise-grade AI application. Using Noodle.ai's solution, the company realized an approximately 30% average reduction in downtime across assets with a 4% positive impact on gross profit.

Source:
Case Study: Asset Flow in Steel. (n.d.). Retrieved May 20, 2022, from Noodle.ai website: https://bit.ly/3lw3LO0

QUESTIONS

1. Discuss how Noodle.ai's client company reduced operating expenses using the Asset Flow application.

2. How does the Asset Sentinel module identify anomalies in real time?

3. How does the application predict the time of the future component or asset failure?

4. Search online and list at least three similar platforms or applications that help decision-makers optimize their decisions through predictive modeling.

QUESTIONS FOR DISCUSSION

1. Distinguish between decision-making technologies, tools, and techniques.

2. Explain why and how data is becoming more powerful and significant for decision-making.

3. List at least three decision analysis applications not mentioned in this chapter.

4. How do companies use decision analysis for strategic decisions?

5. What is Hurwicz's criterion or criterion of realism?

6. How a decision-maker behaves differently while following maximax, maximin, and minimax regret criteria? Discuss with examples.

7. With the help of a real-life example, discuss the five steps in the decision analysis process.

8. What types of decisions should decision tables be used for?

9. Search online and find a problem that can be solved with decision trees. Discuss how you will use decision trees to solve this problem.

10. What are the different nodes in a typical decision tree and what do they represent?

11. List five types of decisions that decision modeling is most suitable for.

12. Explain predictive modeling and its application areas.

13. How are regression models different from classification models? What are the similarities between the two?

14. Discuss different types of time series techniques with the help of examples.

15. What are the major applications of outliers models?

16. How do outlier models identify anomalies? Give a technical overview of this process.

17. What types of problems do clustering algorithms solve?

18. What are the five key application areas of prescriptive modeling?

19. Search online and list at least three examples of using optimization by real-world companies. Use examples not included in this chapter.

20. With the help of an example, explain how text analysis helps organizational decision-making.

REFERENCES

1. Big Data – Statistics & Facts. (2022). Retrieved from Statista website: https://www.statista.com/topics/1464/big-data/
2. Data, BI & Analytics Trend Monitor 2021 – A BARC Research Study. (2021). Retrieved from BARC website: https://barc-research.com/research/bi-trend-monitor/
3. Sherman, R. (2014). *Business Intelligence Guidebook: From Data Integration to Analytics* (1st edition). Waltham, MA: Morgan Kaufmann.
4. Howard, R. A. (1988). Decision Analysis: Practice and Promise. *Management Science, 34*(6), 679–695.

5. The examples discussed in Decision Tables and Decision Trees sections are adapted from: Joshua Emmanuel. (2015, May 11). Decision Analysis 1: Maximax, Maximin, Minimax Regret. Retrieved from https://www.youtube.com/watch?v=NQ-mYn9fPag

6. Taylor, J., Purchase, J., & Soley, R. (2016). *Real-World Decision Modeling with DMN*. Tampa, FL: JTonEDM.

7. What Is Unsupervised Learning? (2021, June 29). Retrieved February 3, 2022, from IBM website: https://www.ibm.com/cloud/learn/unsupervised-learning

8. Buecker, A., Ageeva, Y., Bloom, J., Candas, M. F., Blanchard, V., Chaves, J., Feng, G., Raman, A., & Schlenker, H. (2012). Optimization and Decision Support Design Guide Using IBM ILOG Optimization Decision Manager. ibm.com. Retrieved from https://www.redbooks.ibm.com/redbooks/pdfs/sg248017.pdf

9. Zhang, X. (n.d.). CISC5835, Linear Programming Algorithms for Big Data. Retrieved from https://storm.cis.fordham.edu/zhang/cs5835/slides/LinearProgramming_handout.pdf

CHAPTER 6

Decision Intelligence Market

Vendors and Solutions

In previous chapters, we discussed four forms of DI: decision assistance, support, augmentation, and automation. The DI solutions available in the market today are mainly designed for decision augmentation. However, some of them even offer automation of certain tasks. In this chapter, you will learn about the DI market and key vendors offering cutting-edge solutions for DI.

You will see how the concepts, technologies, tools, and techniques discussed in previous chapters can be applied in building solutions that solve real-world business problems. DI platforms discussed in this chapter are built using various tools and techniques such as predictive and prescriptive modeling, optimization, simulation, automation, and MDP models, combined with technologies such as AI, ML, AutoML, and computer vision (sensors), among others.

Some vendors offer similar solutions but each platform has something unique. You will explore the essential information about each of these companies, the technological details of their platforms, and how they help decision-making. Several application cases are provided with each company's information to help you better understand their platforms and capabilities.

DOI: 10.1201/b23322-6

Large companies such as Google and Microsoft also offer solutions to support decision-making but since they are not purely DI solution vendors, we will exclude them from this chapter. The portfolios of these companies are huge and their solutions (Google's Google Data Studio and Looker, and Microsoft's Power BI) are still highly focused on BI. Instead, we will cover new and emerging providers that are shaping the DI market with their innovative solutions and platforms.

DI SOLUTIONS

Decision intelligence solutions can be considered as a new category of software that helps businesses apply AI to one of their most important functions – decision-making. With a tremendous increase in technological capabilities, businesses can collect massive amounts of data and harness its power using AI-based analytics. Building and managing a DI system in-house requires changing and introducing multiple capabilities. This means you don't only need to develop a highly sophisticated technological infrastructure but also the teams and the talent pool that can help you achieve your goals for DI implementation and adoption. Businesses usually find a huge gap between the scale of AI investment and the tangible returns it delivers. Therefore, investing in solutions created and managed by third-party providers who could take care of your intelligence needs while managing all your data and information sources is a good idea.

DI solutions enable businesses to democratize AI. They make AI accessible and usable to everyone within the organization, not just data scientists or analysts. Another benefit of adopting a ready-made solution is creating a centralized platform that connects and combines all the business data in a single system. The implemented solution then allows decision-makers quick visibility of the hidden patterns in data while also making recommendations on the best course of action in a given scenario.

Organizations are quite prone to building silos that affect businesses' ability to build collective intelligence. When each department or team uses its different information sources and separate pieces of analytics software, the silos only get tougher to break. DI solutions aim to centralize an organization's data and provide AI capabilities to drive organizational outcomes through effective, accurate, and fast decisions.

DI, as a category of AI-powered software, is a relatively new value proposition. When you see a company identifying itself as a *decision intelligence company*, they are mostly one of the providers of DI software solutions. The key players in the DI solutions market as of July 2022 are discussed in this chapter. You will notice some of these vendor companies, such as Noodle.ai and Xylem, provide DI services for a specific use case or a functional area. Others have a broader umbrella that includes solutions for a wide range of industrial applications and decision problems.

It is important to note that the information about these vendor companies is collected from online sources and included in this book for educational purposes only. This book doesn't intend to do promotions and the author is not earning any commissions or monetary compensation to include product information in this book.

DI VENDORS

Peak[1]

Peak, one of the leading decision intelligence companies, is a UK-based enterprise founded in 2014 by Richard Potter, David Leitch, and Atul Sharma. Peak's vision is to "put Decision Intelligence in the hands of every business." The company's key partners include AWS, Snowflake, and Intel. It offers DI services such as customer intelligence, demand intelligence, and supply intelligence for retail, consumer goods, manufacturing, and construction companies. They also offer DI solutions for inventory optimization, price optimization, supply chain, and asset allocation.

As their business is growing, so is their scope and scale. It is a SOC 2 certified company that has earned a few significant awards as a technology company engaged in innovation and one of the best companies in the UK to work for. Some of Peak's client companies include PepsiCo, KFC, AO, Marshalls, Nike, and Aludium.

Peak's decision intelligence platform claims to provide everything decision-makers need to realize DI across their businesses, all in one place. Peak platform offers its clients the following benefits:

- Speed: businesses can get AI models into production in days, not months.

- Flexibility: the solutions are built to fit the user's ways of working. They can choose the amount of support they need from Peak, build what they need, and work exactly how they want to.

- Empowerment: peak provides tools to shorten the time it takes to get data ready for AI. It eliminates the burden of self-creating models and enables teams to focus on tasks they love.

- Connectivity: it connects data, teams, and solutions together as a unified, single platform. Decision-makers can make every decision with full visibility of the impact on the wider business outcomes.

The three core capabilities of Peak's DI platform are as follows:

Dock: a data management toolkit that lets users integrate, prepare, clean, transform, deduplicate, catalog, and organize their data. It is a centralized data warehouse where users can get all the data they need in one place that is ready to be used for AI applications. You can independently ingest the data and also access it from both internal and external sources. Dock's functionalities enable you to connect to Snowflake, S3, and many other data sources to rapidly integrate your data into Peak's system without needing technical support. You can also organize your data in a structured format that allows you to query and validate data, model it, discover and identify patterns, and generate valuable insights to inform decisions.

Factory: this capability allows users to manage the full AI workflow to create centralized intelligence for their business. Factory offers workspaces where you can write scripts in Python, R, or any open-source coding language. Users can build their desired solutions and reports, explore data, adjust models that are already created, or link models from across the business. You can also use Factory's workflow feature to solve complex problems by seeing the visualization of the steps needed to engineer a business decision. Through app deployment, businesses can open up their work to non-technical users who can help drive business outcomes. Different departments and users can deploy dashboards, visualizations, and web apps for interaction and collaboration.

The Factory also allows you the freedom to control the version of code you want to use. You can integrate your files from Github, Bitbucket, and GitLab to access your code. Model management is another great feature that can be used to save, monitor, compare, and revert models. Finally, with API deployment functionality, you can easily deploy APIs, communicate solutions to other users, and get effective models that help your business drive outcomes without any technical or engineering support.

Work: this is the final step where decision-makers get to interact with the results or outputs of Dock and Factory. One of the greatest features of this capability is its built-in explainability which allows you to build trust in your decisions. Even non-technical users can rapidly visualize, interact, and make sense of intelligence for effective decision-making. API deployment allows serving AI-driven recommendations straight to the systems that are already being used. Using the data access feature, users can download intelligence and recommendations in CSV files that are very convenient. Users can choose their desired interface on Work which could include a dashboard, an app, or API deployment to their existing system, or they can just download a file consisting of all intelligence. It is quite flexible.

APPLICATION CASE 6.1: GSK NLP CLASSIFICATION POWERED BY PEAK'S DI PLATFORM[2]

One of the largest pharmaceutical companies in the world, GlaxoSmithKline (GSK) is a global healthcare company based in London, UK. When GSK develops new products, all the products have to go through a rigorous testing process through drug trials. Information related to these trials is collected from healthcare professionals by GSK's Medical Science Liaisons, who input the information and send it to GSK in the form of raw, unstructured text data. It is not an easy task to manually make data AI-ready. GSK wanted to improve its methods to classify open-text field data. They hired Peak's services to achieve this goal.

Using its DI platform, Peak developed a unique natural language processing (NLP) classification model for GSK. The model helps label a controlled set of sentences that can also provide up to two or three labels to any comment included in the datasets. The model also allows determining how valuable or accurate a particular comment is by comparing the number of labels each comment is given. To standardize labels and remove a lot of subjectivity, the model can run through all the company's historical responses and responses that will be received or inputted in the future.

GSK tested Peak's model on a controlled dataset that delivered results with 80% accuracy. One of the most exciting features of this model is that it can assign more than one label to each comment or sentence. While testing, 70% of all sentences had a second label, whereas 30% had a third label. This allowed GSK to label their data, the comments, and the sentences more effectively, helping them perform a more in-depth analysis of their text data. The deeper the analysis, the better the decision.

Tellius[3]

Headquartered in Reston, Virginia, Tellius was founded in 2016 by Ajay Khanna, who now serves as the company's Chief Executive Officer (CEO). The company is led by a team with deep expertise in automated intelligence and big data analytics. Tellius offers services across multiple industries, including pharmaceuticals and life sciences, financial services, e-commerce and retail, healthcare, communications, insurance, consumer goods, technology, and across many functional areas such as marketing, sales, and operations. Its key partners include AWS, Snowflake, Looker, Google Cloud, Databricks, and Azure.

Tellius aims to create solutions that help businesses move seamlessly and effortlessly between exploring data, discovering unseen yet critical insights, generating hypotheses, and acting on data-driven answers to drive business outcomes. With intelligence generated by Tellius' platform, users can get a rich and profound understanding of the business context. Businesses can rapidly analyze billions of data points across various sources with no required maintenance to manage their performance.

It is quite easy to use the Tellius platform. The first step is to connect to your cloud data warehouse, databases, data lakes, applications, or files. Next, it cleanses your data combined from disparate sources, transforms it, and sets up the data pipeline for automated processing. You can now ask questions, visualize your data using natural language, and share findings in interactive vizpads, and get automated insights to uncover important findings with embedded ML. Also, you can easily build, tune, evaluate, and operationalize models into the business workflow.

Tellius is the first DI platform to handle ad hoc queries and compute AI-ML workloads that are too intensive for traditional systems. It raises the data scale by 100 times and speeds up the discovery of insights from hours to seconds. Using its Dual Analytics Engine, you can accelerate the entire analytics process from ad hoc data exploration to advanced insight generation to automated and visual ML modeling. Users can utilize three modes simultaneously to achieve a balance between performance, cost, and speed:

1. In-memory mode caches data to boost performance. It is ideal for databases, application sources, and combining data from multiple sources.

2. Live mode pushes queries down to the data source for processing. This mode is suitable for analytical data warehouses and fast SQL sources.

3. Data lake mode runs search and ML processing on Hadoop nodes as Spark jobs. This mode is ideal for utilizing shared resources in existing data lakes.

Key capabilities of the Tellius platform include guided insights, NLP, data preparation, and automated ML. *Guided insights* help decision-makers uncover the root causes of problems, key drivers of change, and underlying trends and patterns with a single click in seconds. With the help of explainable AI (XAI), they can discover what new problems are on the horizon, why metrics are changing, and keep a pulse on performance indicators without spending hours on manual analysis. Moreover, they can compare differences between different cohorts and discover new segments that need the business's attention. Users can also get push notifications on significant changes to Key Performance Indicators (KPIs) and unexpected anomalies in their data. By obtaining root cause analysis, they can get actionable intelligence and an instant diagnosis of the problem.

Tellius platform generates analysis using natural language explanations to help users interpret results conveniently. Also, you can ask questions in natural language without writing lines of complicated codes. You can literally talk to your data through interactive voice and contextual conversations. Its NLP capability also helps you personalize your search by adapting vocabulary and sharing your stories with your teams in natural language. The platform also generates proactive intelligence and pushes insights about problems you might not be aware of.

Businesses can manage their data conveniently and unify all the *data preparation*, which would help avoid informant silos. It simplifies data preparation and processing for ad hoc queries and AI-ML-driven insights. Its intuitive visual interface helps blend, transform, and clean data with dozens of pre-built, code-free data prep capabilities. These automated capabilities also help in profiling tasks, aggregations and pivots, custom calculations, and feature engineering.

Automated ML capability helps model and transform data using easy point-and-click tools or with custom Python and SQL. You can build, evaluate, and tune ML models for custom analysis and share them with other users. You can apply highly advanced ML models using your preferred approach with single-click AutoML or Point & Click mode for full feature/model/hyperparameter selection granularity. The platform can also automatically choose the most appropriate algorithms and ML models to uncover insights relevant to your decision context. Best fit models are presented to the decision-makers in standard Local Interpretable Model-agnostic Explanations (LIME) methodology that explains the model's metrics and performance. You can embed search, automated insights, and predictive analysis in your custom applications using a full suite of APIs.

APPLICATION CASE 6.2: EMPOWERING LIFE SCIENCES ORGANIZATIONS WITH DI[4]

On May 12, 2022, Tellius announced a partnership with Indegene, a technology-led healthcare solutions provider. Where Tellius specializes in offering AI-driven decision intelligence, Indegene has deep domain knowledge in life sciences and expertise in advanced data and analytics. Together, these two companies have developed an analytical framework that uses AI and ML models to help life sciences organizations read, visualize, and analyze patient data at scale. As a result, decision-makers will have the right tools to quickly uncover valuable insights from the root cause of the problem to business drivers hidden across a large volume of healthcare data and scattered silos. The aim is to help life sciences organizations become future-ready and truly data-driven.

Life sciences companies have access to much larger amounts of data in different formats and types. Traditional BI tools are not sufficient to handle such complexity. They make data access, exploration, and sharing more challenging. Consequently, these companies miss out on extremely valuable insights they might need to make important business decisions. The new analytical framework will help decision-makers in health sciences companies generate granular insights into the patient journey. It analyzes large datasets on prescriptions, diagnoses, medical history, and other information around various patient touchpoints. The analysis helps companies identify patients' reasons for switching to other companies while also helping them to identify new segments of the patients who could be benefitted from a specific drug or treatment.

Tellius has created a platform for life sciences companies that simplifies the complexities of analytics and accelerates the generation of insights across different functions of the organization. DI functionalities offered by the Tellius platform will allow users to search and query across diverse datasets. They will build an understanding of what is changing, why it is changing, and what actions should be taken to improve the situation. This will help companies make better, effective data-driven decisions in the areas of market access, commercial effectiveness, payer analytics, and much more. Indegene will leverage this platform to deliver advanced patient analytics and real-world data (RWD) solutions while also supporting onboarding, implementation, and success. It will ensure that every customer leverages the full power of DI based on patient, prescriber, and market data.

Xylem[5]

Xylem is one of the most inspiring DI solution companies due to its ability to make a positive change in a highly critical area – water management. Xylem is the spinoff of ITT Corporation's water-related businesses that was launched in 2011. It is a leading global water technology company headquartered in Rye Brook, New York. As a Fortune 1000 global water technology company, Xylem is committed to creating advanced technologies and other trusted solutions to help the world solve different types of water challenges. The company is a global provider of innovative, efficient, and sustainable water technologies that help improve the way water is used, reused, managed, and conserved.

Since the pressures and complexity of utility companies are increasing, digital adoption is no longer an option. Xylem Vue, Xylem's digital solutions platform, combines smart and connected technologies, intelligent systems, and services with their extensive expertise in problem-solving to create transformative outcomes for the communities. The solutions are designed to help reduce water loss and increase safety, resiliency, and affordability while providing excellent customer service, improving performance, and lowering costs. Xylem's propositions are the nexus of water expertise, engineering, data, and decision science. It focuses on uniting hydroinformatics, a relatively new area of decision science, with traditional civil engineering and hydrology to leverage their existing data, develop thousands of potential scenarios at scale, and deliver the best insights and outcomes for their clients.

Xylem offers a variety of DI solutions to help their clients visualize network behavior, optimize system performance, and proactively protect assets. These digital insights help make more data-informed decisions and plan for a better future. Xylem's DI solutions are already making a huge impact in making our water systems more efficient, safer, and more affordable.

Xylem offers DI solutions in the following critical areas:

Water Network Optimization: it is a real-time monitoring solution designed as a single platform that integrates sensor data, hydraulic modeling, geographic information system (GIS) data, and (supervisory control and data acquisition (SCADA) to support operators and help clients discover critical insights from their water network. The technology uses a combination of algorithms, ML capabilities, and hydroinformatics to calibrate and optimize the existing hydraulic model, which enables the creation of a digital network twin. It can help in visualizing operating conditions even in areas with no sensors. Decision-makers use this information to correct drinking water distribution in real time. It provides a clear understanding of water age, pressure, and plant mix by combining multiple data sources for maximum visibility.

Wastewater Network Optimization: more and more utility companies are turning to advanced visualization technologies to increase system visibility, gather and utilize real-time sensor data, and improve their capacity to forecast. Wastewater network optimization from Xylem helps these companies visualize, predict, and control their specific wastewater networks highly efficiently. This real-time digital monitoring and modeling solution uses DI to analyze sensor data, hydraulic monitoring, and ML capabilities to provide visibility into a company's complex environment. You can also predict future activity and apply actionable, data-driven decisions to optimize system capacity utilization while reducing flooding events and combined sewer overflows (CSOs).

Treatment System Optimization: utilities need to improve their operational procedures, reduce the overconsumption of resources, identify influent changes, improve effluent stability to meet regulatory requirements, predict future conditions, and reduce response time by developing more efficient systems. Xylem's treatment system optimization provides all these benefits and much more. It uses the DI approach to help maximize a plant's data to deliver highly actionable and quantifiable outcomes. The data updates in real time and is immediately fed into the system for continuous refinement and improvement.

Water Loss Management: the cost of real water loss (water produced but lost before reaching the customer) is estimated at $14 billion annually worldwide. Xylem's water loss management combines DI with multiple technologies to build a single, intuitive user experience to bring together leak, burst, and pressure transient detection. Utilities can quickly identify flow anomalies and quickly address leaks, breaks, and bursts in transmission and distribution mains. They can also detect pressure and pipe stress to prolong asset life. For overall network efficiency, they can monitor water loss more accurately and in a timely manner.

Revenue Locator: utilities lose millions of dollars in revenue each year due to water that has been consumed but not billed. They suffer further monetary losses due to increased penalties for failing to meet water regulatory requirements and struggle in managing meter stock and billing practices. To help utilities identify the root cause of their losses, Xylem's revenue locator uses a machine learning analytics platform to offer an intelligence-based, data-driven method to prevent revenue losses. Using Xylem's revenue locator, utilities can pinpoint meter issues and other causes of apparent loss, eliminate excessive use of sampling and testing practices that cause inefficiencies, avoid premature meter replacement, and reduce the frequency of work orders. Revenue locator software has analyzed over one million meters and identified an estimated four billion gallons of water loss equal to $31 million in unbilled revenue.

Asset Performance Optimization: utility companies often struggle with asset management and allocation when asked to meet or exceed the target level of services with limited resources and information available to them. Xylem's asset performance optimization helps utilities identify high-risk pipe segments, predict asset risk levels, and develop more cost-effective and efficient asset management strategies. It uses ML and DI capabilities to help utilities significantly reduce operational failures and reduce the cost of maintenance and replacement. They can understand risk better, conserve resources, prioritize asset intervention, and improve customer satisfaction by unlocking the potential of their data to support data-driven decision-making.

APPLICATION CASE 6.3: REAL-TIME DECISION SUPPORT SYSTEM TO CUT COMBINED SEWER OVERFLOW BY 100 MILLION GALLONS[6]

Parts of Evansville's sewer system are more than 100 years old. The city is located on the north bank of the Ohio River in southwest Indiana (USA) and serves a population of 163,000, with combined sewers making up almost 40% of the total sewer area. These sewers experience operational and system capacity problems during heavy rainfall. These combined sewers are located in Evansville's historic downtown district and could not transport all the combined sewage to the wastewater treatment plants. Evansville was discharging 1.8 billion gallons of untreated sewage annually across 22 CSO outfalls into the Ohio River and Pidgeon Creek, receiving tributaries.

Evansville entered into a consent decree with the US Environmental Protection Agency in 2011, according to which the city was required to increase the capacity of its sewer system to minimize and, in many cases, eliminate these overflows. The city, as part of the settlement, agreed to take immediate action to upgrade the treatment capacity of its two wastewater treatment plants. Evansville partnered with Xylem to implement Xylem's Wastewater Network Optimization solution. Based on real data, Evansville first wanted to understand how the sewer system behaved. They wanted to leverage this information to build a system model with the goal of maximizing their existing facilities and infrastructure to control overflow volumes in the early stages.

Xylem's solution is based on a data-driven SENSE-PREDICT-ACT methodology that helped in creating a real-time decision support system. SENSE helps use real-time monitoring of the sensor networks to gather and integrate all critical level, flow, and rain gauge data. PREDICT uses AI and ML to integrate collected data with previously existing hydraulic models to develop a digital twin of the City's sewer network. Using both real-time visualization and a forensic review of collection system operations, Evansville was able to see a real-time holistic view of the hydraulic dynamics for their entire collection system. ACT, the real-time operational model, finally began forecasting future outcomes by performing thousands of calculations on their real-time data. The predictions were easy to review and Evansville's staff could now make proactive decisions to optimize their resources and existing sewer infrastructure.

The partnership between Evansville and Xylem resulted in more than 100 million gallons of annualized CSO reduction for the city. The adoption of Xylem's solution allowed operators to have real-time situational awareness of critical data points from throughout the collection system. The system shows wet well levels and capacity available at the treatment plant 30–60 minutes into the future while also providing pumping rate recommendations that help achieve efficiency in decision-making during significant wet weather events.

Noodle.ai[7]

Headquartered in San Francisco, California, Noodle.ai was founded by Stephen Pratt in 2016. Noodle.ai uses XAI and advanced data science capabilities to build solutions that support supply chain decision-making. The solutions are designed to take in vast amounts of data, detect patterns, predict outcomes, and restore the flow of business. This is another company that focuses on addressing problems of a specific industry or functional area of business. Noodle.ai's solutions are built for the supply chain and operations management market. Led by executives from top firms in data science, enterprise software, consumer goods, manufacturing, and AI, Noodle.ai was ranked the number one B2B startup by LinkedIn in 2018.

The company specializes in developing Flow Operations solutions, also known as FlowOps, a category of AI software that aims to eliminate operations entropy across the entire supply chain, from raw material to shelf. According to the founder Stephen Pratt, operations entropy is the seeming randomness, uncertainty, unpredictability, and general fog that can be seen daily in complex factory settings and distribution networks. It increases with complexity. The good news is that we can reduce this entropy by finding patterns in randomness. With advanced technologies, we can make predictions and manage flow – a systematic elimination of entropy in factories and supply chains.

FlowOps are created with the integration of human intelligence and machine intelligence to eliminate waste and friction. They are created by seasoned professionals and with the most advanced machine intelligence tools available today. Noodle.ai has invested over $100 million in research and development to become the leading provider of FlowOps software.

The Noodle.ai FlowOps product suite is proven in production to deliver measurable results in weeks, not months. For manufacturing, the suite includes two applications: Asset Flow and Quality Flow. For supply chains, the suite offers *Inventory Flow, Production Flow, and Demand Flow.* The three supply chain applications are part of the Noodle XAI platform. The human brain inspires the design of XAI engines.

Inventory Flow helps predict supply-demand gaps within the 0–12 weeks' execution window and expedite decisions using recommendations based on patterns previously hidden in supply chain data. It also helps organizations align their teams across functions and regions with a single source of truth to eliminate siloed decision-making full of problems and holes. Production Flow predicts network-wide supply-demand imbalances to diagnose the gaps between the production plan and demand, and avoid fill rate hits, lost sales, and overages. As a result, decision-makers can understand the tradeoffs in inventory and fill rates when making changes to production schedules. Demand Flow feeds supply planning, helping teams reach a consensus faster with less bias and noise. It detects demand patterns, systematic bias, consumption, and plan adherence with dynamic data-driven forecasting. Operating at a very granular level, Demand Flow provides complete, high-quality, long-term plans.

An open XAI platform powers the suite, making each app seamless to integrate, fast to scale, and smooth to deploy. The XAI data engines normalize, correlate, and enrich vast amounts of enterprise data allowing decision-makers to discover patterns, predict and diagnose risks to flow, access recommendations for task-specific actions, and get an explanation of the how and why behind those recommendations. They enable each application to explain how the system detected a pattern and why it made a particular recommendation so decision-makers can understand the root cause and run scenarios before making the final decision.

APPLICATION CASE 6.4: LEADING CPG IMPROVES SUPPLY CHAIN WITH FLOWOPS[8]

Consumer packaged goods (CPG) were facing multiple challenges during the 2020 pandemic due to extreme volatility in the market. The company turned off its existing demand forecasting system because it was wildly inaccurate. Even prior to the pandemic, the system wasn't functioning well enough to make accurate predictions on inventory. Regarding technology, the company was struggling with multiple data silos leading to different versions of the truth, ineffective legacy systems, and long deployment times. This resulted in ever-increasing product obsolescence costs and potential On-Time In-Full (OTIF) penalties.

With Noodle.ai's Inventory Flow, the company was able to predict supply chain KPIs, including demand, inventory, fill rate, and stockouts. They were also able to translate risk predictions to dollar terms and Value at Risk (VAR) to help planners stay focused on critical issues. The system generated recommended mitigation strategies so planners could quickly change deployment allocations, production, and shipment schedules. It also helped track the value of the mitigated risk and capture what portion was a direct result of taking the recommended action.

All planners shared one dashboard with every risk measured in dollars, described in terms of probability, explaining root cause, and simulated with actionable workflows. The statistical comparison performed by the company showed that Inventory Flow provided better predictions of their demand and supply compared to legacy applications. After some initial fine-tuning, data ingestion, and model training, Inventory Flow was ready to go to work. In just three months, they went from start to integrating, running, and getting returns on investment. Inventory Flow comes with deep domain expertise in balancing supply and demand. Moreover, it is capable of knowing how to consume vast amounts of data about every action in a manufacturing company's operations and identifying patterns that no one can see due to data and information complexity.

For the first time, the company could proactively make highly targeted inventory deployment decisions with the help of prioritized recommendations.

It mastered an entirely new level of performance in three critical areas – product flow: getting the right products in the right locations with predictive signals; cash flow: driving revenue by improving order capture and reducing costs associated with inventory and expedites, and team flow: promoting natural team collaboration by creating a single version of truth around predictive VAR. In only three months and even amid the pandemic, the company saw three times return on investment, $1.3 million in value.

Aera Technology[9]

Another Decision Intelligence company, Aera Technology, is a relatively new venture founded in 2017 by Shariq Mansoor, who now serves as Aera's Chief Technology Officer (CTO). The company is headquartered in Mountain View, California. Aera Technology aims to help companies to transform by operating at internet speed and scale in the age of DI. Aera's innovative cognitive technology, Decision Cloud™, enables DI and helps businesses autonomously orchestrate their operations.

The company believes that it is essential for businesses to adapt to the digital transformation causing shifts in financial models, business models, and social structures. Their technology is designed to help groups and individuals access the data succinctly and collaborate on important decisions. It allows businesses to move quickly, make more informed decisions, and execute strategic initiatives more effectively.

Aera Decision Cloud™ is the primary platform that helps you make and execute intelligent business decisions in real time. This cloud-native platform works as the digital brain of your organization that delivers the agility, velocity, and intelligence required to make decisions in today's complex environments. It goes beyond simple reports and KPIs and gives high-level recommendations on actions to optimize business objectives. Three important components of Decision Cloud™ are Cognitive Operating System™, Cognitive Skills™, and Aera Developer™:

1. **Aera's Cognitive Operating System™** is a cloud platform that powers the Decision Cloud™. This open, scalable platform provides a comprehensive set of capabilities that enables users to develop, deploy, and manage DI at scale across the enterprise. These capabilities are the pillars of Decision Cloud™ and are categorized as follows:

   Data: for effective management of data, the system offers: *Data Crawlers* that automatically discover and extract data from enterprise system; *Data Workbench* that helps transform and process billions of rows of data into a unified decision data model; and the *Cognitive Data Layer* that represents the real-time state of the enterprise. It provides access to real-time information extracted by Data Crawlers and Data Streams in a fully integrated digital twin of the organization and helps businesses create a single source of truth.

With a high degree of automation, users can process, refine, and enrich large volumes of transactional and unstructured data in real time. Once populated, it becomes a library of information that teams can use to perform analytics, train ML models, share information, and automate decisions.

Intelligence: to help businesses harness the full power of intelligence, Aera offers tightly integrating *Analytics* capabilities to augment decision-making with an easy-to-use, self-service experience. Users can easily create dashboards and reports and get democratized and governed access to data and insights with useful recommendations for decision-making.

The *Cortex AI/ML*™ capability helps develop, train, and operationalize AI and ML models for decision-making. It is the data science engine inside the Aera Cognitive Operating System™ that enables users to develop and deploy data science workflows efficiently and makes ML available to be embedded in Aera Cognitive Skills™. It is directly integrated to live harmonized datasets coupled with domain-specific algorithms, optimization, and AutoML techniques. Users can also operationalize their proprietary models trained with other tools and make them available to Cognitive Skills™.

Aera's *Modeling* is a purpose-built, embedded capability that helps in what-if analysis. It provides tools for building live, multidimensional models, simulations, and planning capabilities within Cognitive Skills™. Users can build models with ML-enabled, Excel-like user interfaces and formulas without requiring coding or technical expertise.

Automation: this is probably one of the most innovative sets of capabilities that includes *Process Builder*, a low-code graphical environment that allows Skills Builders to use Aera's patented visual programming framework to connect, compose, and orchestrate all the data, engines, services, and user experiences. *Automation Rules* allow businesses to implement decision automation by adding a layer of configurable logic on top of Cognitive Skills™ capabilities. These rules are automatically layered onto the Skill to determine what actions will take place in any given scenario. *Write-Backs* is another capability in this set that helps execute decisions at the data level, automatically writing changes into the relevant underlying transaction systems. It enables full decision automation by providing a path toward the eventual end-to-end automation of decisions.

Engagement: to allow teams and individuals to access information effectively, this set of capabilities includes the *Cognitive Decision Board* that gives you a high-level view and deeper understanding of how decisions are made in the Aera environment. You can familiarize yourself with the context, understand how teams operate, how effective the recommendations are, and how they affect the key metrics. *Search, Voice, Mobile* enables you to access Aera on your mobile devices supported by both iOS and Android. You can access it in any location, any time you want. The dynamic user interface enables machines to do the work, helping you to get proactively engaged when needed. It acts like an augmented digital assistant to drive faster, more intuitive actions. A conversational voice interaction system allows users a rapid way to interact with digital recommendations using natural language.

Finally, it offers the *Cognitive Workbench*, an intuitive interface to deliver prioritized and personalized decision recommendations. These recommendations are generated by Aera Cognitive Skills™, which uses data, intelligence, and automation capabilities. You receive these recommendations in a configurable prioritized list that allows you to understand the context, evaluate the tradeoffs of your decisions, and take action immediately. It also keeps a record of your actions and allows the system to continuously learn, improve over time, and become more effective at taking autonomous actions.

2. **Cognitive Skills**™ are composable capabilities built on top of the Cognitive Operating System™ that help enhance the Decision Cloud™ to address business decision flow for a specific domain or use case.

It contains not only the data model mapping and extensions, decision flows, analytics, metrics, and so forth but also supports user engagement across desktop, mobile, and voice-related functionalities.

3. **Aera Developer**™, another important component of Aera Decision Cloud™, is a purpose-built development environment that helps you integrate the data, intelligence, automation, and engagement required for DI. It is a self-service integrated development environment (IDE) for creating, deploying, and managing DI at scale. For AI-powered enterprise solutions, it is the next-generation cloud development platform. With Aera Developer, you can start with a low-code builder with its included frameworks, libraries, and nodes and then extend the capabilities by integrating your own models and functionalities with Java, SQL, R, Python, and other toolsets in a complete DevOps environment.

Aera offers solutions for various use cases, including procurement, demand, inventory, order, logistics, digital control, tower, finance, and revenue management. This highly innovative company holds great potential to transform the world with the power of decision intelligence.

APPLICATION CASE 6.5: UNLOCKING THE POWER OF DECISION INTELLIGENCE IN SUPPLY CHAIN TRANSFORMATION – EY AND AERA ALLIANCE[10]

EY (Ernst & Young), a multinational professional services network, is one of the largest professional services networks in the world. Headquartered in London, England, EY aims to build a better working world, helping to create long-term value for clients, people, and society and building trust in the capital markets.

In over 150 countries, EY teams empowered by data and technology provide trust through assurance and help clients grow, transform, and operate. On April 6, 2022, EY announced an alliance with Aera Technologies and Ernst and Young LLP (EY US) to help organizations leverage DI to accelerate their supply chain transformation.

Supply chains today face growing pressures from consumers who are increasingly demanding while trying to handle environmental disruptions. Furthermore, increased volume and velocity of data are making decision-making more complex. As a result, organizations are turning to DI to address these issues, become more agile, and react effectively to frequent changes in their environments.

The EY-Aera alliance delivers leading-edge technology and end-to-end digital transformation tailored to customers' business needs while providing them with a roadmap to reimagining their processes and deriving value from their data. Through this alliance, businesses can recognize the value of DI in their supply chains, and they will see the impact in weeks, not months or more. Aera's unique cognitive decision-making technology plays a key role in empowering continuous planning and execution improvements which is at the core of EY's approach to supply chain transformations. Businesses will be able to implement leading supply chain practices without costly IT overhauls. Moreover, they can rapidly synchronize reactions to unprecedented changes and automate decision-making, driving operational and financial improvement. This alliance holds incredible potential to help businesses reach new levels of supply chain innovation.

Diwo[11]

Diwo was founded by Krishna Kallakuri in 2014 and is headquartered in Northville, Michigan. The company offers DI services to empower users to make their decisions faster and better. Diwo's DI platform uses contextual intelligence by continuously monitoring the company's data and combining it with AI-ML capabilities to produce actionable recommendations. Using Diwo's patented knowledge graph technology and unique contextual intelligence, businesses can discover opportunities hidden in their data and access the recommendations that help make decisions more accurately and effectively. In addition, the platform allows easy access to all decision-makers in your business, enabling them to solve complex problems by understanding the tradeoffs of making different choices, business constraints, and the consequences of different decisions.

Diwo's DI platform closes the gap between insights and actions. It combines descriptive and prescriptive analytics to provide decision-makers with a 360-degree view of their decision context and the information needed to make the most optimal decisions. Results can be generated dramatically faster than traditional visualization and BI tools. The platform uses AI, which enables the system to learn constantly from users' interactions, decisions, and incoming data to make predictions, tailor insights, and generate recommendations. Their natural language interface and tailored graphical interface help users reduce their cognitive load by simplifying the most complex analyses and ML models.

To enable 360-degree decisioning, Diwo's platform offers two modules[12]:

DECIDE: this module continuously senses the patterns in data to sense any potential risks or opportunities. It is a unique prescriptive analytics capability that quantifies the business impact and recommends the best strategy for the decision in a timely manner. The module also allows users to evaluate alternatives by understanding their decisions' consequences. Diwo's system generates decision recommendations as *"opportunities,"* each based on the continuous analysis of incoming data streaming from various sources and sensing business trends and anomalies. The opportunities are time-sensitive and, if not addressed, might affect the business's financial performance.

The system also explains the potential impact of these opportunities and makes recommendations on the most optimized solution or strategy depending on the decision context. As the decision-maker approves a strategy, Diwo formalizes and initiates the tasks that are required to be performed to implement the strategy while passing them on to the operational system or the downstream workflow.

ASK: this module provides a guided conversational interface to the users that understand their decision-making context and intent while directing them to the most relevant insights and recommendations. NLP allows the use of natural language while reducing complexity and enhancing conversational capabilities. ASK accelerates the pace of decision-making by making decision-making easier and faster. It uses Business Context Graph (BCG), prior user interactions, and access rights. As the system traverses to BCG, it performs causal inference calculations and identifies and ranks insights.

BCG, the system's brain, is a dynamic probabilistic graph automatically generated from historical data, business requirements, and predictive insights. It analyzes and evaluates relationships between entities and KPIs to discover new patterns and trends while performing anomaly detection and time series forecasting. Its customized probabilistic graphical models use highly sophisticated mathematical algorithms, including Bayesian Networks and Markov models, to evaluate the strength of multi-level relationships and conditional probabilities.

Diwo's Adaptation Studio enables you to embed business contexts, data elements, and maps and set up different opportunities to customize the platform to the business's needs. Using simple English language, decision-makers can feed business requirements, KPIs, metrics, data and business definitions, and configuration parameters related to business processes. Using preferred colors, themes, and visuals, you can customize the user interface based on your brand identity.

Diwo offers businesses an intelligent and highly adaptive system that is designed to continuously optimize business decisions. Diwo's *decision-centric architecture* combines the latest technologies in AI, ML, NLP, statistical inferencing, and distributed data management. It enables deep personalization, real-time analytic response, ease of setup and configurability, and fast time to evaluate with the rapid deployment of applications. Moreover, it combines multiple analytic stacks into a single architecture that allows the faster deployment, rapid management of any changes, and the automation of more structured and streamlined processes.

Businesses can manage data effectively through the integrated architecture that allows ingestion of data from multiple sources covering all key warehouses and operational systems. Data schemas are generated automatically from business requirements to load data into the system. The ingested data is stored in a distributed in-memory database, allowing faster computations and aggregations. The system also learns from users' queries and as new data is ingested, it computes the predictions, KPIs, and other metrics to keep information and insights refreshed.

Another important component of Diwo's technical architecture is its *Model Server* which offers a centralized and scalable infrastructure to deploy and execute AI-ML models. The server has the ability to integrate models from different sources, including R, Python, and AutoML tools. First, the model is developed and when it is ready for deployment, the server fetches the associated metadata related to the model while also loading its artifacts into a database. The adaptation studio then maps this model that is represented as an opportunity and creates a pipeline for model execution.

Diwo's system is built on a cloud-agnostic architecture. It is highly scalable and enterprise-ready. The system is straightforward, easy to deploy, and can be managed through Diwo's *Administration Studio*. It continuously monitors health metrics, usage patterns, and error logs to business KPIs and sends proactive alerts to the administrators. Diwo also uses enterprise-grade data security and access control mechanisms to ensure system safety and security.

Quantellia

Quantellia was founded in 2008 by Dr. Lorien Pratt, who first coined the term decision intelligence. It is, therefore, one of the very first companies to start building solutions around decision intelligence. Headquartered in California, the company offers applied AI-ML and DI-related services. It is a trusted partner for dozens of large and small organizations in multiple sectors. Some of Quantellia's clients are Cisco Systems, SAP, The Carter Center, Ericsson, The Royal Bank of Scotland, Charter Communications, and the US government.[13]

From the information on its website, it seems that Quantellia is more a DI consulting company than a DI software provider company. It doesn't offer sophisticated DI software solutions like Peak, Aera, Diwo, or Tellius. There is a mention on the website regarding DI orchestration software and solutions. Still, there are no details available on the functionality of these software/solutions or what type of technologies or capabilities they are built on. Their key services include decision intelligence training, company-wide presentations, decision-specific workshops, data assessment, decision visualization, and decision orchestration, and data services such as data modeling, cleansing, and enterprise architecture integration.

One of Quantellia's solutions is Agile AI™ which offers support for the client's entire AI lifecycle or only part of that lifecycle, such as project support. This includes executive review, technical review, AI project plan, and risk analysis, analyzing the expected return on investment (ROI) of the AI project, consultation on what actions will change with the implementation of the AI project, and how a business can measure, manage, and maximize business outcomes. Agile AI™ can help companies mitigate risk in the following ways:

- Checking goals, KPIs, and ROI at every step in the lifecycle.

- Applying DI to help connect outcomes of AI systems to organizational goals, actions, and environment.

- Assessing the maturity of data, business objectives, and human expertise available to the business.

- Implementing a formal process to quickly detect changes, monitor ROI, and initiate suitable actions.

- Using proofs of concept (POCs) to make sure that the promise of the models in the lab will also be fulfilled in production.

Overall, the services and solutions are quite consulting-heavy. This, however, doesn't say that they are not a good company. On the contrary, in many cases, companies need nothing but a trusted partner who could help them get started and navigate a high stake, new pursuit such as DI adoption. Quantellia has been in business for about 32 years and has completed 45 projects successfully! It tells a lot about their expertise and excellence in DI-related services.

CONCLUSION

DI market is in its nascent stage, where old and new companies are trying to find new opportunities to sell their innovative solutions and platforms. The companies included in this chapter have built innovative DI services enabling companies to democratize AI. However, they are not the only vendors offering DI solutions. Here are some more companies and what they offer:

- *Exponential AI*'s platform Enso helps build, orchestrate, and manage decision agents at scale. It is designed to serve the needs of healthcare organizations.

- *SAS Intelligent Decisioning* software enables you to make the best decisions while interacting with your stakeholders. You can deliver relevant interactive and real-time decisions based on sophisticated analytics at scale.

- *Pace*'s Pace Revenue platform provides industry-leading decision intelligence in the area of revenue management. Their decision engine is designed to optimize prices and restrictions for better commercial outcomes.

- *Cerebra*, another no-code DI solution, enables marketing and merchandising teams to optimize their tasks and supercharge productivity with insights and actions that have the maximum impact. The software pushes timely recommendations with predicted business impact, making decision-making faster and more effective.

- *Planning Force*'s solution combines human experience, modeling databases, and AI to provide a layer of DI to help decision-makers steer decision-making with incredible speed and precision. The solution offers optimizing complex and nonlinear decision-making processes and simulation capabilities to enhance decision-making.

- *metaphactory*'s metaphacts platform transforms data into consumable, contextual, and actionable knowledge that helps drive continuous DI making organizations more agile. It is a low-code, intuitive interface for searching, browsing, and exploring the so-called knowledge graph.

- *Oracle Real-Time Decisions* offers real-time intelligence that combines both rules and predictive analytics. Their high-performance transactional server generates and delivers real-time decisions and recommendations. Companies can implement processes that self-adjust based on feedback.

Many more vendors, including Sisu, Pyramid Analytics, TransVoyant, Busigence, SharpCloud, Federal Compass, Decisions, and Domo, are making their way into the DI market with their unique solutions, software, and platforms.[14] More and more existing technology companies are diversifying their portfolios and entering the DI domain. New companies see DI as one of the most promising propositions for future markets. They are not wrong. DI is revolutionary and is already becoming one of the most valuable technologies helping almost all types of companies make better decisions.

CASE STUDY: SISU HELPS SAMSUNG JUMPSTART A $1 BILLION PRODUCT LAUNCH

Founded in 2018 by Peter Bailis, Sisu is headquartered in San Francisco, California. Sisu's platform monitors all the organization's information continuously, recommends meaningful acts automatically in seconds, and tracks all the changes to data over time. Sisu helps organizations diagnose what's happening to their business, why it is happening, and how to take action. Samsung is one of the most valuable consumer brands in the world, known for its innovative products, including consumer electronics, mobile devices, and medical equipment. Samsung launches a billion-dollar product – mobile phones at least twice a year.

Over the last ten years, Samsung has sold over two billion Galaxy phones. Every quarter, it sells around 80 million new handsets. These launches require a critical understanding of market complexity and variables that can impact success. Their marketing and analytics teams had access to enough dashboards and reports but digging levels of complex information takes weeks to answer a single question. Another challenge Samsung was facing was scale. Their market segments are huge and diverse. To make optimal decisions, their teams required information on which customer segments were likely to upgrade, which were more interested in older models, and what factors influenced their decisions the most. Traditional systems, including BI tools, couldn't handle the volume and complexity of Samsung's data, which involved many complex variables, including customer demographics, location, device preference, and past interactions with other Samsung products.

Samsung partnered with Sisu, and today, Sisu is deployed globally at Samsung serving critical insights to help every part of Samsung's business. Sisu engine starts with their client's critical business metrics and automatically explores all their data to identify the highest impact populations. Those highest impact drivers are surfaced in order of importance. Next, it applies novel search algorithms to prioritize analysis areas, scans the schema, data types, and other features, and then performs automated transformations to expose critical factors. In addition, the model and feature search is performed to identify statistically significant factors. For accelerated decision-making, Sisu finally generates the top insights with clear explanations on different aspects, such as population behavior and the impact on each metric.

With Sisu, Samsung can continuously track changes in key metrics, including retail sales and campaign performance. They can find answers to their most important questions rapidly as ad hoc queries are handled in real-time. Their analytics workflows are far more collaborative now and it saves them hundreds of hours of time every month. Moreover, they are able to answer ten times more questions than before.

Sources:

Finding Upgrades in a Galaxy of Possibilities. (n.d.). Sisu. Retrieved from https://sisudata.com/static/b14c0e6b98751900b303147b1b60bd4a/Sisu-Case-Study-Samsung.pdf

Samsung: Jumpstarting a $1B Product Launch. (n.d.). Retrieved August 10, 2022, from https://sisudata.com/customers/samsung

Technology Index. (n.d.). Retrieved August 10, 2022, from https://sisudata.com/product/technology

QUESTIONS

1. Would you consider Samsung's decision environment for mobile phone marketing highly complex? Why?

2. Samsung had access to a wealth of dashboards. So why were they not able to find answers to their business questions?

3. Can Samsung use the Sisu engine to optimize decisions outside of marketing? Discuss how.

QUESTIONS FOR DISCUSSION

1. Why is it a good idea to partner with other companies to manage DI more effectively?

2. How does DI help in democratizing AI?

3. What are the problems that organizations face when information silos are created?

4. Search online and list all the DI solutions offered by large companies such as Google, Microsoft, and IBM.

5. List the benefits of Peak's platform for its clients.

6. What are the three core capabilities of Peak's platform? Discuss in detail.

7. How does Tellius' DI platform use AutoML?

8. What three modes can users utilize with Tellius' platform?

9. Discuss Xylem's different water management solutions.

10. What are the FlowOps? How do they help reduce or eliminate operational entropy?

11. What does the open XAI platform do for Noodle.ai's clients?

12. What are the three key components of Aera Decision Cloud™?

13. How can companies mitigate risk using Quantellia's Agile AI™ solution?

14. List five to seven other companies offering DI solutions that are not mentioned in this chapter.

REFERENCES

1. Peak – The Decision Intelligence Company Using AI to Drive Growth. (n.d.). Retrieved May 12, 2022, from Peak website: http://peak.ai/us/

2. GSK Case Study: NLP and Intelligent Decisions. (n.d.). Retrieved May 12, 2022, from Peak website: https://peak.ai/hub/success-story/gsk/

3. AI-Driven Augmented Analytics & Decision Intelligence | Tellius. (n.d.). Retrieved May 13, 2022, from Tellius website: https://www.tellius.com/

4. Tellius and Indegene Partner to Help Life Sciences Companies Enhance Patient Journeys with Faster Data-Backed Decision Making. (2022, May 12). Retrieved May 13, 2022, from Tellius website: https://www.tellius.com/tellius-and-indegene-partner-to-help-life-sciences-companies-enhance-patient-journeys-with-faster-data-backed-decision-making/

5. Xylem Water Solutions & Water Technology | Xylem US. (n.d.). Retrieved May 16, 2022, from Xylem website: https://www.xylem.com/en-us/

6. Real-Time Decision Support System Cuts CSO Volume by 100 Million Gallons | Xylem US. (n.d.). Retrieved May 16, 2022, from Xylem website: https://www.xylem.com/en-us/support/case-studies-white-papers/real-time-decision-support-helps-cut-combined-sewer-overflow-volume-by-100-million-gallons-and-reduces-capital-needed-for-regulatory-compliance/

7. Noodle.ai. (n.d.). Retrieved May 16, 2022, from Noodle.ai website: https://noodle.ai/

8. Leading CPG Runs a Smarter, Faster, Better Supply Chain with Noodle.ai. (n.d.). Retrieved May 16, 2022, from Noodle.ai website: https://explore.noodle.ai/customer-success/cpg-better-supply-chain-with-noodleai-inventory-flow

9. Aera Technology – The Decision Intelligence Company. (n.d.). Retrieved May 17, 2022, from Aera Technology website: https://www.aeratechnology.com/

10. EY Announces Alliance with Aera Technology to Unlock the Power of Decision Intelligence in Supply Chain Transformation. (2022, April). Retrieved May 17, 2022, from Aera Technology website: https://www.aeratechnology.com/announcements/ey-announces-alliance-with-aera-technology-to-unlock-the-power-of-decision-intelligence-in-supply-chain-transformation

11. Diwo: Decisions, Not Dashboards. (n.d.). Retrieved May 13, 2022, from Diwo, LLC website: https://diwo.ai/

12. Diwo Decision Intelligence Platform Technical White Paper. (2021). Diwo, LLC. Retrieved from https://f.hubspotusercontent40.net/hubfs/7625696/diwo%20Technical%20White%20Paper.pdf

13. Assured Agile AI – Quantellia. (n.d.). Retrieved May 13, 2022, from Quantellia website: https://quantellia.com/agile-ai-2/

14. Best Decision Intelligence Software of 2022. (n.d.). Retrieved August 10, 2022, from SOURCEFORGE website: https://sourceforge.net/software/decision-intelligence/

CHAPTER 7

Decision Intelligence Framework for Organizational Decision-Making

AI is game-changing but most AI projects fail to deliver expected results for various reasons. One of these reasons is that organizations adopt AI without a proper need analysis. Many companies implement AI systems just because their competitors have done that, among other reasons. The most important question companies should ask themselves before deciding to adopt such technologies is *"why do we need AI or DI?"* Start with *why*.

In this chapter, we will explore the Decision Intelligence (DI) framework for organizational decision-making. The purpose of the framework is twofold. It aims to help organizations:

1. Make business decisions more effectively by allocating and using resources (people and AI) more efficiently.

2. Understand the DI capability needs of the organization (*why do we need DI?*).

An organization's decision-making system includes both people and technology components. The seven-step DI framework proposed in this

DOI: 10.1201/b23322-7

chapter will help you determine the perfect mix of people's involvement and AI required for each important business decision. In addition, it lays the foundations for an effective DI needs analysis for DI adoption and implementation (which we will discuss in the next chapter). DI adoption in this context means developing a full-fledged DI infrastructure that includes all the necessary DI capabilities at your organization.

DI adoption decisions are made at the strategic level of the organization. However, the DI framework works mostly at tactical and operational levels of decision-making. It provides a structured decision-making process and insights on using the right degree of people and AI collaboration for the success of critical business decisions.

WHY WE NEED A FRAMEWORK FOR DECISION-MAKING

The core idea of this framework is to help people channel their time and energy into making decisions that *they* should focus on – important decisions that require human intelligence and involvement and cannot be handled by technology only. It is about prioritizing the decision-making tasks people need to perform. This might sound obvious but not many people practice prioritizing their decisions. It is not uncommon to see managers who waste their resources on petty tasks focusing on matters that are not significant for business or their own success. They forget that humans can only utilize so much time and energy. Our brain capacities are limited and we must use them wisely on tasks that have some significance in our lives. Let's see the following example:

Dr. Arthur Chappell is the director of online learning at a university. One of his key responsibilities (written clearly in his contract) is ensuring that all the online courses are set up correctly on the university's learning management system (LMS) and are running well without any discrepancies and issues. Dr. Sheila Simons is a new program manager at the School of Education and is working with Dr. Chappell to set up her new program courses on the LMS. She is responsible for working with her team of course developers (the subject matter experts) to develop course content and materials, receive completed courses from them, and finally forward all the course materials to Dr. Chappell for online setup. Since the responsibilities are clear, the process should go smoothly. Right? It didn't.

Dr. Chappell is not someone who prioritizes his decisions. Upon receiving course materials for each course, he would dive deep into the course contents, including textbooks, specific course assignments (such as discussion questions on discussion forums), exercises, and even the due dates for the assignments. Among other things, he asked course developers to change their discussion questions several times. He was so nitpicky that two course developers resigned due to the frustration of revising their course materials for unjustifiable reasons.

Wait! What is his position? He is the director of online learning. It is not his job to go into the details of courses developed by subject matter experts. He is a history professor and isn't even qualified to review education courses. His concerns might be valid but he was not responsible for ensuring the quality of assignments and course content.

Anyway, the program was launched after a year of preparation. As courses began, Dr. Simons started to receive several complaints about online functioning and the setup of the courses on the system. Some courses had grade book issues, some had email and notification problems, and others didn't even have syllabi and necessary resources uploaded. Dr. Chappell failed to fulfill his primary responsibility – ensuring that courses run well on the system. He was spending his resources, time, and energy on the wrong tasks.

This is just one example. You can see a lot of people making the same mistake. They do not prioritize their decisions and tasks. Today, we are surrounded by so many distractions. Each decision has too many alternatives and choices. The more information and choices we have, the more complex our decisions become. It is quite easy to get overwhelmed with the decision burden. It is, therefore, essential to stay focused on tasks that are of great significance in our lives. Also, if we are deliberate, we can share this burden with something quite good at mimicking human intelligence – AI.

Tech advocates suggest collaborating with technology. We, humans, are the creators of technology and if we keep it under control, use it strategically, deliberately, and ethically, it will only help us improve our lives. The framework in this chapter promotes the idea of using the most suitable people involvement-artificial intelligence (*PI-AI*) mix – people and AI collaboration to make effective decisions efficiently. Above all, it helps you decide – how to decide!

Deciding How to Decide

One of the primary decision-making tasks is to decide the *process* we are going to use to make a critical decision. One key question we might ask while facing a decision problem could be: are we going to use intuition or a step-by-step process that leads to more deliberate decision-making or mix both approaches? Decision-making ability is gifted to us and as discussed in

Chapter 2, our brains are wired to make decisions using both intuition and deliberation. In order to use deliberation and rationality, we need resources, information, and a well-structured decision-making process or framework.

As a rational decision-maker faces a significant decision problem, first, they try to figure out how they will make the decision – the process they will use. Since we make so many big and small decisions every day, we mostly do this subconsciously. As discussed in Chapter 2, our brains constantly try to save energy and prompt us to use intuition instead of deliberation, cognition, sense-making, and deeper analysis, which are time- and energy-consuming activities. Business decisions involve risk and some of these decisions affect our business's overall performance and success. Therefore, decision-makers must adopt the right methodology and a systematic approach to make critical business decisions.

The DI framework proposed in this chapter aims to make individuals, teams, and organizations decision-smart. It will guide you through the process of determining how much AI support vs. *people involvement* (we will call it *PI* from now on) you should use in making business decisions of different kinds. Among other benefits, it helps you answer important questions about DI adoption, including:

1. Why do we need DI?

2. What decisions will DI capabilities be used for?

3. What specific DI capabilities do we need as an organization?

The framework emphasizes using human potential (PI) for suitable types of decisions only. Of course, AI cannot make all decisions in our stead. However, it can share our decision burden and sometimes make more accurate and faster decisions than humans. DI framework informs people on how to collaborate with technology to enhance the potential of each decision. As rightly said by Lorien Pratt,[1] DI is about putting humans back into the loop.

DI FRAMEWORK

The DI framework is a seven-step process that helps managers establish a systematic approach to decision-making in their respective departments and at a wider organizational level. It is shown as a flowchart at the end of this chapter (see Figure 7.6). This framework doesn't consider decisions that use intuition only. Let's be practical: many daily decisions can be made successfully using intuition only. You shouldn't analyze decisions that need no analysis – you will be wasting your resources. However, all critical (important) business decisions in today's complex world require a systematic approach to decision-making, a deeper analysis performed by people, supported by advanced AI capabilities. The DI framework can be seen as an essential component of your decision-making system that emphasizes using DI. It starts with preparing your organization for DI adoption.

Most business decisions are made in a team environment. Therefore, you must involve everyone in your team while preparing, planning, and implementing the framework. The core principle of this framework is to use as much technology as reasonably possible so that your people will only be used for the most critical and complex decisions. The examples used in this chapter are straightforward but could be highly complex in real life. Therefore, use your team's knowledge and expertise to improvise on these steps based on your project needs. So, without further ado, let's discuss the framework in detail now.

Preparation and Planning

The first step in preparation is getting together with your team and communicating your organization's intent or decision for DI adoption and its benefits to the organization. But, wait! Are we not talking about the DI framework here? So, why focus on DI adoption? Well, the purpose here is to lay the foundation for building a powerful DI culture where people trust DI. They will not be willing to use this framework if they don't trust DI is good for them and the organization. More details on building a DI culture are covered in the next chapter.

Next, discuss the DI framework and its benefits in improving decision-making. You need to familiarize yourself first with the framework to be able to communicate its value and how it helps in making high-impact decisions. Once your team is comfortable with the idea, start discussing the plan ahead. In the beginning, it might feel like a lot of work, just like how we feel when any new, transformative change is introduced to our lives. However, with time and more repeated attempts, you will start to master this framework, which will significantly improve your entire organization's decision-making potential. In addition, the framework will help you see the bigger picture of how a structured decision-making approach helps you improve your decisions' quality. Know that you don't have to adopt the framework as is. There is a great scope to make changes to the steps your team finds necessary.

Your first attempt at using this framework should be a pilot project, so you can assess this framework's viability for your department or organization. With your team, select an actual project, for example, a marketing project at hand that requires a series of decisions of different types. Now, let us dive deeper into the steps of the DI framework.

The Seven-Step Process

Step 1: Setting Key Goals

It's a little repetition but it is essential to restate that this framework emphasizes that people's involvement should only be used for the most critical decision-making tasks and cannot be delegated to AI entirely. Setting key goals for your project is one of those tasks that *people* should spend a reasonable amount of time on. Most of the time, project managers list these goals in a specific project plan or strategy. If you already have that task completed, eliminate this step and move to the next. If not, then proceed further and do the following:

First, review your project's purpose (it could be your project's mission statement) and list all the tasks you need to complete to accomplish that purpose. Now, combine the tasks of similar nature into a few specific goals. Make sure to put the most important goals first on the list. The goals should be SMART: specific, measurable, attainable, relevant, and time-based. A few examples of SMART goals are as follows:

1. Grow local market share of our product by 15% by the end of the year.

2. Conduct three training sessions for customer service representatives by the second quarter.

3. Increase website traffic by 150% by the end of September 2023.

Having key goals listed will help you stay focused on the most important tasks. You should also determine how the success of each goal will be measured. Define each goal's success criteria or key performance indicators (KPIs) with clearly identified measurement tool(s). For example, the KPI for goal#3 could be:

150% increase in website traffic by the end of September 2023

The measurement tool for these criteria will include the traffic reports from the website.

Step 2: Defining the Decision

This step requires defining the decision by gaining clarity on its context: all the decision's details, including outcomes and constraints. To understand this, let's imagine you are considering focusing on goal#3, "Increase website traffic by 150% by September 2023." Discuss with your team what would be the key decision(s) you will need to make to achieve this goal. Again, it is likely that the project manager has already listed these decisions in the plan using some other terminology, such as project objectives. If you have the objectives or specific tasks (decisions) listed, use them. If not, you can create your own list. For example, one of your key decisions to achieve goal#3 might be:

> Select the three best social media platforms to help generate more traffic for our website.

The task of defining a decision starts (again) with identifying the outcome of the decision and how it will be measured. The decision is successful if it helps achieve the goal. Hence, the success of a decision can be measured based on the success of the goal. As you promoted your website on the three social media platforms, people started visiting your website more. This will result in a 150% increase in website traffic by the end of September 2023.

It is important to note that sometimes, we must think about different versions of the outcomes we seek to achieve. Think about these two variations of the same outcome:

> Outcome 1: Increased website traffic by 150% by the end of September 2023. The purpose is to spread awareness; visitors include everyone who finds our promotion attractive.

> Outcome 2: Increased website traffic by 150% by the end of September 2023. Only potential clients who are likely to buy your products visit the website.

You will formulate different strategies to achieve each of these two outcomes. For example, for outcome 1, you might select any social media platform combination to target the general public. However, for outcome 2, you will only target specific social media platforms where you find most of your potential clients (you find different populations on Facebook, Twitter, Instagram, and LinkedIn!).

Also, you will choose different social media pages or promotion settings for two different outcomes. When you create a promotion campaign on social media, they ask you to personalize your campaign with your preferred settings. For outcome 2, you will select the settings where only the audience matching your customers' demographic and psychographic profile should see this promotion.

Now, think about the constraints and inputs you will need for this decision, given your chosen outcome. For both outcomes, the availability of funds for social media promotion, social media expertise, and technological capabilities are some of the primary requirements. They can become limiting factors or serious constraints that could hinder the success of your decision.

For example, one of your constraints could be the lack of talent – you do not have social media specialists on your team. In this case, instead of determining the most suitable social media platforms yourself, it might be better to outsource this task entirely to a social media marketing agency. Upon having this clarity, write down your decision statement.

If all the constraints are satisfied, the decision can be defined as follows:

Select the three best social media platforms to help generate more traffic for our website.

However, if the constraint is the lack of talent, the decision statement could change to:

Find a suitable social media marketing agency to help increase our website traffic.

Define your decisions after analyzing the outcomes and constraints for each decision. Create a list of all the decisions required to achieve your goal. For goal#3, your decision list might look like this:

1. Select the three best social media platforms to help generate more traffic for our website.

2. Send existing customers a new discount offer to persuade them to return to our website and shop more.

3. Know what people say about the new design of our website on social media to determine if we need to make changes to the design.

4. Train the marketing staff for the website's social media promotions to ensure the availability of the required talent.

5. Launch a PR campaign on the website to attract a different audience.

6. Find out who (market segment) visits our website most frequently to determine the type of customers our website attracts.

Step 3: Rating the Decisions on Importance and Complexity Levels
Once your decisions are clearly defined, you will rate these decisions on two scales: importance and complexity. The first few decisions in your list may also be of high importance. You are a team of rational and intelligent people, and your brains might already be prioritizing these decisions. But it is also important to determine the level of complexity for each decision to understand what class they belong in. Decision classes will be discussed in the next step.

Rate each decision on a scale of a *low, medium, and high on* importance and complexity levels using the two-dimensional, 3×3 matrix shown in Figure 7.1. We have the importance scale on the vertical axis and complexity on the horizontal axis. IL stands for importance level and CL stands for complexity level. On the horizontal axis, the bottom row represents low

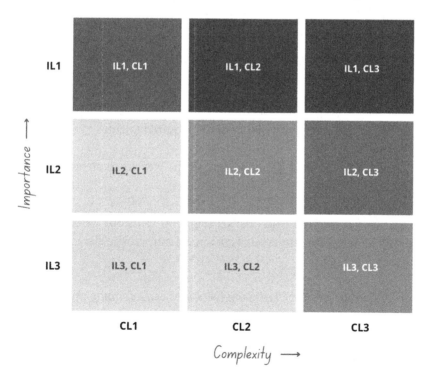

FIGURE 7.1   Decision importance vs. complexity matrix

importance (IL3), the row in the middle represents medium (IL2), and the top row represents high levels of importance (IL1). Similarly, on the vertical axis, the column on the left shows low complexity (CL3), the column in the middle shows medium (CL2), and the one on the right shows a high level of complexity (CL1).

Let us practice this with the decisions we listed in the last step. The ratings here might seem very different from how your team would rate the same decisions depending on your specific context.

Decision 1: select the three best social media platforms to help generate more traffic for our website.

Rating: IL1, CL2

On importance, it is a high-priority decision. The complexity level is rated as medium, considering that some constraints might be involved and add some complexity. This is the reason why we analyzed constraints in the last step. If you don't have clarity on the actual decision context, you will not be able to understand its actual complexity level.

The ratings for other decisions might look like this:

Decision 2: send existing customers a new discount offer to persuade them to return to our website and shop more.

Rating: IL2, CL1

Decision 3: know what people say about the new design of our website on social media to determine if we need to make changes to the design.

Rating: IL2, CL2

Decision 4: train the marketing staff for the website's social media promotions to ensure the availability of the required talent.

Rating: IL1, CL2

Decision 5: launch a PR campaign on the website to attract a different audience.

Rating: IL1, CL3

Decision 6: find out who (market segment) visits our website most frequently to determine the type of customers our website attracts.

Rating: IL1, CL1

Step 4: Prioritizing and Classifying Decisions to Determine the PI-AI Mix
In this step, you will go through a series of discussions with your team on prioritizing and classifying your decisions. Where prioritizing will use the importance level of each decision, classification will be done based on the PI needs to ensure that we use our most critical resource, people, most efficiently. This step will help us determine the most suitable PI-AI mix – what proportions of PI vs. AI we need for each decision. For example, a

high-priority, highly complex decision might require 90% PI and only 10% AI. Here, 90:10 is the PI-AI mix.

Assigning proportions this way might sound like a daunting task. Know that these proportions are approximate weights that can be determined by a little bit of guesswork. They don't have to be the exact values or weights. It is perfectly fine to use rough estimates. We use these weights for the sake of allocating resources effectively, not precisely.

Pareto's 80/20 principle should be used for both prioritizing and classification tasks. The principle states that roughly 80% of consequences come from 20% of the causes. It has successfully been applied to a large number of problems and issues in multiple domains, including economics, sports, marketing, business, technology, and healthcare. For example, Microsoft used this rule and discovered that by fixing 20% of the most reported bugs, 80% of the crashes and errors in a given system could be eliminated.[2]

Many examples have validated the 80/20 principle in business outcomes and processes. Discoveries such as 20% of the products in your product line account for about 80% of dollar sales value and 20% of the customers account for about 80% of an organization's profits have been validated many times in different scenarios. Today, many companies use this principle as a key commandment for decision-making.

According to Pareto's rule, 20% of your most important decisions should account for 80% of your project's success. This means that 20% of decisions are *vital few* and 80% are *useful many*. There are other terminologies that represent the same idea. Some call it a *vital few vs. trivial many*. If a particular decision has made it to your list, it has to have some significance. Therefore, using the term *trivial* might not be appropriate.

Let's start working on this step. First, we will work on prioritizing decisions. List your decisions in order of their significance for your project's success. Most important decisions should come first on your list. Now, highlight your vital few decisions, so they stand out. They are your high-priority decisions and shouldn't exceed 20% of the total decisions on your list. For example, if you have 20 decisions on the list, only four should make it to the top 20%. Here is a caveat – isn't it obvious that all the IL1 decisions from the previous step will make it to the top 20%? Not necessarily. Priority and importance are two different measures here. Priority also includes urgency and other factors, such as the leaders' push to pursue a specific decision first.

Since we will also use this list for further steps, it is a good idea to create a four-column table in a word document and start listing your decisions in the first column in order of their priority. Table 7.1 shows an illustration of how you should list your decisions and record PI-AI requirements for each

TABLE 7.1   PI-AI Requirements

Decision (Numbered Based on the Priority)	Decision Class/ Decision Rating	People Requirements (Specific Human Skills Required)	AI Requirements (Specific Areas That Need AI-Powered Solutions)
1. Launch a PR campaign on the website to attract a different audience.	Class A/ IL1, CL3	Leading, strategizing, communicating, conducting background research, designing the campaign, implementing, monitoring, and evaluating the campaign	Predictive analytics, content search, social listening, customer profiling, copywriting, sentiment analysis
2. Send existing customers a new discount offer to persuade them to return to our website and shop more.	Class D/IL2, CL1	Writing and drafting	Email automation, customer contact (data) management, predict optimal send times, optimize email subject lines, trigger messages based on real-time customer behavior

decision. At this point, focus only on column 1 from the left. As this is just an illustration, it lists only two decisions, one top priority (highlighted) and another, not the top priority decision.

Now, we will classify decisions into four distinct classes – classes A, B, C, and D. You might notice that the classification is done using a 3×3 matrix. If you seek more precision, you can also use a 5×5 matrix which sounds more appropriate for the 80/20 rule. After running a few trials, it was found that a 3×3 matrix produces results that are as satisfactory as results produced by a 5×5 matrix. By using a 3×3 matrix, we trade off precision for efficiency, which is one of the key purposes of DI. Also, since you are using this grid as a visual aid for classification, consider printing out the main grid shown in Figure 7.1. You can also draw and print an empty grid if you want.

So, what are you exactly doing in this step? First, read the description of all decision classes provided shortly in this section. Then using the grid, determine the class of each decision in your priority list. In the second column from the left (Table 7.1), write down which class each decision belongs in. Consider adding decision rating in the same column (this will help determine the PI-AI mix). Also, write down all your people and AI requirements for each decision.

This exercise will help you gain more clarity on your top priority decisions and your PI and AI needs. Where listing human skills will help you assign responsibilities to the right people, knowing your AI needs will help you plan your DI adoption strategy, which we will discuss in the next chapter. So, let's move on and start classifying our decisions.

The four decision classes are as follows:

Class A decisions: these are the decisions that made it to the top 20% on your priority list. They require high-level PI – roughly 80% of your total people potential. AI level will be based on the needs of the decision. Since the complexity levels of these decisions are moderate to high, you cannot wholly automate them. You might require either one or a combination of the decision assistance, support, augmentation, and even some automation technologies.

Figure 7.2 shows where these decisions might sit on the matrix (IL1, CL2, and IL1, CL3). Decision 5 in our list, "launch a PR campaign on the website to attract a different audience," is an excellent example of a class A decision. It is a task of high importance and carries moderate to high levels of complexity.

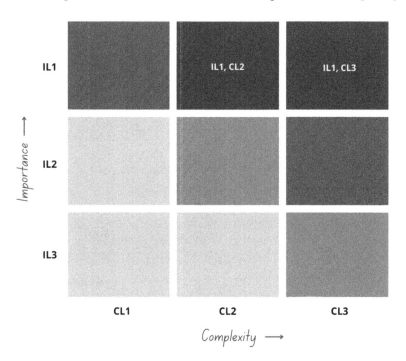

FIGURE 7.2   Class A decisions

Class B decisions: these require moderate-level PI, roughly 10% of your total people potential. Ten percent might seem low but it is enough for the decisions that did not make it to the top 20% of your priority list. The complexity level for these decisions might vary from low to high. Some of these decisions with lower complexity can easily be automated. Those with moderate to lower complexity can be tackled with decision assistance, support, or augmentation technologies with a bit of human intervention.

IL1, CL1, and IL2, CL3 decisions in Figure 7.3 are good examples of the decisions under this category. Decision 6, "find out who (market segment) is visiting our website most frequently to determine the type of customers our website attracts," illustrates IL1, CLI decisions. The decision is highly important but finding out who visits our website is not very complex. Website analytics and traffic reports can quickly inform this decision. Even when complexity is high but the decision is not the top priority, such as the IL2, CL3 decision, you should not use more than a moderate level (roughly 10%, overall) of PI. Consider employing advanced AI technologies to support these decisions.

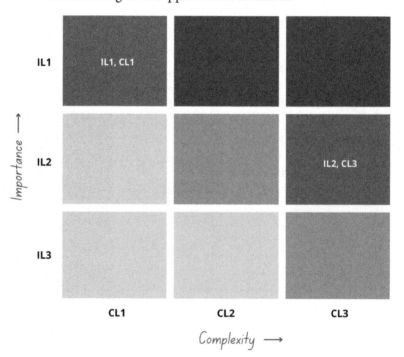

FIGURE 7.3   Class B decisions

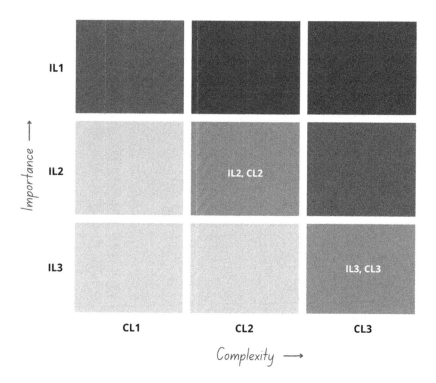

FIGURE 7.4   Class C decisions

Class C decisions: they should use low-level PI, roughly 5% of your total people potential. These decisions are of lower importance levels and should be left mainly to AI regardless of complexity levels. If they are highly complex and call for high PI, it might be better not to pursue them. Figure 7.4 highlights class C decisions. Decision 3, "know what people say about the new design of our website on social media to determine if we need to make changes to the design," is an excellent example of an IL2, CL2 decision. For IL3, CL3 decision, even though the complexity is high, it is one of the least important decisions where you shouldn't be using much of PI.

Class D decisions: they should use the lowest level of PI, less than 5% of your total people potential. As highlighted in Figure 7.5, these decisions are mostly low priority and since the complexity level is also low to moderate (mostly low), we can automate these decisions completely and handle them with very little, lowest

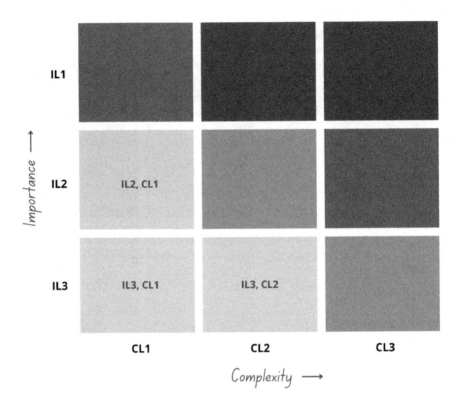

FIGURE 7.5   Class D decisions

levels of PI. Decision 2, "send our existing customers a new discount offer to persuade them to return to our website and shop more," is an excellent example of IL2, CL1 decisions. One person can create a standard promotion email (they can even choose pre-built email templates). Then, this email could be successfully sent to all the existing customers using an automated AI-powered solution. Not quite complex. Many business decisions fall into this category; they can easily be automated.

Step 5: Formulating Decision Implementation Strategy
Some crucial aspects of your decisions are now clear to you. You also have an idea of how you will deploy most of your critical PI-AI capabilities. In this step, you will formulate a detailed strategy on how to successfully implement your top priority and highly important decisions with the right PI-AI mix.

We recommend starting with your vital few – class A decisions. These decisions usually represent moderate to high levels of complexity. Take this class A decision, for example: launch a PR campaign on the website to attract a different audience. Launching a campaign could be cumbersome since it requires many different types of tasks. The dynamics of public relations change pretty frequently, and so do the constraints. This decision is a type of non-programmed and unstructured decision. Since the information to support such decisions is usually incomplete or ambiguous, they require decision-makers' knowledge, experience, thoughtful judgment, creative thinking, and high involvement in the decision-making process.[3]

Imagine you are the team leader to launch this marketing campaign. You already learned a lot about this decision from the previous steps. Now you will lay out the blueprint for implementing this decision. Break down the decision into various tasks that must be completed to execute it. Take one task at a time, and with your team, brainstorm (or use similar techniques such as brainwriting) to generate multiple alternatives on how this task could be performed in the best possible manner. Shortlist three to five best alternatives. In the next step, perform research to analyze each alternative's viability and overall strength. Based upon this analysis, choose the best alternative. This is similar to the decision-making process we discussed in Chapter 1.

Alternatively, you can also delegate these tasks to others. With the table you created in the last step, you know what people skills you need for this decision. So, identify talent who possess those skills and can deliver successful outcomes. Then, delegate them the responsibility to complete those tasks. This is why this framework is so crucial. As you know which decisions are your top priority and which carry high importance-high complexity, you can employ the right people and the right level of PI to implement the decision successfully. At this step, you will also need to start making arrangements to acquire the required AI capabilities.

You only need to do this much work for your vital few, top 20% decisions, and some of the other highly important decisions that are also highly complex. Once you have this step completed for class A decisions, move on to class B and then to class C decisions. Ensure you are not spending too much time strategizing implementation for less important decisions (although some of them might still need a brief strategy). Class D decisions mostly involve low complexity, are repeated over time, and fall under the programmed decisions category. The decision context of these decisions is relatively straightforward. Determine if your class D decisions can be automated. If yes, then do it. If they cannot be automated, consider aborting them completely. In case you cannot do either (automating or aborting), consider implementing these decisions with some quick plans instead of detailed strategies.

Step 6: Implementing the Strategy

So, you have your decision implementation strategies all figured out. Now, you will implement these strategies in executing actual decisions. There are certain things you should keep in mind at this step. The first-time implementation of your strategy will require more time and attention. In dynamic systems where decisions are usually non-programmed, things sometimes change at a swift pace. Make sure the decision strategy you created fits the most current problem context. The strategy created six months ago might become redundant if the context has already changed.

During implementation, you will also utilize the AI capabilities you finalized in the last step. If your team is using these solutions for the first time, the process will be slow and they will likely make some mistakes. Solution providers usually offer team and individual training and demonstrations. Ensure your team has acquired the necessary skills before working on the actual tasks. Nevertheless, your people will derive greater satisfaction in executing tasks since they are more focused on the few most important decisions.

Step 7: Evaluating the Strategy

This is the time to evaluate the success of your decision-making strategy. Keep in mind that success comes in increments when you work with technology and there is always an evolution over time. It is likely that the approach you engineered failed at the first implementation. In this case, go back and create a new strategy with the required variations in the PI-AI mix and the methodology of the process. If you succeed, congratulations! You have devised a good strategy. You should consider using the same strategy or approach for all future, similar decisions. Still, it is essential, especially for non-programmed decisions, that you review your decision context every time before finalizing your decision-making strategy.

CONCLUSION

To conclude this chapter, we can say that people, one of the most crucial business resources, should be involved only in critical decisions related to organizational goals. Decisions that are unimportant must either be automated or left with other technology solutions. It's not a secret that prioritizing decisions is essential. Everybody knows that. What is interesting (and unfortunate) is that although everybody knows that, many teams and organizations do not do it consistently. They keep repeating the same mistake of wasting critical resources on less important matters because they don't know or at least they don't realize how it damages their organization's overall efficiency.

This framework allows you to train yourself and your team on how to make decisions that produce the best outcomes, most efficiently, with the right PI-AI mix. Even though you can use this framework before, during, and after DI adoption, it is recommended to start working on it before the adoption. While going through the seven steps of the framework, you will learn what types of AI capabilities you actually need. This will help you to determine AI needs for DI adoption. Then, continue using this framework to prioritize your decisions and allocate your most important resources (people) most efficiently. As mentioned before, it might feel like a little too much work initially but as you start seeing the results and the impact on the quality of your decisions, you will not regret it.

As you keep using this framework for some time, you will notice that it will become your *way* of making decisions. With repeated attempts, your team will become programmed to make decisions systematically. You don't have to follow the steps strictly as they are explained. Get creative and find out better ways you and your team can leverage this framework. Regardless of whether you follow the exact steps, all you need to ensure is that your approach is systematic and that you:

- start with a goal in mind

- define your decisions (considering their outcomes and constraints)

- prioritize and classify your decisions

- use most of your people's potential for important and complex decisions

- formulate and implement a good PI-AI strategy

- evaluate the performance of your decision.

For a quick reference, you can use Figure 7.6, which is the representation of the DI framework as a flowchart. In the next chapter, we will discuss how to implement DI successfully in your organization and how to handle critical ethical issues related to DI.

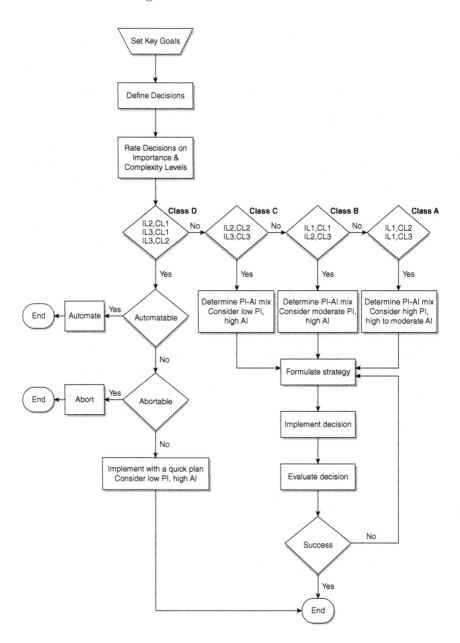

FIGURE 7.6 DI framework – flowchart representation

CASE STUDY: DRÄGER IMPROVES CUSTOMER SERVICE WITH STARMIND – LESS TIME SEARCHING, MORE TIME FOR CUSTOMERS

Dräger is an international company leading in medical and safety technologies fields. Founded in 1889, this German company is headquartered in Lübeck. It is currently present in more than 190 countries and has more than 13,700 employees worldwide. It partnered with Starmind to enhance customer service and increase employee productivity and satisfaction. Starmind offers AI-powered solutions to help connect employees to the expert knowledge they need. It is based in Zürich and was founded in 2010.

Dräger serves clinicians and emergency responders to help them support, protect, and save lives. It is committed to ensuring that clients get the right Dräger technologies most suitable for their needs. Dräger's sales teams work hard to provide their clients with up-to-date information on various products, applications, and services. Things got a little concerning when surveys of the sales teams revealed that the salespeople were often spending several days tracking down answers to clients' questions from more than 6,000 colleagues in sales, production, marketing, and other departments. The time these sales experts were wasting could have been spent on more valuable interactions with their clients.

Starmind's AI-powered solution provided Dräger's salespeople with relevant information and high-quality answers to their questions more efficiently. Starmind's powerful AI analyzes millions of data points teams create every day. The results of this analysis are then used to build a real-time network of the organization's knowledge. When someone asks a question, the system connects them to colleagues with the exact knowledge regardless of their title, location, or department. As questions go to the right people instantly, it allows salespeople to save a lot of time and energy.

Not only the salespeople but it also helps other people save their time who were otherwise contacted for inquiries. In just five months of pilot implementation, the number of questions that had to be answered more than once decreased by 64%. Moreover, the employee survey informed that 94% of users were very satisfied with Starmind's solution and would recommend it to other colleagues. Salespeople saw a 12% point increase in working time as they now spend 48% less time searching for experts and know-how. Today, the workload at Dräger is distributed more evenly throughout different departments. In addition, more people across the business now have the opportunity to share their expertise and create collective intelligence for the organization. By accessing Starmind on different devices, salespeople can get answers to their questions faster. They can also get access to instant expertise if the question has already been answered from a previous inquiry.

In the first 15 months of implementation, 6,369 questions were asked and answered on Starmind. Each answer was reused on an average of 5.2 times. Currently, only 18% of questions are raised and answered multiple times compared to 50% shortly after implementation. With time, the system will only improve. Dräger's salespeople are saving a significant amount of time and energy with Starmind's proprietary AI solutions. They can redirect these resources to more valuable activities for their clients and ensure much better customer service.

Sources:

How Dräger Reduced Complexity with Starmind. (2021, October). Retrieved August 11, 2022, from Starmind website: https://www.starmind. ai/customers/drager

Starmind. (n.d.). Retrieved August 11, 2022, from Starmind website: https://www.starmind.ai/how-starmind-works

QUESTIONS

1. What challenges was Dräger facing regarding the performance of its salespeople?

2. How did Starmind's platform connect salespeople to other colleagues with relevant information in real-time?

3. How did AI-powered solutions help salespeople save their time and energy?

4. What was the overall impact of this partnership on Dräger's efficiency in customer service?

5. Search online and discuss two more examples where organizations took their success to another level using people-AI augmentation.

QUESTIONS FOR DISCUSSION

1. What is the significance of adopting a step-by-step, systematic approach to decision-making?

2. Why is it important to prioritize your decisions and tasks?

3. What is the purpose of the DI framework proposed in this chapter?

4. Why do business decisions require more deliberation? Discuss with examples of some real-life business decisions.

5. Why is it important to keep humans in the loop when it comes to making important business decisions? What can humans do in this context that machines cannot?

6. Before starting to work on the DI framework, what tasks do you need to consider for preparation and planning?

7. Explain the importance of setting key goals at the beginning of the process.

8. How do you define decisions considering their outcomes and constraints? Discuss with the help of suitable examples.

9. With the help of examples, discuss how to rate decisions on importance vs. complexity levels.

10. According to the DI framework, what are the four classes of decisions?

11. Is it important to formulate a detailed decision implementation strategy for all types of decisions? Why or why not?

12. Discuss things to consider while implementing your decision or operationalizing your strategy for important decisions.

13. Why is it essential to evaluate the success of your decisions?

14. How can the DI framework help organizations improve their overall decision-making at the team, departmental, and organizational levels? Discuss in detail.

REFERENCES

1. Pratt, L. (2019). *Link: How Decision Intelligence Connects Data, Actions, and Outcomes for a Better World.* Warrington, UK: Emerald Publishing.
2. Rooney, P. (2002, October 3). Microsoft's CEO: 80-20 Rule Applies To Bugs, Not Just Features. Retrieved June 20, 2022, from CRN website: https://www.crn.com/news/security/18821726/microsofts-ceo-80-20-rule-applies-to-bugs-not-just-features.htm

3. Bright, D., Cortes, A., Gardner, D., Hartmann, E., Lambert, J., Ludec, L., ..., White, M. (n.d.). *Programmed and Nonprogrammed Decisions – Principles of Management*. Houston, TX: OpenStax.. Retrieved from https://openstax.org/books/principles-management/pages/2-3-programmed-and-nonprogrammed-decisions

CHAPTER 8

Recommendations for DI Implementation and Ethics

Decision intelligence is in its nascent stage as a disciple. Nevertheless, it has the potential to shape the future of this planet by significantly improving our businesses and lives. As a result, more and more companies will soon strategically adopt DI. The idea of DI adoption looks promising but implementing such technological capabilities does not come without challenges.

In this chapter, we will list recommendations for successful DI implementation. The two terms *adoption* and *implementation* are used synonymously. You cannot adopt a technology until you implement it! These recommendations are made considering your organization wants to implement DI in either one or the combination of the three forms – decision support, augmentation, and automation. If you only need AI for decision assistance, then your existing systems and some basic tools such as third-party apps and internet search should be sufficient. After recommendations, DI readiness assessment and DI readiness audit will be discussed in detail.

We hear many people, including experts and scholars, voice their concerns over AI taking too much control over our lives. There are a large number of ethical issues that need to be addressed before we venture into newer AI fields and disciplines. This chapter also covers critical ethical

DOI: 10.1201/b23322-8

considerations for DI and what we can do to ensure that it is used for the well-being of people and organizations without hurting anyone's interests.

RECOMMENDATIONS FOR DI IMPLEMENTATION

Various big and small companies are adopting DI technologies as a significant source of their competitive advantage. DI in action can be seen as a full-fledged organizational system made of several components working interdependently to accomplish common goals. Different components of an organization's DI system might include the guiding documents (DI strategy and DI policy), participating or relevant individuals and teams, key and supporting technologies, technological infrastructure, DI solutions, processes, and more. This system needs to be managed just like any other entity focusing on four essential management functions: planning, organizing, leading, and controlling.

Note that the requirements of DI implementation are not the same for all organizations. You don't need significant changes if your organization already uses AI capabilities in one or more business functions. AI is the foundation of DI, and if you have basic AI capabilities in place, you might only need to upgrade the new data stack to make DI work. However, you will still need to make certain adjustments or take additional actions to establish it as an organization-wide practice.

Key recommendations for successful implementation of DI system(s) are as follows:

Start Early, Start Small

Have you ever heard about the first mover advantage? It describes the advantage a company gains by being first to market. Entering the market first enables a company to establish its brand and business before other entrants. Similarly, early DI adopters are likely to report a much better profit outlook than their competitors, who are not investing in such capabilities. These systems take time and experimentation to succeed like any other revolutionary change. People in the organization need time to hone skills specific to any technology. Skill-building has its unique learning curve. So if you start early, your teams will learn quicker, and you will have the talent prepared to harness the power of DI before your competitors. You will also have more time to develop a robust system that gives high returns on your investment.

Many organizations that started to adopt AI early are the leaders in their specific industries today or market leaders have bought them for a handsome price. For example, consider how Google acquired DeepMind Technologies in 2014 to strengthen its technological capacity, especially in artificial neural networks. Today, Google uses these technologies to serve the market of billions of users worldwide. So start your DI adoption early. Start it now.

Instead of adopting DI on a large scale, try implementing it at a smaller level first. For example, you might consider implementing recommendation engines for some of the tasks first, and from there, you can scale at your desired pace. A slow change in little increments is always better than radical change that disturbs the order and challenges the status quo people generally like to maintain.

Develop a Business Case

Building a DI system requires a significant investment of various resources. Therefore, assessing the need for DI in your organization is essential. For example, many companies do not even have enough data to power the ML or AI systems.. Many others might only need a decision support system and no augmentation or automation solutions. Still, the first question you need to address is *why* you need DI. Then, how will you justify that your organization needs DI system implementation to your stakeholders, especially project sponsors? Developing a business case and communicating it as a compelling story might help accomplish that. The sponsors will want to know what problems DI solutions will solve for your company. This is why you should work on the DI framework before DI implementation. The framework allows you to list the decisions that require specific AI-powered DI technologies.

You also need to properly assess the factors responsible for creating urgency for DI adoption. Your story should communicate the DI system's benefits and the consequences of not adopting it. For example, DI helps organizations improve operational efficiency through effective decision-making and responsiveness to the market. Tell your stakeholders about all the problems it will solve, opportunities it will bring, the most important beneficiaries, and other processes that will benefit from this project.

Make It a Strategic Initiative

DI adoption is crucial for any organization and should be considered an important strategic initiative. Each organization has its different DI strategy based on several factors such as type of business, need for specific DI form, capacity to invest, and availability of necessary resources. As a result, a DI system in one organization might look completely different from the DI system in another. An organization's DI strategy should be created as a plan that includes:

- Organization's vision for DI adoption

- The purpose of DI adoption

- Values concerning DI

- How DI adoption aligns with organizational goals

- DI standards (or KPIs) that guide all the DI practices and help assess DI outcomes

- Description of critical projects and initiatives; prioritization and timelines

- Requirements – finance, infrastructure, and talent

- Risk assessment

- Business process alignment

- Performance management

- Impact tracking

The list is not all-inclusive. You can add aspects critical for your organization's success to the plan. Make sure to anticipate barriers to adoption and list the solutions to prevent or overcome them. Do not forget to account for resources spent on workflow redesign, training, and communication. Again, the strategy must explain how DI will be used to create a system that produces effective decisions and increases decision-making process efficiency.

Use Project Management Approach

Managing a high-magnitude pursuit such as AI or DI adoption requires making many complex decisions. Its implementation should be designed as a project led by a manager with adequate knowledge of project management methodologies, DI concepts, and how the capabilities are acquired, maintained, and used. In the beginning, you should determine the portfolio of DI initiatives, the projects your organization needs, and then list the deliverables for each initiative.

It is a good idea to create a plan consisting of the details of all the essential activities that need to be performed before, during, and after DI implementation. Rick Sherman[1] recommends that before developing your project schedule, consider defining your work breakdown structure (WBS). Considering project deliverables, WBS helps incrementally decompose the project into smaller and more manageable components. It provides a well-designed framework to plan, schedule, and manage different projects. A DI project, according to Sherman, will have the same phases as a typical BI or IT application development project with the following phases:

Scope and plan: determine high-level requirements such as timeframe, resources, and costs. Key activities include building teams, creating budgets, obtaining sponsorships, and performing DI needs assessment, readiness assessment, and audit (see DI Readiness Assessment section for details).

Analyze and define: analyze the requirements in the previous phase and define detailed business, resources, data, and quality requirements for the project.

Architect and design: develop a DI solution blueprint containing information, data, technology, and product architectures. This can be done while the last step is still underway.

Build, test, and refine: DI system components (technologies, platforms, and solutions) start to build in this phase. It is recommended to construct multiple prototypes that could be tested for quality and effectiveness. You can quickly identify flaws and bottlenecks through prototyping, which makes refining easier.

Implement: software, platforms, and products are migrated first into testing and then to the production environment. System testing is performed. The teams collaborate with in-house production support as well as off-premise support such as cloud service providers.

Deploy and roll-out: business users start to use the system for their daily tasks. The project team ensures clarity of communication with multiple stakeholders. Business users are also offered training on using the new system and its components. The support process, including help desks, is established.

Build Capacity, Capabilities, and Infrastructure

Most companies that have successfully adopted AI and DI are already highly digitized. These companies invested early in digital capabilities such as big data and cloud infrastructure. Cutting-edge technology is a mandate for this project to be successful. As mentioned before, if you are already using AI capabilities, you might have the basic infrastructure ready. Many legacy systems and AI platforms can be repurposed for DI use with a few changes, updates, and upgrades. Perform research on what type of infrastructure other successful companies in your industry use. This kind of benchmarking helps you understand what form of DI and practices you need to succeed in your industry. After considering your particular needs and situation, list down all your infrastructural needs for DI.

You also need a well-designed, modern data architecture that we discussed in Chapter 1. The architecture allows real-time data management capabilities such as data sourcing (structured, semi-structured, and unstructured), automated pipelines for data ingestion, data storage, data transformation, workflow management, AI-ML-powered analytics, insights generation, and data visualization. Most successful and modern companies are moving to operate entirely on the cloud. If you are considering that, then make sure you are partnering with the right providers. If you are already using cloud services, you should check the status of your cloud resources, especially if you are looking to scale up. They might not be suitable anymore since your workloads and other requirements are changing. Also, check your network to see how much burden they can carry and the network bandwidth that AI's data flow requirements can tax.

Data is crucial for DI. ML algorithms require massive amounts of data to generate insights. Consider adding more and more data from different sources to your architecture. The use of synthetic data is a new trend gaining more popularity today. Instead of using real historical data, you can utilize synthetic, artificially generated data to fuel your ML systems. Make sure the quality of all data remains one of your primary concerns. Inaccurate, unreliable, and outdated data will only result in poor and unreliable insights. Know that information silos in the organization can affect access to essential data. Think, plan, and discuss with your team how you will break those silos to access the data that is being housed in insulated, restrictive environments.

Another component you must consider is DI tools – the software, platform, or solution that will enable the actual functioning of DI. Intelligent systems created with AI and AutoML technologies are replacing traditional DSSs. The market is booming with new DI solutions (discussed in Chapter 6) that make valuable recommendations for decision augmentation. Your chosen tool should deliver the DI solution end to end. Some of these tools will need integration with other data management and visualization systems. They should also be able to scale beyond the initial testing and evaluation stages. Many decision automation tools, such as InRule, Sapiens, and Decisions, are available in the market. Cloud adoption is accelerated as technologies are getting advanced, and the nature of work is changing. Today, various cloud services offer tools that support DI. From basic analytics (such as Domo and Google Analytics) to advanced tools (such as Google Big Query and Microsoft Azure), even some edge applications (such as Google Cloud's Edge TPU and AWS for Edge) could make it to your ensemble of essential DI tools.

You need a team that helps design and develop the most suitable DI system for your organization's needs. Also, business users must be able to use these systems without any problems. Identify and understand the talent gap within your enterprise. If required, train existing people or hire new talent. As a team, they will be making a massive amount of decisions in this project. It is crucial to account for the dynamics of team decision-making that we discussed in Chapter 2. It is also essential to ensure that your DI system is integrated with other business processes. Often, integration problems become the root cause of the failure of the entire system. Finally, consider building (or reengineering) processes that facilitate scaling.

DI Education and Training

Adopting DI is going to be a massive technological shift for your organization. It is a new discipline and many people in your organization might not be aware of what it is, why it is crucial, and how to use it for their daily tasks. It might also instill fear among employees regarding the safety of their jobs. Like AI, DI will also take away or change some jobs. It is, therefore, essential to first help them build trust in DI. Tell them the overall benefits of DI – how it will help them and the organization achieve their goals. You will also need to inform them how each employee's daily work will change as the project is implemented and running. Different training programs should be organized to educate people on fundamental concepts of DI, DI technologies, critical skills required, end-user experience, analytics, DI leadership, and how to use DI solutions to make better decisions.

You can choose to launch an internal training program that incorporates online or in-person classroom work, symposiums, workshops, seminars, or on-the-job training. In addition, many organizations hire external trainers or faculty to develop and deliver different training programs.

Partner for Success

While strategizing for DI, you will need to decide whether to develop DI capabilities in-house or use partners. Building and maintaining a highly sophisticated, fully functional DI system in-house is not a simple feat. On the contrary, it can be a complicated process that requires significant technical expertise and other resources. The good news is that you can find partners outside your firm who could help you transition smoothly into your DI journey. Partnering with outsiders is not an uncommon practice. For example, large companies like Amazon and Google partnered with outside talent, providers, and companies to develop their AI systems and procedures.[2]

In order to find the right partner, it is essential to have your needs analysis done beforehand. You will need to perform in-depth research comparing different DI providers in the market. Working with partners can be a long-term commitment and you don't want to commit to someone who cannot deliver on their promises. As discussed in Chapter 7, more and more companies are venturing into offering DI solutions and services today. Before getting into a long-term contract or subscription, use their free trials. It will extend the time for research but you will save significant amounts of resources that you would spend if you chose the wrong partner.

Use Design Thinking

Design thinking is one of the most effective techniques that help designing products or services using a process including empathizing with users, defining the problem, ideation, prototyping, and testing stages. Using this approach, you can build systems and solutions that minimize decision-makers' mental-technical effort (such as writing cumbersome codes) and maximize results by providing valuable recommendations for various decisions. Design thinking focuses on designing solutions that ease users' pains and increase their gains.

The designing process starts with empathy – knowing what causes pain for your user. You can use different techniques such as journey mapping, interviews, and shadowing to probe deeply into their problems. Based on this information, you then define their actual personas, pain points, and challenges they are facing. With your team, you can now do some ideation using brainstorming, brainwriting, and divergent and convergent thinking exercises.

Using ideas from the previous steps, you now create a prototype of your solution. Proper testing is performed in the next stage to determine whether this prototype will work or if your design has any flaws. This information can be extremely useful in iterating and building the best solution for your users. Design thinking uses experimentation and helps you create an agile and adaptable system. Many large and small companies use this framework to produce products and services that their customers value. With design thinking, you can create DI solutions that decision-makers *actually want*, not those *you think they want*.

Focus on Collaboration

DI is an interdisciplinary approach that involves both technical and managerial decision-making aspects. Technology teams should never be solely in charge of DI initiatives. They cannot see decision contexts and nuances that business managers can. Therefore, DI initiatives should be co-managed by interdisciplinary teams. Democratizing AI is the very purpose of DI. A successful DI practice requires the team to have people with multiple skills who could perform different necessary functions. Diverse team members can generate better ideas together and solve execution problems more creatively.

It also requires all the management levels to work together to ensure DI investment success. Executive leadership support is crucial in DI adoption since the top management, the C-level officers, are the ones who approve finances and decisions of such importance and magnitude. Without their support, it will be difficult or impossible to succeed in this pursuit. As a best practice, the entire project should be led by a coalition of business, IT, and data analytics leaders.[3]

Build a DI Culture

DI is not just a bunch of technologies. Instead, it is a value that focuses on making data-driven decisions for higher efficiency and effectiveness. From leaders to employees, each individual and team should be involved in making DI work for your organization. Therefore, building a culture that encourages DI use is essential. One of the most significant barriers to technology adoption is reluctance from people. Change is never comfortable, and that's why people resist it. Organizations need change agents, leaders, and managers who can communicate the value of DI to the people. Key individuals, including those who have the potential to influence most people, should be involved in making DI-related strategic decisions.

As mentioned before, it is essential to help people build trust in DI. People at all levels should understand that DI is for good and that algorithms can produce better results than humans in many decision scenarios. Moreover, they should be willing to augment their intuition, creativity, and judgment with what algorithms suggest. Efficiency in decision-making is one of the critical benefits of DI. Moreover, it helps you make more accurate decisions. Your people will be less likely to resist if they know all the benefits DI brings for them and the organization. By building a climate where everyone values what is essential for organizational success, you can also break silos that result in the compartmentalization of information and several other problems.

Monitor Performance, Assess Impact, and Modify DI Solutions

Once deployed, the DI system will start to perform and produce results. Performance monitoring is essential to ensure that your systems are working per the standards. It helps you identify the gaps between the standard and actual performances of the system. You can find out the sources of deviation and correct the course as needed. This is the control function of managing DI.

Assessing the impact of the system on the organization's profits is essential. However, measuring the financial impact or the return on investment for pursuits like DI adoption is not always easy. Therefore, you should consider using KPIs that help assess your new system's impact on overall efficiency, people, and productivity. Suppose the overall impact is not positive (or is insignificant). In that case, you might consider modifying your DI solutions and making changes to improve the system's performance. You must ensure that DI positively impacts the overall organizational functioning and outcomes.

DI READINESS ASSESSMENT

DI adoption is not merely a change. It is a transformation that alters the ways you make day-to-day decisions. It is about putting your trust in AI, algorithms, and machines. Moreover, you need the proper infrastructure, processes ready to align with new technologies and systems, and much more. Therefore, one of the most critical tasks in adopting DI is determining whether your organization is ready for such a vast transformation. Unfortunately, many organizations fail in similar pursuits because they are not ready for a change of such a high magnitude in the first place. Therefore, starting your DI project with a readiness assessment is a good idea.

The assessment can be done using DI Readiness Audit Tool, which we will discuss shortly. The tool is based on the following three readiness criteria:

Strategic and Leadership Readiness

As a first step, assessing if DI adoption aligns with the organization's vision and mission, serves strategic priorities, and helps the organization achieve its short-term and long-term goals is crucial. An organization's strategy guides most of its actions and decisions. The purpose of the strategy is to inform stakeholders about the goals the organization wants to achieve that are aligned with its vision and mission. Of course, the bottom line of every business is profit. Profit is generated when your revenues are higher than the costs incurred. DI adoption can be costly and organizational leaders might not find it worthwhile if it doesn't help the organization increase its profit.

The C-level executives and organizational leaders must be convinced of DI's value to approve its adoption. Often, leaders just don't have the mindset that supports adopting something this revolutionary. Among other reasons, the fear of failure might prevent them from accepting this idea. Determining whether or not they are ready for DI adoption is necessary. The project will not even start if the leaders on the top disapprove of this investment.

Infrastructural and Operational Readiness

To a great extent, infrastructure readiness depends on whether you want to build your solutions in-house. For in-house development, you need much more advanced and sophisticated facilities, including a well-maintained data center that, among other things, can support the massive processing required for ML and AI. We discussed these requirements in the previous section.

It is also essential to ensure that you can manage all the processes and operations directly or indirectly related to this project. The processes need to be adaptable to the changing requirements. In addition, they should integrate smoothly with the new system and its components. Ensuring data security, privacy, and other cybersecurity concerns is also crucial. Moreover, you will need to make changes to your policies for governance, compliance, and risk. DI adoption will definitely bring some additional and concerning ramifications in this context.

Talent and Cultural Readiness

Talent is a critical resource for the success of any IT, AI, or DI project. It is people who make these systems work and use them. Since DI requires a new set of capabilities, you might not yet have people with the necessary skill set. You will also need a team to oversee this project and manage all the tasks, including monitoring and tracking DI-based continuous improvement. One of the most important pieces is the culture of the organization. You will need a deep assessment of whether or not your organization is culturally ready for this transformation.

DI Readiness Audit

You can use the DI Readiness Audit Tool in Exhibit 8.1 to assess DI readiness for your organization. It is a form consisting of 30 questions covering three assessment criteria discussed in this section. Considering the weighted significance of each criterion, the tool includes nine questions (30%) from strategic and leadership readiness, 12 questions (40%) from infrastructure and operational readiness, and nine questions (30%) from the people and cultural readiness area.

The questions should be answered "Yes" or "No." To generate better insights from this assessment, you should evaluate each response individually to determine if some deficiencies need to be fixed or opportunities you can leverage for successful DI adoption. Each "Yes" counts for one point. If you get a score equal to or greater than 24, you are in good standing to start your DI adoption journey. It is also possible that you earn a lower score but if it is still under the 50th percentile (equal to or above 15 points), it is quite possible to change some things around that change your current standing. A score below 15 might not be the ideal situation to initiate this change.

EXHIBIT 8.1 DI READINESS AUDIT

Answer the following questions "Yes" or "No."

1. Does your vision for DI adoption align with the overall organizational philosophy, vision, and mission?
   a. Yes
   b. No

2. Will your DI strategy be focused on your organization's strategic priorities?
   a. Yes
   b. No

3. Do leaders in your organization value data-driven decision-making?

    a. Yes

    b. No

4. Are your organization's leaders open to adopting revolutionary technologies for business success?

    a. Yes

    b. No

5. Is your business facing problems related to decision-making that led you to consider adopting DI?

    a. Yes

    b. No

6. Do you have a compelling business case defining the problems DI will solve?

    a. Yes

    b. No

7. Have you identified and listed all the needs for the proposed DI implementation?

    a. Yes

    b. No

8. Have you listed all the key performance indicators to evaluate the performance of this project?

    a. Yes

    b. No

9. Have you assessed the risk associated with this project?

    a. Yes

    b. No

10. Will you be able to have enough financial resources available to fund this project?

    a. Yes

    b. No

11. Will all the necessary data be available in a machine-readable format for ML and AI?

    a. Yes

    b. No

12. Have you chosen the DI solutions you will require in this project?

    a. Yes

    b. No

13. Will your chosen solutions scale beyond testing and evaluation at the initial stage?

   a. Yes
   b. No

14. Have you allocated time for different project activities and tasks?

   a. Yes
   b. No

15. Do your facilities and data centers have sufficient resources to support DI adoption and maintenance?

   a. Yes
   b. No

16. Are your business processes designed to support the use of DI?

   a. Yes
   b. No

17. Are all your processes ready to be integrated with the new DI system?

   a. Yes
   b. No

18. Do you have a mechanism in place to prevent and tackle cybersecurity-related risks?

   a. Yes
   b. No

19. Do you have a realistic plan created for deployment?

   a. Yes
   b. No

20. Have you identified all the governance needs for implementing and managing a DI system at your organization?

   a. Yes
   b. No

21. Have you performed adequate research on partnerships you will need to develop in the future to implement and maintain the DI system?

   a. Yes
   b. No

22. Do you have a team of individuals with diverse, necessary skills to oversee this project and manage essential functions, including organizing, leading, monitoring performance, and assessing the project impact?

   a. Yes
   b. No

23. Do you have a skilled workforce, or will you have the talent available in the future required for the success of the DI project at your organization?

    a. Yes
    b. No

24. Have you identified training and education needs for this project?

    a. Yes
    b. No

25. Are all the important people involved in planning this new pursuit?

    a. Yes
    b. No

26. Have you identified individuals whose work will be directly impacted by this project?

    a. Yes
    b. No

27. Is your workforce aware of all the benefits of DI for them and for the organization?

    a. Yes
    b. No

28. Does your workforce now, or will it in the future, trust in the ability of algorithms to improve decision-making?

    a. Yes
    b. No

29. Will your organizational culture support the implementation of the new DI system?

    a. Yes
    b. No

30. Have you identified change agents and influencers who will help you navigate this change successfully?

    a. Yes
    b. No

ETHICS FOR DI

Decision intelligence, as a more focused implementation of AI, helps us improve our decision-making. However, certain ethical challenges or concerns must be discussed concerning DI use. It is essential to determine the extent to which we should allow AI to control our decisions or make decisions on our behalf. Ethical concerns for DI are the same as some of the common ethical concerns for AI. Nevertheless, we need to familiarize ourselves with them. Let's discuss some of the key ethical challenges related to DI and how *you* – someone responsible for the ethical implementation of DI systems at your organization can help address them.

Biased Algorithms

Algorithms running in systems today are ruling our choices and lives. These systems decide which movie or content recommendations we receive and which advertisements we see and predict which products we are going to buy next. Do you know that these algorithms, like humans, could be biased? Humans are the creators of algorithms. They choose the data that is fed to the algorithm, how it is used, and how its results should be applied. It is quite possible that human developers' bias may creep into the algorithms and their foundational assumptions might affect the credibility of the programs they develop. AI and ML industry in the West is dominated by men. Moreover, the underrepresentation of women, black and Latinx people can be seen clearly throughout various technology disciplines. Recent studies inform that facial recognition systems developed by large companies like IBM and Amazon were found to be less accurate at identifying features of people with darker skin color.[4]

The major concern here is the effect – the treatment of people and securing their fundamental rights. If law enforcement agencies use these biased algorithms, it could increase the risk of unjustly apprehending people of color. Financial service companies are using AI on a large scale now. A study from UC Berkeley[5] found that several mortgage algorithms have systematically (however wrongfully) charged black and Latinx borrowers higher interest rates than the borrowers who were white. The researchers at Stanford University[6] found that large racial disparities were demonstrated in automated speech recognition systems where the voice assistants misidentified 35% of words from black users. Only 19% of words from white users were misidentified. Various studies[7] inform of inherent biases attached to certain races, genders, and people from specific professional backgrounds.

Catastrophic consequences occur when unethical governments and their leaders are given the power of such significance. Chinese government authorities are using a vast system of advanced facial recognition technologies to track the Uighurs, a largely Muslim minority in China's western region. Uighurs resemble closely to people from Central Asia and often look different from China's majority Han population. As of April 2019, China held as many as a million Uighurs in detention camps. Demand for such capabilities in China is only increasing, which tells us that it will only worsen.[8] Such automated racism with racial profiling of this magnitude can pose serious challenges for humanity and must be controlled.

One of the key factors behind algorithmic bias is insufficient or unfair data. ML models are fed a bunch of data for training. Through an algorithm, the computer processes that data to learn to identify, judge, predict, or decide. For example, suppose you feed the system an image dataset with five million images of white people's faces. Since the pictures only include the white population, the system will only learn to identify features in white people's faces. Now, if it sees a new image of a person from Central Asia, it will likely make a mistake. Facial features of humans vary depending on race, age, ethnicity, gender, and geographical location, among other factors. Therefore, controlling your data and ensuring that you feed algorithms data points representative of the real, diverse population is essential. You should have a firm data governance policy that all business and technology users can access and understand. The team responsible for building and deploying algorithms must include people from diverse backgrounds. This will prevent individual biases from creeping into the system. You can also consider hiring a third party to continually analyze your system, data, and algorithms for fairness. Consider using tools and frameworks, such as Bias Analyzer, REVISE, FairML, IBM AI Fairness 360, and Microsoft's Fairlearn, to mitigate bias from your datasets, models, and algorithms.

Data Privacy and Protection

AI capabilities installed within most companies' systems use tons of data related to various aspects of people's personal and professional lives. Results generated by this data mostly become the basis of different types of crucial business decisions in marketing, advertising, and hiring. The 2016 presidential campaigns of Ted Cruz and Donald Trump will always be remembered for the scandal of swaying the 2016 elections in the United States. A British consulting firm Cambridge Analytica harvested millions of Facebook users' data without their consent. The information was used to target political advertising created to influence users' opinions regarding their votes. They performed a psychological analysis of users' Facebook profiles for patterns and built algorithms to predict how to best target them. According to a report from Britain's Channel 4 News,[9] a Cambridge Analytica database identified Black voters disproportionately for "Deterrence." The database contained information on nearly 200 million American voters and sorted likely Democratic voters into several categories. It put 3.5 million African Americans into a category called "Deterrence." It was an apparent bid to dissuade people of color from supporting Hillary Clinton, who ran as the Democratic nominee. Channel 4 informed that Donald Trump's 2016 presidential campaign used this database, but the campaign denied this allegation. According to Federal Election Commission data, Trump's 2016 campaign paid $5.9 million to Cambridge Analytica.

There are multiple pieces of evidence quoting different instances of companies using people's personal information for unethical purposes. Privacy policies from the organizations such as Facebook are lengthy, sometimes unclear, and difficult to understand by a common user. As a result, people hardly read all the content in the policy and consent to it without knowing the consequences. Although we have a legislative framework in place to protect individual privacy, we still need a better protection framework against discriminatory algorithmic decision-making and online data privacy and protection.

Large datasets are prone to breaches, running a higher privacy risk. AI technologies can deanonymize even seemingly anonymized personal data. This poses a risk of individuals being identified, having their data leaked, and being used for unethical purposes. It might mean little to many people, but we need transparency on how companies and businesses use our information. To address this concern, you can provide people with relevant information (such as privacy policy) in multiple, easy-to-understand formats. You should only collect data that is necessary for a particular AI or DI analysis. It should be kept secured and maintained only for as long as required to accomplish your goals. Consider adding data privacy, transparency, and protection guidelines to your governance strategy so the developers can minimize these challenges well before production in the development stage.[10] For DI, you will, at some point, need to work with people's personal data. Around the world, people and the public have lost trust in AI and technology due to businesses' unethical practices, data breaches, leaks, and scandals. In order to restore their confidence, you must take deliberative steps to ensure their information is safe and will not be used for any projects with unethical implications.

Accuracy of Data and Information

According to Statista,[11] global data creation is projected to grow to more than 180 zettabytes by 2025. We are creating massive amounts of data every second, a lot of which is being recorded, stored, and used somewhere for purposes we might not even be aware of. Analytics performed on the data power the most critical business decisions today. So, how much of your data is accurate and reliable? Data quality has been a severe concern to analysts since the quality of the outcome and the results depend significantly on the quality of the input – the data. Misleading data will only generate misleading insights. Poor data quality increases the complexity of data ecosystems resulting in poor decision-making.

Data inaccuracy is not just about the wrong form or format of the data. It is also about the content and the message it delivers. Today, uncountable deepfake content is streaming on our social media platforms, affecting our thoughts, opinions, and choices regarding important decisions in our lives. Deepfakes are synthetic media or content created with AI technologies such as deep learning that replace one person's likeness with another. Developers can create fictional photos, audios, and videos to mislead audiences on different platforms. For example, a LinkedIn fake, "Katie Jones," who is thought to be a deepfake created for a foreign spying operation, claimed to work at the Center for Strategic and International Studies. In 2017, a Reddit user posted doctored porn clips that swapped celebrities' faces, including Gal Gadot, Taylor Swift, and Scarlett Johansson, onto porn performers. These are just a couple of examples. Several deepfakes of political leaders, business leaders, and celebrities have been streaming online, influencing millions of users worldwide. Unfortunately, fake information and inauthentic data are becoming more prevalent.

A study from IBM[12] estimated that America loses $3.1 trillion of its gross domestic product (GDP) due to bad data. One in three business leaders doesn't trust their own data. The poor preparation of data often causes data inaccuracies. In addition, poor data entry practices and not regulating data accessibility from different sources make the problem worse. Okay! Ensuring data quality can be taxing, and we accept that. You can consider remediating only a relevant portion of your data that will be used for important analysis and decisions. Focus on expanding your data management team with some employees dedicated to ensuring data quality. There are also ML technologies that you can use to derive a data quality index score that assesses the quality and reliability of your dataset. Additional recommendations to improve your data quality can be found on Gartner's website: https://www.gartner.com/ smarterwithgartner/how-to-improve-your-data-quality

Job Loss

One of the most critical concerns about the growing use of AI is the loss of jobs and employment. Automation has already eliminated millions of jobs worldwide. Moreover, competent AI systems, including DI solutions, can now handle a wide range of knowledge-based, white-collar work. Concerns about AI causing huge disruptions to the job market have been around for a long time. As the cost of smart technologies and devices falls over time, these technologies become accessible to even small businesses. Some industries, such as banking and financial services, and manufacturing, will face more disruptions in this area. It will also depend upon the nature of the work itself. Jobs that require more structured, programmable, and repeatable tasks can be codified into standard steps and will be automated sooner or later. As a result, millions of workers across the globe will be displaced by AI-driven technologies, including DI. Fukoku Mutual Life Insurance company in Japan uses the IBM AI software to save roughly $1.1 million per year on employee salaries. Other companies in Japan are also testing and implementing AI systems to automate work and save costs incurred on salaries.[13] Similar trends are reported in other countries, including Israel, the United States, and China.

According to the World Economic Forum's Future of Jobs Report 2020,[14] job demand will be decreased for certain jobs, including data entry clerks, administrative and executive secretaries, accounting-bookkeeping and payroll clerks, accountants, auditors, and assembly and factory workers. However, job demand will grow for data analysts and scientists, AI and ML specialists, big data specialists, digital marketing and strategy specialists, and process automation specialists, among others. The report provides an optimistic picture informing 97 million new jobs will be created while 85 million jobs will be displaced across 26 countries by 2025. In short, AI will create more job opportunities than displacing jobs.

Companies should focus on reskilling and upskilling their workforce to help employees prepare for new types of jobs. You should try new job training methods and emphasize building AI-ready culture. Consider collaborating with other parties such as government, educators, and nonprofit organizations on multi-sector training for upskilling and reskilling. A multi-sector partnership, Generation Unlimited aims to help 1.8 billion young people transition from school to work by 2030 worldwide.[15] Workers, on their part, should also take responsibility for their futures. Furthermore, you can hire career counselors to help your employees create actionable plans for career development. Helping them build a better future for themselves and their families is a good thing to do.

INITIATIVES OF LARGE CORPORATIONS TO PROMOTE AI ETHICS

Even though some people call it a post-trust era when we have lost trust in businesses, some of the world's largest companies are working together to make business practices more ethical. Partnership on AI (PAI), a nonprofit coalition committed to making the use of AI more responsible, was announced in 2016. PAI works on creating actionable resources that help the AI community translate critical insights into a positive impact on the world. Amazon, Facebook, Google, DeepMind, Microsoft, and IBM started the coalition as founding members in 2016, and Apple joined the coalition as a founding member in 2017.[16] Another tech giant, Baidu from China, joined the coalition in 2018. Baidu develops AI technologies such as autonomous driving, voice-enabled digital assistants, and smart cloud.[17] The coalition works with 100 partners in 14 countries, with 56 nonprofits, 13 industries, 27 academics, and four media groups.[18] PAI's resources are already making a difference by influencing the way large tech companies work. Meta's researchers used PAI's recommendations to responsibly publish their research on OPT-175B, a large language model with 175 billion parameters. The recommendations help them determine what information was appropriate to disclose and how to publish it responsibly.[19] Other companies using AI can use PAI resources to ensure they use AI applications ethically.

These large tech giants also have individual practices in place for the ethical use of AI and related technologies. For example, Microsoft has established a set of principles to ensure its AI systems are developed and used responsibly. Their central effort is led by the Aether Committee, the Office of Responsible AI (ORA), and Responsible AI Strategy in Engineering (RAISE), which work closely with teams to uphold Microsoft's responsible AI principles in their daily tasks. Microsoft's principles for responsible AI are as follows[20]:

1. Fairness: AI systems should treat all people fairly

2. Reliability and safety: AI systems should perform reliably and safely

3. Privacy and security: AI systems should be secure and respect the privacy

4. Inclusiveness: AI systems should empower everyone and engage people

5. Transparency: AI systems should be understandable

6. Accountability: people should be accountable for AI systems

Recognizing the ethical challenges of technology, Google has also listed objectives it uses to assess its AI applications. The objectives are as follows[21]:

1. Be socially beneficial

2. Avoid creating or reinforcing unfair bias

3. Be built and tested for safety

4. Be accountable to people

5. Incorporate privacy design principles

6. Uphold high standards of scientific excellence

7. Be made available for users that accord with these principles.

IBM is taking AI ethics to the next level. Grounded in commitments to trust and transparency, IBM has followed its core principles for decades. These principles guide IBM in handling its client data and insights with responsible development and deployment of new technologies. Their principles include:

1. The purpose of AI is to augment (not replace) human intelligence

2. Data and insights belong to their creator

3. New technology, including AI systems, must be transparent and explainable

Each principle has a detailed description of several practices that IBM employs for more responsible use of AI.[22]

With a quick Google search, you can see several corporate initiatives that promote AI ethics today. DI is an AI application and all the initiatives discussed above will also help in promoting the responsible use of DI.

You can combine the principles and objectives listed by Microsoft, Google, and IBM, to create your own framework to establish an ethical DI practice at your organization.

CONCLUSION AND THE FUTURE OF DI

Depending upon your current AI profile, DI adoption at your organization could either be a small project or a large-scale pursuit requiring transformational leadership. Top management's support is crucial for DI adoption. Besides profits, they must consider other benefits of this investment, including business growth opportunities it will unlock, the competitive advantage it will build, operational efficiencies it will improve, and customer lifetime value increased by this project. Make sure you have all the necessary resources, capacity, capabilities, and infrastructure. If you face problems developing talent for DI, consider sourcing talent or skills externally. Some organizations even use outsourcing to spare all the hassle that comes with projects of this size.

For various reasons, some organizational cultures do not appreciate revolutionary ideas such as DI. If that's the case with your organization, you might find it difficult to implement DI successfully. However, it is always possible to change the culture if you have inspiring leaders and change agents who can effectively communicate the project's benefits to the people and navigate them successfully through this change. Identify individuals who believe in DI, and have some kind of influence over others. They might become change agents who can influence people to drive this transformation in the right direction. Do not forget to assess your organization's readiness for DI adoption.

Another important DI aspect discussed in this chapter is ethics. Following the lead of large corporations, your organization should create a proper DI and AI governance system implemented at all management levels and across all functional areas. Decision-makers must consider the well-being of the people while implementing any system that might affect their interests. In addition to the practices listed in this chapter, you and your team should always follow the three general principles of ethics for any technology-related decisions:

- Respect for all persons
- Beneficence: not inflicting harm and promoting well-being where possible

- Distributive justice: fair treatment of all persons considering all have equal moral worth.

Businesses are not responsible for earning profits for their investors only. They also have a responsibility toward their people. Here, people means all stakeholders.

The future of DI is promising. With businesses becoming more open to using AI solutions and increasing access to massive amounts of data and technologies, DI will gain more popularity in the future. In fact, it will become one of the most common management practices in all types of organizations. Due to the efficiency benefits it brings, decision-makers will use DI for a variety of big and small decisions. It is already happening. Many businesses are using DI without calling it DI. You are using DI even when using AI at the most granular level to aid a simple decision. The trend will only go upward. The major innovations will be seen in decision augmentation and automation areas.

DI solution providers are launching revolutionizing technologies, enhancing their portfolio daily. Through decision augmentation, these solutions will change the ways how business decisions are made. More and more decisions in the future will be based on the recommendations provided by AI. Intelligent systems will be used at a larger scale to create value for all stakeholders, including our planet. They are already making significant contributions to improving our overall well-being. The case study at the end of this chapter illustrates how AI and DI can be used for the greater good.

Intelligent automation, also called hyperautomation, has already been adopted by more than 50% of the world's largest companies. These companies include JP Morgan, ADP, Lloyds Banking Group, Netflix, and Unilever. As Bornet et al.[23] explain, hyperautomation combines various methods and technologies to execute business processes with minimal human intervention. It works on behalf of knowledge workers and increases process speed and process resilience, enhances compliance and quality, reduces costs, and optimizes decision outcomes. With advancements in IoT, we will see more autonomous agents helping us solve our day-to-day problems while making our lives easier and more comfortable. As research in other areas, such as swarm intelligence, advances, new systems will emerge, mimicking and surpassing human capabilities at different levels and scales.

Despite all the glowing possibilities, these innovations will surely disrupt various aspects of our lives. In addition to job loss, the nature and methods of work will change significantly, requiring us to develop new skill sets. In addition to higher-level technical skills, workers will also need other competencies critical for effective decision-making. These competencies include creative problem-solving, critical thinking, system thinking, envisioning, strategizing, communicating, leading, adapting, and using emotional intelligence. The good news is that it is all achievable and manageable. As humans, we grow, adapt, improve, and keep thriving. We hope to see this world becoming a better place with some remarkable DI innovations in the future.

"You are either controlling the technology, or the technology is controlling you."

CASE STUDY: AI FOR GREATER GOOD – STANFORD MEDICINE USES GOOGLE GLASS TO HELP KIDS WITH AUTISM SOCIALIZE

Stanford Medicine, a leader in the biomedical revolution, integrates research, medical education, and healthcare at Stanford School of Medicine, Stanford Health Care, and Stanford Children's Health. Their close proximity to the parent organization – Stanford University, and their ongoing associations with the entrepreneurial endeavors of Silicon Valley help them translate new knowledge into tangible health benefits.

Researchers at Stanford Medicine developed an app that can be paired with Google Glass to help children with autism understand human emotions conveyed through people's facial expressions. According to the Centers for Disease Control and Prevention, about 1 in 68 children in the United States have autism. Children with autism spectrum disorders struggle with reading and understanding social cues, including identifying facial expressions. As they often cannot make eye contact, it affects their response to other people, including friends and family members.

Google Glass, manufactured by Google, is a headset, motion-controlled android device that offers a unique augmented reality experience. First launched in 2013, Google Glass was considered one of Google's failed innovations. Nevertheless, this device is revolutionizing the ways AI can be used for the greater good.

Stanford researchers named the prototype *Superpower Glass*. It is an ML-assisted software system that runs through an Android app on the Google Glass headset. It is designed to recognize eight basic and primary emotions – happiness, sadness, anger, surprise, distrust, fear, neutral, and contempt. The app was trained with hundreds of thousands of photos of human faces showing the eight emotions (or expressions). It also had a mechanism to allow people (involved in the study) to calibrate it to their own neutral faces if necessary. The Superpower Glass literally provides children wearing the device with real-time cues about other people's facial expressions.

In the pilot study, 14 families were given Superpower Glass to be used at home. The device was linked with a smartphone through a local wireless network. It was equipped with a camera that recorded the wearer's field of view, a small screen over one eye, and a speaker to give the wearer visual and audio information. As the child interacted with others, the app identified and named their emotions through the Google Glass screen or speaker. Despite such a sophisticated design, the headset can be worn conveniently as regular eyeglasses.

The researchers designed three unique ways to implement this program. In *free play*, the software provided the child with visual and auditory cues each time it recognized an emotion on the face of someone in the field of view as the child interacted or played with their families. The two others were game modes. In *guess my emotion*, a parent acted out one of the eight facial expressions, and the child tried to identify it. Finally, in *capture the smile*, the child would give another person clues about the emotion they wanted to show until the other person acted it out. These methods helped researchers measure children's overall improvement in recognizing social cues and improving their relationships.

Children used Superpower Glass for ten weeks. After one to three months of regular use, parents started to notice that the children made more eye contact and related better to others around them. Researchers studied parent surveys and lab reports to conclude that the severity of children's autism was decreased and social skills were improved. Superpower Glass can work as an effective decision support system to help professional therapists tailor better behavior learning plans for children with autism. These wearable AI systems have great potential to help people with brain-related challenges improve their quality of life and overall well-being.

Source:
Digitale, E. (2018). Google Glass helps kids with autism read facial expressions. Retrieved August 12, 2022, from Stanford Medicine News Center website: http://med.stanford.edu/news/all-news/2018/08/google-glass-helps-kids-with-autism-read-facial-expressions.html

QUESTIONS

1. What challenges do children with autism face when bonding with others?

2. How does Superpower Glass work? Discuss its design and functioning in detail. Do more research if necessary.

3. Search online and discuss why Google Glass failed in the first place.

4. Discuss the methodology of testing the efficacy of Superpower Glass.

5. List at least three AI innovations that positively change people's lives and contribute to the greater good.

QUESTIONS FOR DISCUSSION

1. List five companies that adopted AI technologies early and are using AI as their competitive advantage today.

2. How will you convince your investors to invest in a major DI project?

3. What should be the various components of your DI strategic plan?

4. What is the significance of using a project management approach for DI planning and implementation?

5. List the key infrastructure needs that must be satisfied for DI adoption.

6. Why is data crucial for DI?

7. Search online and list five types of education and training programs you can use to prepare your workforce for DI. Be specific about the contents covered in each program.

8. Why is it a good idea to partner with outside parties to implement DI systems successfully at your organization?

9. What is design thinking?

10. How will you use design thinking to build a successful DI system or solution for your organization? Discuss with the help of an example. Also, explain each step of design thinking in detail.

11. Why do people resist revolutionary changes such as AI and DI adoption?

12. How can you build a culture that supports and encourages DI?

13. How can you modify DI solutions that do not deliver desired outcomes?

14. Why is DI readiness assessment important?

15. What are the three key criteria of DI readiness assessment?

16. With the help of real-life examples, list various ethical considerations for DI adoption. Use examples that are not already used in this chapter.

17. Search online and list five companies using AI ethically that are not mentioned in this chapter. Explain their practices in detail.

18. What challenges and opportunities do you see as DI becomes more commonplace?

REFERENCES

1. Sherman, R. (2015). *Business Intelligence Guidebook: From Data Integration to Analytics* (1st edition). Waltham, MA: Morgan Kaufmann.
2. Bughin, J., McCarthy, B., & Chui, M. (2017, August 28). A Survey of 3,000 Executives Reveals How Businesses Succeed with AI. *Harvard Business Review*. Retrieved from https://hbr.org/2017/08/a-survey-of-3000-executives-reveals-how-businesses-succeed-with-ai
3. Fountaine, T., McCarthy, B., & Saleh, T. (2019, July 1). Building the AI-Powered Organization. *Harvard Business Review*. Retrieved from https://hbr.org/2019/07/building-the-ai-powered-organization
4. Metz, C. & Singer, N. (2019, April 3). A.I. Experts Question Amazon's Facial-Recognition Technology. *The New York Times*. Retrieved from https://www.nytimes.com/2019/04/03/technology/amazon-facial-recognition-technology.html
5. Public Affairs, UC Berkeley (2018, November 13). Mortgage Algorithms Perpetuate Racial Bias in Lending, Study Finds. *Berkeley News*. Retrieved from https://news.berkeley.edu/story_jump/mortgage-algorithms-perpetuate-racial-bias-in-lending-study-finds/
6. Koenecke, A., Nam, A., Lake, E., Nudell, J., Quartey, M., Mengesha, Z., Toups, C., Rickford, J. R., Jurafsky, D., & Goel, S. (2020). Racial disparities in automated speech recognition. *Proceedings of the National Academy of Sciences, 117*(14), 7684–7689. https://doi.org/10.1073/pnas.1915768117

7. PwC. (n.d.). Understanding Algorithmic Bias and How to Build Trust in AI. Retrieved July 14, 2022, from PwC website: https://www.pwc.com/us/en/tech-effect/ai-analytics/algorithmic-bias-and-trust-in-ai.html

8. Mozur, P. (2019, April 14). One Month, 500,000 Face Scans: How China Is Using A.I. to Profile a Minority. *The New York Times.* Retrieved from https://www.nytimes.com/2019/04/14/technology/china-surveillance-artificial-intelligence-racial-profiling.html

9. Chan, R. (2019, October 5). The Cambridge Analytica Whistleblower Explains How the Firm Used Facebook Data to Sway Elections. Retrieved July 15, 2022, from *Business Insider* website: https://www.businessinsider.com/cambridge-analytica-whistleblower-christopher-wylie-facebook-data-2019-10

10. 4 Ways to Preserve Privacy in Artificial Intelligence. (n.d.). Retrieved July 15, 2022, from Booz Allen Hamilton website: https://www.boozallen.com/s/solution/four-ways-to-preserve-privacy-in-ai.html

11. Total data volume worldwide 2010-2025. (n.d.). Retrieved July 15, 2022, from Statista website: https://www.statista.com/statistics/871513/worldwide-data-created/

12. Gherini, A. (2016, November 2). You're Approaching Data Wrong – and It's Costing the U.S. $3 Trillion. Retrieved July 15, 2022, from Inc.com website: https://www.inc.com/anne-gherini/why-your-bad-data-is-creating-a-3-trillion-problem.html

13. Gershgorn, D. (2017). Worried about AI Taking Your Job? It's Already Happening in Japan. Retrieved July 15, 2022, from World Economic Forum website: https://www.weforum.org/agenda/2017/01/worried-about-ai-taking-your-job-its-already-happening-in-japan/

14. The Future of Jobs Report 2020. (2020). Retrieved August 17, 2022, from World Economic Forum website: https://www.weforum.org/reports/the-future-of-jobs-report-2020/

15. Kande, M., & Sonmez, M. (2020). Don't fear AI. The tech will lead to long-term job growth. Retrieved August 17, 2022, from World Economic Forum website: https://www.weforum.org/agenda/2020/10/dont-fear-ai-it-will-lead-to-long-term-job-growth/

16. Vincent, J. (2017, January 27). Apple Joins Research Group for Ethical AI with Fellow Tech Giants. Retrieved July 15, 2022, from The Verge website: https://www.theverge.com/2017/1/27/14411810/apple-joins-partnership-for-ai

17. Taylor, C. (2018, October 17). Baidu becomes the first Chinese firm to join US-led A.I. body. Retrieved July 15, 2022, from CNBC website: https://www.cnbc.com/2018/10/17/baidu-becomes-the-first-chinese-firm-to-join-us-led-ai-body.html

18. Partnership on AI. (n.d.). Retrieved July 15, 2022, from Partnership on AI website: https://partnershiponai.org/

19. Bremner, P. (n.d.). Recommendations in Practice: Meta Researchers Apply PAI Guidance. Retrieved July 15, 2022, from Partnership on AI website: https://partnershiponai.org/resource/recommendations-in-practice-meta-researchers-apply-pai-guidance/

20. Our Approach to Responsible AI at Microsoft. (n.d.). Retrieved July 15, 2022, from Microsoft website: https://www.microsoft.com/en-us/ai/our-approach

21. Our Principles. (n.d.). Retrieved July 15, 2022, from Google AI website: https://ai.google/principles/

22. IBM'S Principles for Data Trust and Transparency. (2018, May 30). Retrieved July 15, 2022, from IBM website: https://www.ibm.com/blogs/policy/trust-principles/

23. Bornet, P., Barkin, I., & Wirtz, J. (2020). *INTELLIGENT AUTOMATION: Learn How to Harness Artificial Intelligence to Boost Business & Make Our World More Human.*

Index

Note: Page numbers with *italics* refer to the figure and **bold** refer to the table.

Printed in the United States
by Baker & Taylor Publisher Services